Gun Thugs, Rednecks, and Radicals

A Documentary History of the West Virginia Mine Wars
Edited by David Alan Corbin

PM

OAKLAND, CA

W. VA

Gun Thugs, Rednecks, and Radicals: A Documentary History of the West Virginia Mine Wars
David Alan Corbin
© PM Press 2011

ISBN: 978-1-60486-452-6
Library of Congress Control Number: 2011927957

Cover design by Josh MacPhee/Justseeds.org, cover and interior illustration by Chris Stain, "The Battle of Blair Mountain"
Interior design by Lauren Cooper
Transcription by Jacqueline F. Thomas

10 9 8 7 6 5 4 3 2 1

PM Press
PO Box 23912
Oakland, CA 94623
www.pmpress.org

Chapters I-X were originally published in 1990 as *The West Virginia Mine Wars: An Anthology* by Appalachian Editions, Charleston, W. Va.

Chapter XI was originally published in 1971 as *The Socialist and Labor Star: Huntington, W. Va. 1912–1915* by Appalachian Movement Press, Huntington, W. Va.

Map created by Brandon Nida. Credited images courtesy of *Goldenseal*.

Reprint permission kindly granted by the AFL-CIO, The New York Times Company, *The Atlantic*, The Nation Company, Inc., the *United Mine Workers Journal*, and the Baltimore Sun Company.

Printed in the USA on recycled paper, by the Employee Owners of Thomson-Shore in Dexter, Michigan.

www.thomsonshore.com

Contents

To my brother Ronald Corbin,
for his support and encouragement

Preface

Long banished from history books and popular consciousness, the West Virginia Mine Wars of the early twentieth century continue to be the subject of a belated process of historical recovery. This is, in part, undoubtedly because those distant events reverberate in current-day matters.

The ongoing fight over the fate of Blair Mountain is a case in point. In 1921, Blair Mountain was the site of an armed insurrection by thousands of coal miners against a force of sheriffs' deputies and company gun thugs entrenched along the Logan County ridgeline. As the dramatic and culminating action of the Mine Wars, the stakes for both sides were enormous. Either the coal fields of southern West Virginia would remain under the near-absolute hegemony of coal operators or the area would be opened to unionization, making it "safe for democracy," to borrow the rhetoric of the late Great War.

There is today yet another battle over the fate of Blair Mountain. This time the stakes are whether or not the mountain will be devastated and leveled by coal industry giants such as Massey Energy and Arch Coal, not only in order to cheaply extract the mineral wealth beneath its surface, but also, by unhappy coincidence, to eradicate the physical terrain upon which workers engaged their class enemies. In 1921, the West Virginia coal miners fought as resolutely as other workers did in those times—in Munich and Turin and Kronstadt—and met similar defeat. Such an outcome, however, did not resolve the cause of their struggle, but only prolonged it for a later date.

David Alan Corbin is the author of the most definitive study of that period of open and unrelenting class struggle known as the West Virginia Mine Wars. His book, *Life, Work, and Rebellion in the Coal Fields: The Southern West Virginia Miners, 1880–1922*, is as thorough and comprehensive a treatment of its subject as can be found between two covers. That is not to say, however, that it is by any means exhaustive, and the texts reprinted here demonstrate Corbin's willingness to return to the period and issues of his book, as he has in his articles in journals and other collections.

The texts gathered here provide, in fact, a coda to Corbin's continual delving into this much-neglected, but undeniably significant, chapter in the history of American labor. Corbin's essay on the *Socialist and Labor Star* was originally published in 1971 by Appalachian Movement Press of Huntington, West Virginia. Appalachian Movement Press was a cooperative, radical press and very much the product of the student New Left, especially the presence of Students for a Democratic Society (SDS) on the campus of Huntington's Marshall University. Besides contemporaneous analyses of the class structure of quasi-colonial West Virginia, the press also issued several pamphlets by poet and labor activist Don West, already then known for his regionalist radicalism. Corbin's recovery of an important historical moment of West Virginia's "underground" press fit quite nicely with the aspirations of those who brought Appalachian Movement Press into existence.

Corbin would continue to delve into this overlooked but significant era of American class struggle. In 1977, he contributed to a collection titled *Essays in Southern Labor History*. The article, "'Frank Keeney Is Our Leader; and We Shall Not Be Moved': Rank-and-File Leadership in the West Virginia Coal Fields," foreshadows themes that would, in the 1981 publication of *Life, Work, and Rebellion*, reveal the local and self-directed nature of the workers' insurrections.

To challenge longstanding mythology that West Virginians were incapable of autonomous resistance—a perception seemingly shared by both coal industry apologists and professional agitators—Corbin published a scathing indictment of the latter in the *Journal of American History*, titled "Betrayal in the West Virginia Coal Fields: Eugene Debs and the Socialist Party of America, 1912–1914." Building on the division of the state's Socialists between reformist social democrats, predominant in the northern coal fields, and revolutionary syndicalists, more characteristic of unionists in the southern coal fields, Corbin exposed a vein of regional radical history that would be explored by fellow labor historian Fred Barkey in his account of the history of the Socialist Party in early twentieth-century West Virginia. Even as late as 1993, apologists for Debs would be trying to rescue him from Corbin's indictment, most notably Roger Fagge's "Eugene V. Debs in West Virginia, 1913: A Reappraisal" published in *West Virginia History*.

In 1990, Corbin edited the collection also here republished, then as *The West Virginia Mine Wars: An Anthology*. The purpose was to gather in a single place contemporaneous accounts of both the 1912–1913 mine war in Cabin and Paint Creeks and the 1920–1921 events culminating in the Armed March on Blair Mountain. As a compilation of original, long-out-of-print source materials, *Gun Thugs, Rednecks, and Radicals* exhibits the same archeological and historical intentions evident in the present struggle over the status of Blair Mountain. It was and is grounded in the conviction that to save our own time we must also reclaim and save from annihilation our past, along with that of those thousands of nameless working people who nevertheless wrote their own history by risking everything for liberation.

Gordon Simmons
West Virginia Labor History Association

Introduction

During a dozen years of public schooling in West Virginia, I never heard about the great West Virginia Mine Wars. I never heard of the Paint Creek–Cabin Creek strike of 1912, the Matewan Massacre in 1920, or the 1921 Battle of Blair Mountain. I heard nothing about the leaders of these events—Frank Keeney, Fred Mooney, and Mother Jones.

Instead, I was taught happy and pleasant things about our state. This included such bits of information like the location of the world's largest clothespin factory and the world's biggest ashtray. I learned more than I ever needed to know about prehistoric Indian mounds, and I was taught something about Blennerhasset Island.

To be able to counter any disparaging remarks outsiders may have made about our state, my school friends and I learned about every West Virginian who ever achieved national prominence. Our teachers prepared us to repel our out-of-state detractors with highly charged ammunition like the fact that Pearl Buck came from Hillsboro, that Stonewall Jackson was born in Clarksburg, that Don Knotts hailed from Morgantown, while Soupy Sales and Peter Marshall went to Marshall College.

When we were told of the importance West Virginia held in relation to the rest of the nation, we were not informed of the fact that our coal heated its homes, fueled its industries, and powered its battleships for decades. Nor were we told about the thousands of West Virginians who died getting that coal out of the ground. We were not told of the struggle these people underwent for safer working conditions and a better standard of living; that is, the struggle for their union. No, nothing about that.

"The typical mountaineer's historical education has been a process of 'trivial pursuit,'" notes *Charleston Gazette* columnist Rick Wilson. "While we were busy memorizing the counties in alphabetical order, we were certainly not taught about how our ancestors were swindled out of their mineral rights and land by outside coal, rail, and gas interests or any of the unpleasant consequences thereof. Real history, like sex, was something you learned on the streets, if at all."

We were even handed historical disinformation, West Virginia non-facts: The American Revolution began at Point Pleasant, not Lexington. West Virginian James Rumsey, not Robert Fulton, built the steamboat. Amos Dolbear, not Alexander Graham Bell, invented the telephone.

State historian John Williams points out that these alternative histories of our state read like Soviet encyclopedias under Stalin, which established a Russian inventor and context for every important development in the modern world. Williams argues that this historical makeover of West Virginia is an effort to disguise some perceived shame, much like "defensive individuals who seek to mask a sense of inferiority by boastfulness."

Maybe so. On the other hand, there could well be something of an effort, conscious or unconscious, to keep West Virginians from knowing their real history—to bury it under trivia, distortions, and ersatz pleasantries.

The idea of rewriting history to cover unpleasant realities isn't new. It was portrayed in George Orwell's classic novel *1984*, where we found Big Brother destroying old state rationing figures so reduced rations might be labeled "increases" without contradiction. The Soviet Union revised history under Stalin. And, it is being done in China, where a barbaric government is currently suppressing news of its massacre of students and workers. According to that country's official history books, the 1989 student uprisings in search of dignity and democracy never happened. If the Chinese leadership has its way, future generations will not be told of their predecessors' struggle against a tyrannical, corrupt regime that denied them life and liberty.

I didn't have to read Orwell—or travel to the Soviet Union or China—to experience the phenomenon of historical distortion. In Oceania, the tool was the "memory hole." In China, it's been called "the big lie." In West Virginia, it is labeled "history."

In West Virginia, as in China, a vast storehouse of history lies beneath the official fabrication. The stock in this storehouse isn't always neat, nice, and pretty, but it is rich, meaningful, and telling.

It is a story of struggle. It is a story of courageous men and women demanding and fighting for their rights, for their dignity, and for their freedom. It is a rich and proud history, one more deserving of discussion than the world's largest clothespin factory, the source of the first steamboat, or Soupy Sales's alma mater.

Lon Savage, in an important, thought-provoking speech on the sixty-ninth anniversary of the Matewan Massacre, compared the West

Virginia Mine Wars to the Old West; the shootings at Matewan to the gunfight at the OK Corral. This is a good, graphic comparison and it makes the important point that far lesser events in American history have received far greater attention than similar, but more significant events in West Virginia.

Still, it should be recalled that the OK Corral was a local fight over interests peculiar to that time and place. The Mine Wars, however, were battles for timeless and universal values and principles: industrial democracy, social equality, and political rights. Perhaps a better analogy is to relate the West Virginia miners' turn-of-the-century struggle for their union to the civil rights movement among black Americans, five decades later.

Like the civil rights movement of the 1960s, the miners' organizing effort had good and bad characters. Each story involved brutality, destruction, and death. And both movements are stories of oppressed, exploited people fighting for dignity, self-respect, human rights, and freedom. Both are stories of courageous men and women doing heroic things under extraordinary circumstances against extraordinary foes. Each also carries the reminder that the United States has not always been as fair and egalitarian as we'd like to believe.

The West Virginia Mine Wars involved nearly every form of violence and warfare. The Paint Creek–Cabin Creek strike was nothing short of a revolution—an uprising against a brutal, autocratic regime. The Matewan Massacre paralleled an Old West–style shootout on the main street of town. The killings of Sid Hatfield and Ed Chambers on the steps of the McDowell County Courthouse in Welch was a gangland "hit," and the ensuing March on Logan was civil war.

The West Virginia miners' conflict was also fought with much of the advanced weaponry the early twentieth century could bring to bear: automatic rifles, machine guns, grenades, as well as shotguns and handguns. There was a train, the "Bull Moose Special," fitted with guns and armor. There were bombing planes and fully equipped, trained, and prepared armies. There were passwords, spies, scouts, supply personnel, commissaries, sentries, medical units, medics, and officers.

It was also a war fought with legal artillery: injunctions, yellow-dog contracts, housing contracts and evictions, economic sanctions, and deportation. In their effort to win their union, the West Virginia miners were subjected to various forms of persecution and prosecution: 104 court-martial prosecutions, deportations, and indictments charging more than 550 people with murder and treason against the government.

The struggle of the southern West Virginia miners also involved some of the most important and colorful personalities in the history of the American labor movement, including Mother Jones, Frank Keeney, Fred Mooney, and Sid Hatfield. Although they were heroes in their own day, these people have become strangers to the majority of West Virginians and their children.

On a positive note, the West Virginia Mine Wars have been receiving greater attention in recent years. They have been the subject of historical studies including Lon Savage's *Thunder in the Mountains*, Howard Lee's *Bloodletting in Appalachia*, and—for better or worse—my own *Life, Work, and Rebellion in the Coal Fields*. These scholarly, historical studies have provided the backdrop for best-selling novels, including Denise Giardina's *Storming Heaven* and Mary Lee Settle's *Scapegoat*. We have seen some outstanding movies including the PBS documentary *Even the Heavens Weep* and the John Sayles feature film *Matewan*.

It is now time for a volume that allows these historical events and the people involved in them to speak for themselves. In this book, you will hear from generals of the labor movement, like Fred Mooney, Frank Keeney, and Mother Jones, as well as from the foot soldiers, like George Echols and Maud Estep.

This anthology is not offered as a complete history of the West Virginia Mine Wars. Some readers, for instance, might be disappointed that the "other side"—the coal industry's side—isn't better represented. Such critics will have to remain disappointed, for that is not the reason for this book.

The purpose of the volume is to document the history of this important movement through original articles, stories, and testimony—in the actual words of people who either witnessed or participated in these remarkable events. Each account is presented with a brief word of background. Each witness is introduced. Let them tell you about their time. Let them tell you their stories. Let them give you a history full of struggle, of violence and death, but also full of life and hope.

The story of the West Virginia Mine Wars is not always a pretty one. It isn't always a happy story. But it is history—West Virginia's history. It is the story of a people struggling for a better way of life. It is a story worth retelling. I hope you find it as educational and fascinating as I have.

David Corbin

CHAPTER I

CHAPTER I
A Complete and Ruthless Rule:
Emergence of the Company Town

The southern West Virginia Mine Wars of 1912–1921 drew scores of newspaper reporters to the Mountain State to inform America about what was going on in this seemingly primitive and violent Appalachian backcountry.

Upon their arrival, the savviest journalists quickly discovered that the Mine Wars were more than brief, episodic outbreaks of hostility between inherently violent people. They were the culmination of decades of exploitation and oppression, an inevitable result of a brutal way of industrial life and work that had evolved in the coal fields. Foremost, the battles were part of a decades-long struggle for dignity and political and social rights in southern West Virginia.

The intensity of the violence in southern West Virginia can be traced to the oppressive, exploitative nature of life and work in the coal fields there. The heart of that authoritarian system was the company town.

Ownership of the land and resources gave the coal companies enormous social control over the miners. "You didn't even own your own soul in those damnable places," recalled one elderly miner. "The company owned everything, the houses, the schools, churches, the stores—everything."

The coal company town was a complete system. In addition to owning and controlling all the institutions in the town, coal company rule in southern West Virginia included the company doctor who delivered the babies, the mines in which the children went to work, and the cemeteries where they eventually were buried.

Foremost, company rule included the company police in the form of mine guards, who would toss the miners into the company jail when they got disruptive, or administer the company beating when they attempted to unionize.

It was a complete rule and it was a ruthless rule. Consequently, when the miners did go on strike for their union, they did so not for simple wage increases, but for their dignity and freedom.

Winthrop D. Lane was a nationally renowned author and social worker when the *New York Evening Post* commissioned him to go to West Virginia and "make a study of the whole conflict." A graduate of the New York School of Social Work, Lane had devoted his life to social causes. He organized the first international conference on mental hygiene, served as director of the New Jersey Prison Commission, and authored several books. Two of them, *Punishment and Reformation* and *What Makes Crime*, examined the social and economic causes of criminal behavior.

Lane also served as a reporter and editor of several important and prestigious eastern publications including the *Evening Post* and the *Survey*, for which he covered the Mine Wars. In writing about West Virginia, Lane talked to countless people in order "to get at the facts and the psychology, the color, the atmosphere of the conflict." Later, he turned his articles into two books on industrial conditions in the West Virginia coal fields, *Civil War in West Virginia* (1921) and *The Denial of Civil Liberties in the Coal Fields* (1924). All of Lane's writing is rich in information and insight, and serves as an important reference for anyone writing about the period.

Black Avalanche
By Winthrop D. Lane

In this article—published in the March 25, 1922, Survey *(New York)—Winthrop D. Lane captures the transition of southern West Virginia from a pastoral, agricultural society into a fully developed, industrialized economy. In so doing, he catches the essence of the cultural changes industrialization had wrought and how the stage was set for decades of violence.*

Less than twenty years ago parts of those vast stretches of low mountains that cover so much of West Virginia slumbered in solitude. The traveler rode horseback up the stony beds of mountain streams and sought shelter at night in a lonely settler's hut or on the slope of the inhospitable mountain. Forests of oak, ash, cucumber wood and poplar covered the hills. Bears lumbered through the wilderness and wildcats howled at night. No railroad had yet penetrated the region. People lived in small groups here and there in the valleys; life on the whole was simple and devoted chiefly to agriculture. The earth reposed peacefully.

Today, in traversing this region, you pass coal-mining village after coal-mining village. As you ride up the valley of the Guyandotte River, or through McDowell, Mingo and other counties, where the hills stood in untouched quietness two decades ago, evidences of the transformation are on every hand. The houses of those who work in the mines are never out of sight. Large mouths gape blackly at you from the hillsides. Gaunt tipples, head houses and other buildings stare at you from the slopes of the mountains. Railroads send their sidings in many directions. Long lines of squat mine cars run along their narrow gage tracks and disappear around the curves of the hills. The earth is scraped and ugly. The blackness of coal is over everything, and mounds of fine coal stand about. Peacefulness and quiet have departed.

"We think coal and live coal," said a circuit court judge to members of Senator Kenyon's committee visiting the state recently. "If you take our coal from us, we shall go back to the days of the bobcat and the wilderness. Coal is our existence."

This change underlies all that is going forward in that territory today. The conflict over unionism that has invaded these peaceful valleys has made itself familiar through bloody scenes. Another struggle has recently transcended it in the lives of those who inhabit the coal region: the struggle with unemployment. To the miner his employment in the mine is the only way of making a living. Mining operations cover whole counties and ascend river valleys to their sources. They supply whatever opportunity for a livelihood there is. Occasional jobs may be found elsewhere, but they are unimportant and few. If a considerable number of mines close down, whole towns sit around idle. The coal fields of West Virginia comprise an area larger than Rhode Island, Massachusetts and Delaware combined. Any general search for other employment would lead to a small migration.

I have just returned from visiting parts of the state. In some places production has remained nearly normal, but in others the mines have worked little for more than a year. I looked into family cupboards that contained food for only a single meal. I saw the haunted look in the eyes of men who did not know how they were going to provide for the immediate wants of wives and children. Cows have been killed so that there might be fresh meat, although these were the only source of milk for babies. Children are staying away from school because they have no clothes and shoes. Families who have something saved up have helped other families; communities hitherto dependent upon coal have become dependent upon charity.

I

Before describing this situation, let us see what kind of civilization lies back of it. The story of the exploitation of West Virginia's coal resources is dramatic. When Thomas Batts and his few companions pushed their first sturdy way into this fortress of nature, they had no conception of the vast treasures that lay around them. Not until other explorers in 1742 saw "creeks full of coal" was the first record written of the existence of this mineral wealth. George Washington, surveying land in 1770 in what is now Mason County, saw a "Cole hill on fire." Settlement for long was slow. Pioneers, migrating from the eastern valleys and from Maryland, New Jersey and Pennsylvania, found the hills of West Virginia inaccessible and hostile. In the neighboring states of Ohio, Indiana, and Michigan, farms were cleared and towns established before West Virginia became peopled. As late as 1830 or 1840 the inhabitants of the state could still be found tilling their acres, tanning leather for their own shoes, making their own thread and wax, preparing flax and wool for their own cloth and carving dishes and bowls from blocks of cucumber wood and yellow poplar.

No use was made of coal at this time except by crossroads blacksmiths, who employed it in their little shops, and by frontier settlers who dug lumps of it from the outcrops of seams near their cabins and placed these on logs with which they had filled their fireplaces on winter nights.

In 1835 Samuel P. Hildreth published the first observation of the coal strata of West Virginia. Richard Cowling Taylor, the "father of English geology," visited the state in 1848 and described "that magnificent, central, elevated region within whose borders slumber in undisturbed darkness untold millions of acres of coal." Not until the few years just before the Civil War were corporations formed for mining this coal. These were few and unimportant, however, and the war put a stop to their operations.

About 1879 development began in earnest. Then people who knew the great value of West Virginia's coal deposits began to call this to the attention of outside capital. West Virginia advertised her wealth. At the Centennial Exposition at Philadelphia in 1876, she "surprised the world," we read, "with the exhibit of her natural resources; and the thousands of dollars she thus expended resulted in the investment of millions within her borders." In the earlier operations the leading part had been taken by West Virginians. Now outside aid was sought. Companies were formed on every hand. Land was bought in large quantities. Tracts of it were still held by descendants of original grantees from the English crown and these suddenly found themselves wealthy. On a scale hitherto unimagined, corporations sprang into existence. Many of these had no intention of mining the coal themselves, but planned to lease their land to others who would do it; this practice is common in the state today. Some of the land was bought by railroad companies, who wanted it for the coal that it held as well as for rights of way. Manufacturing establishments in northern cities acquired some of it for their own future supplies of fuel; public utility corporations did the same thing. But by far the greatest number of companies planned exploitation for the general market.

This rapid development passed by certain parts of the state. A modern coal mine is useless until a railroad runs to its very door. The first roads into the state, the Chesapeake & Ohio, the Baltimore & Ohio, the Norfolk & Western, left many districts untouched. Logan County had no railroad until 1904; today it is one of the most productive counties in the state. Other regions were almost as late in being opened. Mines, mine towns, mining corporations, labor unions, the problem of unemployment—all are new. Many localities are going through processes today that were typical of the older Pennsylvania regions fifty years ago.

Miners came into the valleys with a rush. Welsh coal diggers from the pits of Kidwelley; Englishmen from Lancashire; Belgians from the coal basins of Hainaut and Liege; these mingled with much larger numbers of Italians, Slavs, Austrians and Poles. The hills of the state resounded to the languages of foreign lands; more than thirty nationalities are represented among the workmen in these mines today. Americans, however, outnumber the foreigners. They have come from the coal fields of Ohio, Indiana, Illinois, Pennsylvania and other states. Negroes from the Southern cotton fields have found employment in the mines. And, not the least, the mountaineers of the state themselves. Watching the mines creep nearer and nearer to their cabins, they have looked with foreboding at first and then, realizing the futility of any effort to stand aside, they have shouldered picks and entered the mouths of the black tunnels.

The romance of the story is in part its size and in parts its suddenness. Take McDowell County, which was described two generations ago as "comparatively unpeopled"; on her hillsides sheep were raised and wool was grown. Today mines line her valleys and her annual production of 18,000,000 tons of coal places her first in output among the counties of the state.

Meanwhile, "much of this country is owned by non-residents," writes the historian. The few facts that are known as to coal land ownership show the magnitude of some of the interests involved. The Norfolk & Western Railway Company owns nearly every share of the Pocahontas Coal and Coke Company. According to the annual reports of the railway for 1902, when this control was acquired, the Pocahontas Coal and Coke Company owned 295,000 acres in the Pocahontas field, or "about four-fifths" of that field. This is a leasing concern. A large number of mining operators are engaged in extracting coal from its land. Another large holder is the United States Steel Corporation. Through subsidiaries this corporation owns more than 53,000 acres of coking coal land and 32,000 of surface coal land in Logan and Mingo counties combined, and leases 63,000 acres in the Pocahontas field.

II

Let us see what kind of civilization has resulted. The typical coal mining town is not a town in the ordinary sense at all. The place where the town stands is the point at which a seam has been opened, buildings have been erected and machinery has been installed. The dwellings that cluster about the tipple or straggle along the bed of the creek are not occupied by the self-dependent citizens of a community which gives many opportunities for employment and presents a variety of facets to the world at large; they are occupied solely by the men who work in the mines. The town is the adjunct and necessary convenience of an industry; if the mines should disappear, it, too, would cease to exist. It is not even called a town in the language of the locality. It is called a camp.

No one owns his own house; he cannot acquire so much title to property. No one runs a store, operates a garage or sells groceries or haberdashery to his fellow townsmen. No one amuses them in a movie theater. There is no Main Street of small independent businesses, owned by different people, and making up that mosaic of commercial life that is typical of villages everywhere. There is little if any participation in common, group activities. No body of elected councilmen ever passes on repairs for roads, no group of people ever gets together and decides that the old school house is too ramshackle for the children or that the old church needs repainting. No family physician builds up a successful practice by competing with other physicians. No lawyer settles disputes over property rights among his neighbors.

It is not accurate to say that that no one does these things. The coal company does them all. It owns all the houses and rents them to the miner. It owns the store, the pool room, the movie theater, and often helps to build the school and the church. It often owns the Y.M.C.A. building, if there is one. The company employs the physician and collects a small sum monthly from each miner to help pay him. Sometimes it supplements the salary of the teacher and assists the minister in making both ends meet.

The company owns all the land and everything upon it. It therefore controls the life and activities of the little community. It is responsible for the sanitation; if sewage disposal is adequate, the credit belongs to the employer. The company's ownership sometimes extends to the roads, so that it can control ingress and egress. In some counties the company is the employer of the deputy sheriffs and is therefore responsible for police supervision. In Logan County the operators paid out $61,000 last year, as the president of the Logan Coal Operators' Association testified before the Kenyon Committee, in salaries for deputy sheriffs.

Miners in West Virginia are not paid as workers elsewhere are paid. They do not receive in cash all that they have earned. On their semi-monthly paydays they are given statements showing how much they owe the company and how much the company owes them. Among the items charged against them in this account is the indebtedness incurred by them at the company store. Other items are rent for their houses, lighting, heating, doctor's services, use of the hospital, the sharpening of tools and occasionally a charge for use of the company wash house in which to clean up after a day's work. The miner pays the same amount for doctor and hospital services whether there has been illness in his family or not. For major operations such as child birth and other important surgical treatment, additional sums are paid. Rent varies according to the condition of the house, usually running from $6 to $10 a month. Lighting costs the miner on an average about $1 a month, coal from heating the house from $1 to $2, the medical charge is about $1 or $2, and hospital service costs from fifty cents to $1 a month. All of these items are deducted by the company from his earnings. The charge for food and other necessaries bought at the company store is likely to be the largest item. If the miner's credit sheet shows $79.31 and his debits come to $26.16, he receives $53.15 in cash. These are averages taken from a company pay-roll for the latter half of November, 1920. If the miner has been out of work part of the period, his debits form a greater share of his earnings. Weeks or months of unemployment, such as are now being experienced, often compel the companies to forego some of these charges and leave the miner nothing.

Miners in West Virginia still use scrip largely in making purchases at the company store. This is issued to them by the company up to the amount of their credit or earnings at the time. Scrip consists either of coupons in perforated sheets or small metal tokens rounded like coins, stamped in various denominations. Some companies accept this scrip in lieu of real money at the pool room, the movie theater and other places beside the company store. The law of West Virginia prohibits companies from issuing scrip in payment of wages, specifying that if such scrip is issued it shall be held to be "a promise to pay the sum specified therein in lawful money"; but companies generally issue the scrip. I have never heard of a case being taken to the courts to settle whether or not its use is lawful. That it encourages spending is undoubted. The general superintendent of a coal company writes: "By giving them [the men] the privilege of handling scrip in this way, much more of it is being spent and the attendance at our theaters would not be so large if we did not allow them to use the scrip for purchasing tickets."

The result of this general mode of life is that many mining towns are unsightly, unhealthful and poorly looked after. Houses are slapped up, seldom repainted and allowed to go unrepaired. The surface privy is nearly everywhere in evidence; it is a prevalent cause of soil pollution and often stands on high ground back of the house, so that its contents are washed toward the bed of the creek. Garbage is collected with indifferent frequency, perhaps once during the hot summer months. There are towns in which tin cans cover the ground in every yard and the whole aspect is one of dreariness and the ugliest of neglect. Children find no playground but the railroad. There is not even a sidewalk. Once in a while you pass belching coke ovens, spewing their fumes and smoke from their open tops directly at the windows and doors of houses close by.

A few towns, on the other hand, are neat, attractive in appearance, well cared for. The houses are substantially built, perhaps even supplied with running water. Garbage and ashes are frequently removed. Some companies offer prizes for the best garden and try in other ways to keep the town pleasant in appearance. Children run in a playground. Here and there a company maintains a dairy herd and sells its employees fresh milk. A bank for savings is sometimes found and men who have been with the company for some time are given free insurance policies. These are the exceptional communities. They prove that it is not necessary to live in the midst of dirt and unsightliness even if you do work for a coal mining corporation.

For all of this strange type of existence there is historical and not ungenerous explanation. The first companies to come into the territory had to bring their civilization with them. Men were needed to work the mines, and men must be provided for if they are to live. Houses were built, therefore, and next the necessaries of life had to be secured. The company built a store in which it sold provisions to its employees. Children became more and more numerous; education being essential, a school was built. Perhaps this was followed by a pool room or a movie theater. By successive stages a community was produced. But each expenditure resulting in an addition to the town's activities was made by the coal company. The company owned the land all around, and when the town was built the company owned the town. What began as a means of taking care of the emergent needs of people became a settled condition everywhere. Today four hundred thousand men, women and children in West Virginia are living this subservient existence. They are caught up in a civilization within a civilization—an alien order imbedded in democracy.

There is no escape from it for them. Its paternalism touches their lives at every point. They cannot initiate or take part in any of those little ways of controlling one's environment that are the common pride of normal small towns from New England to the mountains of the West. Any collective voice among them is smothered; they are the recipients of what others think is good for them. Many might not know what to do at first with a degree of control over their own and their group life if they had it, but the process of learning might be of benefit to them.

One way of exercising some measure of control over the conditions of their life and work has been open to them. That has been through affiliation with the United Mine Workers of America. By belonging to a labor union strong enough to negotiate with the organized groups of their employers, they have been able to find an outlet for those impulses of self-expression that lie dormant in every man, and to improve the outward conditions of their lives. I do not know of any adequate analysis that has ever been made of the psychological forces that lead men to labor unionism, but I do know that to miners pressed down by the pervading dependence of their existence in company towns, the opportunity afforded by unions for joining with their fellows in some kind of collective effort may seem a welcome escape.

Company-Owned Americans
By Arthur Gleason

The following article, appearing in the June 12, 1920, issue of the Nation, *provides a good overview of how the system worked. Writer Arthur Gleason reveals how miners were the tools, as well as the victims, of company rule.*

In the non-union counties, houses are owned by the coal companies. Justice is administered by the coal companies. Constitutional rights are interpreted by the coal companies. Food and clothing are sold (thought not exclusively) in company stores. The miners worship in a company church are preached at by a company pastor, play pool in the company Y.M.C.A.; gain education in a company school; receive treatment from a company doctor and hospital; die on company land. From the cradle to the grave, they draw breath by the grace of the sometimes absentee coal owner, one of whose visible representations is the deputy sheriff, a public official in the pay of the coal owner. As a worker under similar conditions once said: "We work in *his* plant. We live in *his* house. Our children to go to *his* school. On Sunday we go to hear *his* preacher. And when we die we are buried in *his* cemetery."

The employees live in *company houses*. Everything belongs to the mine owners, and home ownership is not permitted. The lease of the Logan Mining Company reads that when the miner's employment ceases, "either for cause or without cause the right of said employee and his family to use and occupy premises shall simultaneously end and terminate." The miners generally pay $8 a month for a four-room house, a dollar for coal, 50 cents to a dollar for lights. Fulton Mitchell, deputy sheriff, states:

> My understanding is that most of the companies have a form of lease, and when they lease to miners they reserve the right to object to any person other than employees coming on their possessions.

They do object. Mr. A. Bays is a traveling salesman who "works" the Logan District. He describes it:

Every operation has its armed guard—usually two. I was served with a little notice by a deputy sheriff in Logan, at Logan Court House, Fult Mitchell, to not go up Island Creek any more, that it was dangerous and I was liable to get shot. I had an option on a piece of coal land. The notice served on me by this man Mitchell forbade me using the railroad going up there and back.

The children of the employees receive *company-aided education*, E.F. Scaggs is Logan County Superintendent of Schools. He says:

We have 250 schools, every teacher counts a school, with a school population of 10,361. Actual enrollment 8,650. There are three districts. In every district in the county the salaries of the teachers are supplemented. The Stone Branch Coal Co. proposed if I would get them a teacher, they would pay $15 on the salary. The Board of Education pays $1,125 for a principal at the Omar Schools. The Main Island Creek Coal Co. made it $2,500. J.W. Miller at Ethel is being paid $15 a month by the Coal Companies. The Coal Companies at a number of places have built schoolhouses, and it cost them from seven down to five and up to eight thousand dollars, and they are waiting on the board until the board is financially able to reimburse them. A lot of medical inspection is being looked after in the schools by company physicians.

The company stimulates *religion*. Mr. W.O. Percival superintends the Island Creek Coal Company, and says he dismissed Dan Chapple for talking unionism. He adds:

We have one Y.M.C.A. located at Whitmans (H.C. Mix) and one at Monaville (J.G. Suttles). We contribute $1,000 a year to each Y.M.C.A. The county employed teachers for six months, and the Island Creek Coal Co. extended this term on all schools for three months, and the expense for teachers was $4,360.50. At the school buildings we also supplied such things as slides, teeter-totters, and such things that cost us $600. I don't believe we mentioned the church game. On the churches, we have one Union Church, one Catholic, one

Greek Catholic, and the two Y.M.C.A.'s are used for Sunday School. One church and two schoolhouses are used by the Negroes. We also operate a sanitary dairy. The company contributes enough to cover the service that they render us.

The Logan Mining Company employs 600 men, and is managed by J.J. Ross. Mr. Ross says:

In 1916 our company paid an 18 per cent dividend; in 1917, 12 per cent. Our company contributes about $50 a month toward the minister at Earling, $40 a month at Dingess Run, and also contributes to the Y.M.C.A. on Island Creek. I have always been opposed to unionization. I object to groups dealing with us to this extent. I don't think they can make their wants known as well as they would individually. We pay the deputy at Monaville. We did pay the man on Dingess Run extra, but I don't know whether we do now or not, and at Earling we pay the man extra. We try to consider our employees and ourselves the same as one large family, realizing that the company must make a reasonable profit if they want to do the best they can for the men in the way of wages and living conditions.

The coal companies subsidize *health*. Dr. R.R. Vaughn states:

The United States Coal and Oil Company of Holden own a hospital. They check off from their men to pay for that hospital or to take care of it. My own employment is by assessment on the men. The married men are assessed $1.20 a month, and the single men 70 cents a month—checked off from the pay roll.

CHAPTER II

CHAPTER II
Revolution:
The Paint Creek–Cabin Creek Strike

In April, 1912, the first of the southern West Virginia Mine Wars erupted in the Paint Creek–Cabin Creek Districts of Kanawha County.

The strike quickly assumed ominous dimensions. The founder and first president of the American Federation of Labor, Samuel Gompers, went to great lengths to explain to his fellow unionists what the Paint Creek–Cabin Creek strike was about. Gompers stressed its importance, not only for the miners involved in it, but also for workers throughout the nation. In so doing, Gompers provided additional historic background on the plight of the southern West Virginia miner in the pre-union company town, and gave us a brief but good description of the 1912–1913 strike.

Russianized West Virginia: Corporate Perversion of American Concepts of Liberty and Human Justice—Organized Labor to the Rescue
By Samuel Gompers

In this article, written for the American Federationist *after the strike was settled, Samuel Gompers describes the spirit of the union movement and the people who propelled it. "Normal human beings possessing a spark of independence and ambition cannot be oppressed beyond a certain limit of endurance," he writes. "The West Virginia miners struck to free themselves from intolerable conditions."*

Gompers was especially critical of the West Virginia government, which he found to be guilty of numerous sins—both omission and commission. It should be pointed out that when Gompers wrote about "Russianized" West Virginia, he was referring to czarist Russia.

The long, hard struggle of the miners of West Virginia still goes on. That statement carries with it little significance to many, but to those who know conditions among those mountaineer miners and who are gifted with some imaginative insight, it brings up a story of a most desolate life and of great social injustice: it leads to dreary little mountain cabins, hardships, and monotonous grinding toil without many of the necessities or the comforts of life and with all the degradation attached to an economic despotism under which the workers were compelled to spend their meager wages at the companies' stores, powerless to influence conditions of work, unable to free themselves from enslaving debts. These men had sunk almost into the depths of despair, down even to peonage and almost to slavery.

For years agitation to organize these miners has been carried on under great difficulties. Officials of the United Mine Workers and representative labor men have gone among them. But the seeds of agitation and education did not fall upon rocky soil, though long dormant yet

they lived to bear fruit. Last year the miners were stirred to despera-
tion by their wrongs. In the beginning the uprising was perhaps not a
concerted action, but as scattered groups rebelled against existing conditions, the movement became unified and insistent. The men in grim
determination united in an effort that entailed suffering and privation.

But normal human beings possessing a spark of independence and
ambition cannot be oppressed beyond a certain limit of endurance.
The West Virginia miners struck to free themselves from intolerable
conditions. This strike raised a constitutional issue of importance not
only to workmen but also to all who value constitutional government.
The Governor of the State declared that district under martial law; civil
law, the writ of habeas corpus, trial by jury, were suspended. The Constitution of the United States denies Congress the power to suspend
the writ of habeas corpus "unless when in cases of rebellion or invasion
the public safety may require it." Those powers which are prohibited
to Congress are also prohibited to the States. The constitution of the
State of West Virginia declares that "the privilege of the writ of habeas
corpus shall not be suspended. No person shall be held to answer for
treason, felony, or other crime not cognizable by a justice, unless on
presentment or indictment of a grand jury." Nevertheless, martial law
was proclaimed and under it the leaders of the strikers were arrested
and brought before a military commission. Through their attorneys
they demanded habeas corpus proceedings, which were denied them.
Judge Littlepage of the Circuit Court of Kanawha County who agreed
with the contentions of the miners, issued an order forbidding the
military court to try the prisoners. The court's order was ignored
and disregarded.

The miners' appeal to the Supreme Court of the State was denied
by the majority decision. Judge Ira E. Robinson wrote a dissenting
opinion in which he said:

> It is claimed that the power given by the constitution to the Gov-
> ernor as commander-in-chief of the military forces of the State,
> to call out the same to execute the laws, suppress insurrection
> and repel invasion, authorized a proclamation of martial law.
> Are these words to undo every other guaranty in the instru-
> ment? Can we overturn the many clear, direct, and explicit pro-
> visions, all tending to protect against substitution the will of
> one for the will of the people, by merest implication from the

provision quoted? That provision gives the Governor power to use the militia to execute the laws as the constitution and legislative acts made in pursuance thereof provide they shall be executed. It certainly gives him no authority to execute them otherwise. In the execution of the laws the constitution itself must be executed as the superior law. The Governor may use the militia to suppress insurrection and repel in invasion. But that use is only for the purpose of executing and upholding the laws. He can not use the militia in such a way as to oust the laws of the land. It is put into his hands to demand allegiance and obedience to the laws. It, therefore, can not be used by him for the trial of civil offenses according to his own will and law; for, so to use it would to subvert the very purpose for which it is put into his hands. By the power of the militia he may, if the necessity exists, arrest and detain any citizen offending against the laws; but he can not imprison him at his will, because the constitution guarantees to that offender trial by jury, the judgment of his peers. He may use military force where force in disobedience to the laws demands it; but military force against one violating the laws of the land can have no place in the trial and punishment of the offender. The necessity for military force is at an end when the force of the offender in his violation of the law is overcome by his arrest and detention. There may be force used in apprehending the offender and bringing him to constitutional justice, but surely none can be applied in finding his guilt and fixing the punishment.

Public interest was diverted from the miners to the conflict between military and civil government. It was not true that the civil tribunals of the State were unable to deal with all offenders against the laws. No invasion had occurred; no civil war existed. If there was it must be classified as a private war of the feudal coal barons. Even in medieval times private wars were forbidden and repressed by the State. Is it wise for a modern State to identify private quarrels of the coal operators or any employers with constitutional government and overturn constitutional law in order to protect them? This is indeed a grave issue. The decision of the State Supreme Court of Appeals caused protesting Judge Littlepage to dissolve his order and the drumhead court-martial was permitted to try citizens even though regular courts were capable of performing that function. Military government had eliminated civil government.

After the present Governor took office, he personally investigated conditions, freed many of the "prisoners of war," but did not then abolish martial law. However, he used his influence to assist the miners to secure an agreement with the operators under which work could be resumed.

On April 26, an agreement was reached between the miners' representatives in convention at Charleston and the mine operators. The basic terms of the agreement were: checkweighmen to be chosen by miners; semi-monthly pay; no discrimination against any miners and the right of miners to purchase necessities at independent stores; nine-hour workday.

But the operators failed to abide by the terms of the agreement. Although they made a pretense of employing the strikers, in a short time they began discriminating against and dismissing them. The situation became so intolerable that another strike was begun in the latter part of June. On July 15, the Paint Creek miners secured an agreement for the West Virginia miners providing recognition of the union with the check-off system, the nine-hour workday, and checkweighmen. July 29, Cabin Creek and Coal Creek miners entered into an agreement with their mine operators containing the following terms: recognition of the union and the right to organize; semi-monthly pay; nine-hour workday; checkweighmen; no compulsion to trade at company stores.

In the New River District a convention of the operators and miners was called to meet in Charleston, but only the miners came. However, a conference afterwards determined upon the terms of an agreement which was ratified. This agreement recognized the right of the miners to organize and to expend their wages wherever they pleased; provided for the semi-monthly pay-day, checkweighmen and arbitration of disputes; and specified that there should be no discrimination against strikers.

In addition, the West Virginia Legislature enacted a law which practically abolishes the mine guard system, thus freeing the miners from the rule of the justly hated regime of Baldwin-Felts brutality. Such progress indicates that the West Virginia miners are entering upon a new era of freedom and opportunity. The present agreements will supply the means of self-protection and the attainment of yet better and fairer terms of employment.

The miners have learned from their experiences of the last ten years and the recent strike, the imperative necessity for organization for strength and for a means of voicing their wrongs and needs. The work of agitation, education, and organization will continue until all the miners are given the opportunity of uniting for the common uplift.

For the public—or more correctly, the other workers and employers—there are more serious and more complex problems of justice. All the constituted forces of government were exerted in behalf of property, material things. To this end civil authority was displaced for military force. Mine operators were permitted to station armed guards upon their property. Wherever disturbances or bloodshed occurred, it was always the miners who were arrested and not the mine owners, their brutal minions, and guards. Yet miners were killed, too—are not their lives as valuable as those of the guards? Are not men struggling for personal rights, economic independence, ideals for a better life, entitled to protection, safety, and liberty under our social arrangements? Shall martial law displace civil authority and shall things override human beings? Wealth, indeed, is necessary and valuable; but wealth should serve the needs of men, not enslave them. Freedom cannot exist where human beings are subordinated to things.

There is another question of vital importance to the miners of the Kanawha Valley that must be solved by the government authorities—the extent and scope of the rights of private ownership. The coal corporations own vast contiguous tracts of land in West Virginia and claim the absolute right to do what they will with one hundred thousand acres. The only roads through this land are those permitted by the companies; the only houses and villages, those constructed and owned by the company; no church or post-office can be erected or used without the approval of the owner; sanitation, school, social intercourse, business transactions, are all subject to the interference of holders of the proprietary rights. No one is allowed on that private soil who has not given a satisfactory account of himself and his mission to the police authority employed and directed by the owners. In short, the coal operators who own this section of the State arrogate to themselves all rights of government except such as must be conceded to the county. To make the situation more vivid and forcible, take another illustration. Suppose the United States Steel Corporation had been in existence in 1800 and had realized the value of the Louisiana Territory. The purchase price the United States paid for that territory would have presented no difficulties to the United States Steel Corporation. After purchasing that immense tract of land, approximately nine hundred thousand square miles in extent, what would have been the property rights of the corporation? Would the Steel Corporation have been permitted the absolute unrestricted right of government over that vast territory, controlling municipal affairs, sanitation, police, locomotion, the privilege of assemblage, the erection of churches and school-houses, and the control of doctrines and theories taught by schools and churches? The difference in the sizes of the two territories does not affect the underlying principle. Because the miners of West Virginia must work for coal operators who own all the adjacent lands, does it follow that these companies can select their clergymen for them, can control sanitary conditions, can regulate their associations, can censor their literature, can deny them the right to walk in certain directions and to band themselves together for legitimate purposes or to make any effort to better themselves and their families?

Until some limitations are placed upon the absolutism of these absentee coal operators in West Virginia, the government of West Virginia will continue to be Russianized and the people can be naught but serfs. Organized labor has forced these conditions and perversions of justice upon public attention and now demands that the wrongs be righted. In West Virginia, as in the world over, the economic movement for freedom will work a mighty transformation in political thought and practices.

REVISED MAP OF THE UNITED STATES
Organizers compared West Virginia coal operators to the Czar of Russia, and the United Mine Workers Journal *took the idea a step further.* COURTESY OF *UMWJ.*

Civil War in the
West Virginia Coal Mines:
The Mine Guards
By Harold E. West

Harold E. West reported on events in West Virginia for the Baltimore Sun. *His articles were considered among the most thorough and insightful written about the Paint Creek–Cabin Creek strike. Consequently, West's articles were reprinted in numerous places. The following first appeared in the* Survey, *April 5, 1913.*

"I went to West Virginia absolutely unprejudiced," the Baltimore reporter wrote, "with the idea of telling the truth about the situation. I found conditions I did not believe could exist in America and I am no novice in the newspaper game, having seen some pretty raw things in my time."

Attached is a section of his reporting that discusses the mine guard system and the role in the strike of the "thugs," as the miners called them. The article allows the reader to begin to understand why the miners hated the company mine guards so much.

These mine guards are an institution all along the creeks in the non-union sections of the state. They are as a rule supplied by the Baldwin-Felts Detective Agency of Roanoke and Bluefield. It is said the total number in the mining regions of West Virginia reaches well up to 2,500. Ordinarily they are recruited from the country towns of Virginia and West Virginia, preferably the towns in the hill country, and frequently have been the "bad men" of the towns from which they came. And these towns have produced some pretty hard characters. The ruffian of the West Virginia town would not take off his hat to the desperado of the wildest town of the wildest West.

These Baldwin guards who are engaged by the mining companies to do their "rough work" take the place of the Pinkertons who formerly were used for such work by the coal companies. Since the Homestead strike in the steel mill years ago when the Pinkertons fired into the strikers and killed a number of them, this class of business has gradually drifted away from the Pinkertons and much of it has been acquired by the Baldwin-Felts agency.

In explanation of the employment of these guards, the operators say that their property must be guarded, that the state does not give them sufficient protection. Men who do service as mine guards cannot be expected to be "lady-like." They deal with desperate characters and are constantly in peril. The guards act on the principle that they must strike first if they are to strike at all, and evidence shows that they have not the slightest hesitancy about striking first. The operators also say that it is necessary to require explanations of strangers in order to keep out labor agitators and to prevent the miners from being annoyed and threatened by them.

No class of men on earth are more cordially hated by the miners than these same mine guards who are engaged to "protect" them from annoyance by outsiders. Before the state troops went into the region and took their rifles away from them, the mine guards went about everywhere, gun in hand, searching trains, halting strangers, ejecting undesirables, turning miners out of their houses and doing whatever "rough work" the companies felt they needed to have done. Stories of their brutality are told on every hand along the creeks. Some are unquestionably exaggerated, but the truth of many can be proved and has been proved.

In spite of the work they do some of these Baldwin men seem to be decent enough chaps to those who are not "undesirable," and they are, for the most part, intelligent. But they are in the mines for a definite purpose. They understand what that purpose is and they have no hesitancy about "delivering the goods." They seem to have no illusions about their work. It pays well and if brutality is required, why, brutality "goes." Whenever possible they are clothed with some semblance of the authority of the law, either by being sworn in as railroad detectives, as constables or deputy sheriffs.

But for all that a number have been indicted for offenses ranging from common assault to murder. In every case, however, bail has been ready and it is rare that charges against them have been brought to trial. Some of the assault cases in which they have figured have been of great brutality, yet rarely has any serious trouble resulted for the guards. They go about their work in a purely impersonal way. If a worker becomes too inquisitive, if he shows too much independence, or complains too much about his condition, he is beaten up some night as he passes under a coal tipple, but the man who does the beating has no feeling against him personally; it is simply a matter of business to him.

Just what the services of the guards cost the coal companies is difficult to learn. The companies contract with the Baldwin-Felts agency for them and the sum they pay is kept a secret. It is generally understood that the guards get about $5 a day, or between $100 to $125 a month. A man in the mines who knows one of them intimately told me he "picked up his gun" for $105 a month. When a man joins the Baldwins he "picks up his gun," and that stamps him forevermore with his former associates, if they were of the laboring class, as an enemy and a man who has turned his back on his class and his kind.

Unless the miners are beaten in this fight, and utterly and completely beaten, there will never be a settlement of the difficulty here until the mine guards are driven from the region. "The mine guards must go," is the slogan of the striking miner everywhere. His going is of more importance than an increase in pay. There will be no lasting peace in the region until they are gone. All over the state when the situation in the Kanawha Valley comes up for discussion you are told that the mine guards are at the bottom of the trouble. They are the Ishmaelites of the coal regions for their hands are supposed to be against every miner, and every miner's hand is raised against them. They go about in constant peril—they are paid to face danger and they face it all the time. But they are afraid, for they never know when they may get a charge of buckshot or a bullet from an old Springfield army rifle that will make a hole in a man's body big enough for you to put your fist in. A number of guards have been killed since the trouble began, and it is generally understood that some of these were buried by their fellows and nothing said about it, there being a disposition down in the mines not to let the other side know when either side scores and gets a man.

Senate Testimony

What follow are some personal accounts of the callousness and brutality of the guards. These stories are taken from testimony before a U.S. Senate committee that investigated the Paint Creek–Cabin Creek strike.

Gianiana Seville, the wife of a Paint Creek miner, and Philip Cajano, a miner from Ohley, describe how they and their families suffered for their union activism at the hands of the Baldwin-Felts agents. Their stories offer additional insight into the miners' fear, resentment, and hatred for the guards.

Testimony of Gianiana Seville to the U.S. Senate

MR. HOUSTON: Where do you live?

MRS. SEVILLE: At Handley.

MR. HOUSTON: Did you ever live on Paint Creek?

MRS. SEVILLE: Yes, sir.

MR. HOUSTON: At what point?

MRS. SEVILLE: Banner Hollow.

MR. HOUSTON: Are you married?

MRS. SEVILLE: Yes, sir.

MR. HOUSTON: How many children?

MRS. SEVILLE: Four.

MR. HOUSTON: Is your husband living?

MRS. SEVILLE: Yes.

MR. HOUSTON: What is his occupation? What was his occupation when he lived on Paint Creek?

MRS. SEVILLE: Always in the mine. He went to Paint Creek when they started the railroad, and then he went into the mines until the strike.

MR. HOUSTON: For what company was your husband working on Paint Creek?

MRS. SEVILLE: I do not know the name of the company.

MR. HOUSTON: On whose property do you live?

MRS. SEVILLE: On the property of the company.

MR. HOUSTON: Were you ever evicted from your home by the company guards? If so, give the circumstances. Were you ever put out of the company's property by the mine guards?

MRS. SEVILLE: No. We left ourselves because we were afraid they would kill us.

MR. HOUSTON: Were you ever mistreated by the mine guards?

MRS. SEVILLE: Yes, sir.

MR. HOUSTON: What was the mistreatment?

MRS. SEVILLE: On the 10th day of June I got out of bed to hear some shooting. When I got out of bed I heard this shooting, and I went to the door to see what was the matter. I saw the guards coming down the hill. Those guards were going into the other neighbor houses there, and they began to pick up the men that they could find in the houses. Then they came into our house, and they opened the door, and then they came in and looked under the bed; and then on the bed was my baby, and it was asleep, and I told the guards to let the baby alone because the baby was on the bed; and they struck me and I fell down, and then they kicked me in the stomach and they hit me with their fists in here [indicating], and then they knocked me down. The first they said when they got in, they turned up the bed, then, and they wanted to get in, and they asked me to give them the keys of the trunk, and I refused to do it, and then they hit me and threw me down.

SENATOR KENYON: How many were there at the time?

MRS. SEVILLE: About 20.

SENATOR KENYON: How many struck you?

MRS. SEVILLE: Two.

SENATOR KENYON: Did they knock you down?

MRS. SEVILLE: He hit me with his fists and then he kicked me.

SENATOR KENYON: Did they knock you down?

MRS. SEVILLE: Yes, sir.

SENATOR KENYON: Ask her.

MRS. SEVILLE: Yes; and then they kicked me and took me by the arm and raised me up.

SENATOR KENYON: Did they kick you after you were down?

MRS. SEVILLE: When I wanted to go on to the bed to get the baby.

SENATOR KENYON: Did they? Ask her this question correctly. Did they kick you after you were down?

MRS. SEVILLE: I have explained that one of them grabbed me by the arm, you know, and I wanted to get the baby, and then one kicked me in the stomach, and one knocked me down and hit me with his fist.

SENATOR KENYON: Now, when was this?

MRS. SEVILLE: The 5th day of June.

SENATOR KENYON: 1912?

MRS. SEVILLE: 1912.

MR. HOUSTON: What was your physical condition at that time?

MRS. SEVILLE: I was pregnant for five months.

MR. HOUSTON: What was the result of this assault made upon you?

MRS. SEVILLE: I will explain it to you that when I received it my husband was in Ohio hunting for a job, and I sent a letter to him that I was very sick and that I might die. And I was sick until the 14th of August, when they took me to the hospital at Hansford and the baby was born dead. (. . .)

Testimony of Philip Cajano to the U.S. Senate

Philip Cajano was called as a witness, and, having been sworn by the chairman, testified as follows:

MR. BELCHER: How do you spell your name?

MR. CAJANO: I don't know.

MR. BELCHER: Where are you from?

MR. CAJANO: Ohley.

MR. BELCHER: Have you had any trouble up there recently with the mine guards?

MR. CAJANO: I have had no trouble with the mine guards, but they brought me—

MR. BELCHER: Speak up loud. What trouble have you had up there in the last few days, if any?

MR. CAJANO: I went up to join the union on the meeting night, and I went to work the next morning and they fired me already.

MR. BELCHER: Who fired you?

MR. CAJANO: The superintendent, M.T. Davis.

MR. BELCHER: M.T. Davis?

MR. CAJANO: Yes.

MR. BELCHER: Did he discharge you for joining the miners' union?

MR. CAJANO: Yes, sir. Well, no; he didn't tell me. I asked him what he fired me for, and he says I know why he fired me; I know what he fired me for.

MR. BELCHER: Then what happened after that conversation?

MR. CAJANO: Then I got fired and at night when I came down to pack my grip to get out of there he put three fellows on me to lick me.

MR. BELCHER: Put three fellows on you for what?

MR. CAJANO: To lick me; to whip me.

MR. BELCHER: Did they do it?

MR. CAJANO: Yes, sir; one fellow by the name of Stump, he jumped on me first, and he says, "I got to lick you." I says, "I don't want any trouble off of you." He says, "Well, I am going to lick you." I says, "What are you going to lick me for?" He says, "You know what I am going to lick you for." And he gave me a punch here [indicating on the cheek] and another here [indicating other side of face], and then he kicked me and hit me on both sides of my face, and then kicked me.

MR. BELCHER: Where was Davis at this time?

MR. CAJANO: Davis was right there with his hands in his hip pockets, ready for the automatic pistol.

MR. BELCHER: Did he try to prevent these men from assaulting you?

MR. CAJANO: No, sir; he says to the boy, "Go ahead, Stump." He says, "If he ever makes a move to hit you, I will fix him."

MR. BELCHER: How much do you weigh?

MR. CAJANO: Me?

MR. BELCHER: Yes.

MR. CAJANO: I weigh about 125 pounds.

MR. BELCHER: Did you have your glasses on at that time?

MR. CAJANO: Yes.

MR. BELCHER: What kind of lenses are those—compound lenses?

MR. CAJANO: Near-sighted glasses.

MR. BELCHER: Had you been guilty of any misconduct or disorderly in any way that caused Davis to discharge you?

MR. CAJANO: No, sir; not guilty at all. I done my work right and everything else, and had been there in my time and done my duty.

MR. BELCHER: When did this happen?

MR. CAJANO: Well, that happened last week.

MR. BELCHER: Last week?

MR. CAJANO: On Tuesday we had a meeting and next day he fired me.

MR. BELCHER: And that night they beat you?

MR. CAJANO: That night they beat me.

MR. BELCHER: Where was this at?

MR. CAJANO: At Ohley.

MR. BELCHER: That is on Cabin Creek?

MR. CAJANO: Yes.

MR. BELCHER: And Ohley is one of the mines of the Cabin Creek Consolidated Coal Co., of which Mr. M.T. Davis is president; or do you know?

MR. CAJANO: Yes.

SENATOR MARTINE: Did you stand still and allow them to punch you?

MR. CAJANO: I had to stay right still, because they were too many and I was alone.

SENATOR MARTINE: A pretty tough situation, to stand still and be punched, even thought you were alone.

MR. CAJANO: Yes; and the super was right there to take the men's part, and with his hand on his automatic and telling them, "Go ahead, boys."

SENATOR MARTINE: Do you know the man's name who said that?

MR. CAJANO: Do I know the man's name who said that?

SENATOR MARTINE: Yes.

MR. CAJANO: It was Davis himself.

SENATOR MARTINE: Did he have military clothes on?

MR. CAJANO: Military clothes on him? He had clothes just as well as I had.

SENATOR MARTINE: But he was not a militiaman?

MR. CAJANO: No.

SENATOR MARTINE: Davis was the superintendent or owner—

MR. CAJANO: Yes, sir.

SENATOR MARTINE: Or coal operator?

MR. CAJANO: Yes, sir; he was the superintendent.

SENATOR MARTINE: No doubt about that?

MR. CAJANO: No.

MR. BELCHER: How far can you see with your glasses off?

MR. CAJANO: I can't see a man from here to the window with my glasses off.

MR. STEDMAN: Indicating 15 or 20 feet.

SENATOR KENYON: How old are you?

MR. CAJANO: Twenty-two.

SENATOR KENYON: Where were you born?

MR. CAJANO: In the old country.

SENATOR KENYON: Whereabouts?

MR. CAJANO: Italy.

SENATOR KENYON: When did you come to this country?

(. . .)

MR. KNIGHT: You say it was Mr. M.T. Davis who told these men to hit you and discharged you?

MR. CAJANO: He discharged me for joining the union, I suppose. I told him, "Why did you discharge me for?" and he says, "You know what you are discharged for"; so I went home in the nighttime, and while I was going home to pack my grip there was the Stump boy and two more boys right there, and the Stump boy came over and says, "I have got to whip you," and I says, "I don't want any trouble with you." He says, "I have got to whip you," and he gave me a punch and made a grab for my glasses once and gave me a punch here and gave me a kick; and Davis was out there with his hands in his hip pocket, with his hand on the automatic, and he says, "Go ahead, boys; if he jumps on you, I will fix him."

SENATOR KENYON: How do you know he had his hand on his automatic?

MR. CAJANO: He showed it to me more than once.

SENATOR KENYON: Was he in the habit of carrying it in his pocket?

MR. CAJANO: He carries it all the time.

SENATOR KENYON: That is why you thought it was in his pocket? You did not see the gun?

MR. CAJANO: He had his hand on his automatic, and I seen the automatic.

SENATOR KENYON: Could you see the hand on the gun?

MR. CAJANO: Yes.

(. . .)

MR. KNIGHT: Was anybody there when Stump assaulted you except Davis, yourself, and these three miners?

MR. CAJANO: There was Kelly and the mine guard there, and the fellow that runs the motor—I don't know what his name is—and there was a whole lot of them right there: there were about seven of them, anyway.

MR. KNIGHT: Where was it?

MR. CAJANO: Right on the other side of the creek it was that I was going over to get my clothes.

MR. KNIGHT: Was it near the store or office?

MR. CAJANO: No, sir; it was on the private road—on the county road.

MR. KNIGHT: How far was it from the house where you lived?

MR. CAJANO: Just about 25 feet.

MR. KNIGHT: What were those men doing there; standing there when you came up?

MR. CAJANO: Well, they were standing there just to beat me, I suppose.

MR. KNIGHT: Were they waiting for you when you came along.

MR. CAJANO: Yes, sir; they were waiting for me when I came along.

MR. KNIGHT: You say Stump opened the conversation by saying he had to lick you.

MR. CAJANO: Yes.

MR. KNIGHT: And while he was licking you Davis told him to go ahead, and if you made a move he would fix you?

MR. CAJANO: Yes. (. . .)

"Solidarity Forever"

In 1912, Ralph Chaplin was an unknown reporter for a labor newspaper in Huntington, West Virginia, the Socialist and Labor Star. While working on that paper, he watched in fascination as the miners' walkout at Paint and Cabin Creeks evolved into a massive strike, full of revolutionary potential. As a reporter, Chaplin not only covered the strike, he helped smuggle news into and out of the strike zone after Governor William Glasscock placed the area under martial law.

Chaplin was eventually driven out of West Virginia for his radical labor activities. The spirit and solidarity of the miners, however, stayed with him as he became a nationally known labor artist, poet, balladeer, and writer. He was also well known as an organizer for the revolutionary union, the Industrial Workers of the World (I.W.W.).

Memories of the 1912 West Virginia strike came to fruition one evening in January, 1915. While lying on a rug in his living room, the labor activist grabbed a pencil and began putting his thoughts and recollections onto paper. Stanza after stanza came pouring out, until he had written what would become the most popular labor song in the United States, "Solidarity Forever." Sung to the tune of "John Brown's Body," the song would be heard on picket lines and in union halls throughout the country for decades to come.

"I wanted a song to be full of revolutionary fervor and to have a chorus that was singing and defiant," Chaplin wrote. And it was. What follows are the stanzas of "Solidarity Forever," labor's anthem inspired by the Paint Creek–Cabin Creek strike.

Solidarity Forever

(Tune: John Brown's Body)

(by Ralph Chaplin, January, 1915, 9th Edition, 1916)

With Power and Dignity

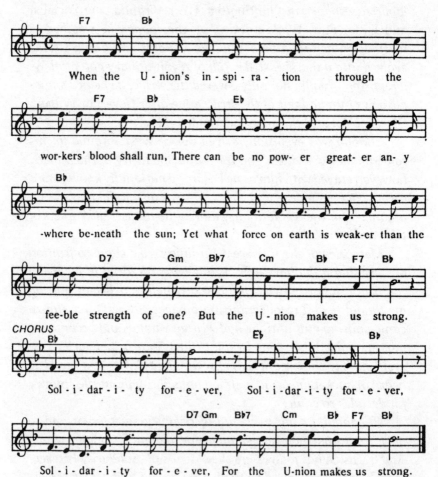

When the U-nion's in-spi-ra-tion through the wor-kers' blood shall run, There can be no pow-er great-er an-y-where be-neath the sun; Yet what force on earth is weak-er than the fee-ble strength of one? But the U-nion makes us strong.

CHORUS

Sol-i-dar-i-ty for-e-ver, Sol-i-dar-i-ty for-e-ver, Sol-i-dar-i-ty for-e-ver, For the U-nion makes us strong.

When the Union's inspiration
       through the workers' blood shall run,
There can be no power greater
       anywhere beneath the sun;
Yet what force on earth is weaker
       than the feeble strength of one?
But the Union makes us strong.

CHORUS
Solidarity forever, Solidarity forever,
Solidarity forever, For the Union makes us strong.

Is there aught we hold in common
       with the greedy parasite,
Who would lash us into serfdom
       and would crush us with his might?
Is there anything left to us
       but to organize and fight?
For the Union makes us strong. [chorus]

It is we who plowed the prairies;
       built the cities where they trade;
Dug the mines and built the workshops;
       endless miles of railroad laid.
Now we stand outcast and starving,
       'midst the wonders we have made;
But the Union makes us strong. [chorus]

All the world that's owned by idle drones
        is ours and ours alone.
We have laid the wide foundations;
        built it skyward stone by stone.
It is ours, not to slave in,
        but to master and to own,
While the Union makes us strong. [chorus]

They have taken untold millions
        that they never toiled to earn,
But without our brain and muscle
        not a single wheel can turn.
We can break their haughty power;
        gain our freedom when we learn
That the Union makes us strong. [chorus]

In our hands is placed a power
        greater than their hoarded gold;
Greater than the might of armies,
        magnified a thousand-fold.
We can bring to birth a new world
        from the ashes of the old.
For the Union makes us strong. [chorus]

CHAPTER III

CHAPTER III
Battle Weaponry:
The Bull Moose Special

On February 2, 1913, a Kanawha County coal operator, with help from the county sheriff and several Baldwin-Felts mine guards, took a small train on a short ride up Paint Creek hollow. The train included the locomotive, two coaches, and two baggage cars, one of which was rigged with a Gatling gun. When the train reached the colony of striking miners and their families camped at Holly Grove, the gunmen on board opened fire.

Miraculously only one person was killed by the murderous train that local people would come to call the "Death Special" and the "Bull Moose Special." To Maud Estep and her family, however, the single casualty—her husband, Cesco—was tragic enough.

Testimony of Maud Estep
to the U.S. Senate

Mrs. Estep told a U.S. Senate committee about the events that led to her husband's death that night. Her story is another personal account of the brutality not only of that particular conflict, but the society created by the coal industry.

Maud Estep was called as a witness, and, having been sworn by Senator Kenyon, testified as follows:

Direct examination:

MR. BELCHER: What is your husband's name?

MRS. ESTEP: Francis Francesco.

MR. BELCHER: And what is your name?

MRS. ESTEP: Maud Estep.

MR. BELCHER: Mrs. Estep, where do you now reside?

MRS. ESTEP: Holly Grove.

MR. BELCHER: How long have you lived at Holly Grove?

MRS. ESTEP: I have lived there ever since last April.

MR. BELCHER: Where did you live prior to April last?

MRS. ESTEP: On Cabin Creek and Acme.

MR. BELCHER: Is your husband living?

MRS. ESTEP: No, sir.

MR. BELCHER: When did he die?

MRS. ESTEP: The 7th of February.

SENATOR KENYON: You had better put the year in.

MR. BELCHER: What year—February of this year?

MRS. ESTEP: Yes, sir.

MR. BELCHER: What caused his death, if you know?

MRS. ESTEP: Well, he was shot from the train, I suppose; the train went up there, and they were shooting from the train at the house.

MR. BELCHER: Is that what is known as the Bull-Moose train?

MRS. ESTEP: Yes, sir.

MR. BELCHER: At what time in the night was this, Mrs. Estep?

MRS. ESTEP: Between 10 and 11 o'clock, some time; I don't just exactly know what time that was by my time.

MR. BELCHER: Where were you living at Holly Grove?

MRS. ESTEP: We lived across over on the other side from the station—across the creek.

MR. BELCHER: Were you living in a house?

MRS. ESTEP: Yes, sir.

MR. BELCHER: What was your husband doing immediately before he was shot?

MRS. ESTEP: He was in the house when the train commenced shooting down on the other side. We were all in the house sitting there carrying on and talking. We heard the train come shooting, and he hollered for us to go to the cellar, and he went out the front door—him and some more boys that were in there; they ran out the front door, and I went through the kitchen way, and I never got any farther than the kitchen door; we were all trying to get to the cellar. He was standing hollering for me to go and get into the cellar. It was dark that I could just see the bulk of him. It scared me so—and I had a little one in my arms—that I could not go any farther. His cousin was there on a visit, and after the train commenced shooting he took hold of me and told me not to fall, and about that time a shot struck him in the leg.

SENATOR KENYON: Struck the cousin in the leg?

MRS. ESTEP: Yes, sir; his cousin.

SENATOR KENYON: You go into the cellar of your house right off the ground, do you not?

MRS. ESTEP: Yes, sir.

SENATOR KENYON: The house was elevated a few feet above the ground?

MRS. ESTEP: Yes, sir; there had been a cellar under there, and it was torn down, and they were fixing it up, so if any trouble started I could go there.

SENATOR KENYON: Was there any shooting in town that night?

MRS. ESTEP: No, sir; not until the train came.

SENATOR KENYON: How old was your baby?

MRS. ESTEP: My baby, one I have now, is 2 months old.

SENATOR KENYON: Your baby was not born at that time?

MRS. ESTEP: No, sir.

SENATOR KENYON: Did you have another child, did you say?

MRS. ESTEP: Yes, sir.

SENATOR KENYON: How old was that child?

MRS. ESTEP: He won't be 2 years old until the 16th of September.

SENATOR KENYON: What time was this?

MRS. ESTEP: Between 10 and 11 o'clock.

SENATOR KENYON: Had there been any shooting in the little settlement there before the train came along?

MRS. ESTEP: No, sir; the first thing we heard was shots from the train. I suppose it started from the train. It was away below our house. We live up above the first town where the station is.

SENATOR KENYON: You live where that bridge is?

MRS. ESTEP: Yes, sir.

SENATOR KENYON: That swinging bridge?

MRS. ESTEP: Yes, sir.

SENATOR KENYON: The bridge across the creek there?

MRS. ESTEP: Yes, sir.

SENATOR KENYON: What time of night was this?

MRS. ESTEP: Between 10 and 11 o'clock—that is, by our time.

SENATOR KENYON: Had there been any disorder in the settlement that night? Had you heard any shooting before that time?

MRS. ESTEP: No, sir.

SENATOR KENYON: Could you hear this train coming?

MRS. ESTEP: We heard it after it commenced shooting. We had not heard it before. We had our doors closed.

SENATOR KENYON: Could you see the train?

MRS. ESTEP: No, sir; I never went out the front way at all.

SENATOR KENYON: When did you know your husband was shot?

MRS. ESTEP: I didn't know he was killed until after the train quit shooting, and I heard some of them speak to him and call his name, and I never heard him answer.

SENATOR KENYON: Did he get into the cellar?

MRS. ESTEP: No, sir.

SENATOR KENYON: The body was outside of the house and near the back corner of the house.

MRS. ESTEP: Yes, sir; right on the outside of the house, pretty near to the back corner of the house.

SENATOR KENYON: Could you tell whether the house was hit by bullets?

MRS. ESTEP: It seemed to me like it was, but I have never been back over there to see. I left there that night in the night and I have not been back.

(. . .)

MR. BELCHER: What was the last thing your husband said to you, Mrs. Estep? Was he trying to get you in the cellar?

MRS. ESTEP: Yes, sir; the last I heard him he was hollering for me to go in and get in the cellar. Hessie Willis was in there with me, and me and her went out the back way, and he was standing there; I could just see him in the dark; I could just see the bulk of him in the dark, and he was saying; "You women get in right quick; get in the cellar."

MR. KNIGHT: If these men had any guns, you didn't see them?

MRS. ESTEP: No, sir.

MR. BELCHER: You never heard them say anything about shooting up anybody, did you?

MRS. ESTEP: No, sir.

MR. BELCHER: And they had just come over there and, so far as you know, were acting in an orderly manner?

MRS. ESTEP: Yes, sir; they had just come in there. It happened so quick after they came in that I disremember them coming in.

MR. BELCHER: Did you hear the train before the shooting give two sharp blasts of whistle?

MRS. ESTEP: No, sir.

MR. BELCHER: You didn't see the train as it went by at all?

MRS. ESTEP: No, sir. (. . .)

Testimony of Lee Calvin
to the U.S. Senate

Lee Calvin was a mine guard on board the "Bull Moose Special" and witnessed the barrage of fire against the unsuspecting gathering of miners. When it was done, Calvin heard the coal operator's order that the train be backed up so they could "give them another round."

So repulsed was he by what he saw and heard, Calvin told the Senate committee about events of that ugly night in Holly Grove. His testimony further documents the bitterness of the strike and gives additional evidence of tactics so brutal that they even offended a company mine guard's sense of decency.

MR. BELCHER: Just prior to your reaching Holly Grove what was done with that train?

MR. CALVIN: When we started up from the junction I was going to explain—

MR. BELCHER: Go ahead.

MR. CALVIN: They were loading guns and every man was getting a rifle, and Walker came over and handed me a rifle and I says, "I don't want no rifle. The sheriff asked me up here tonight. He didn't say I was an officer or what. He says just come up to Mucklow, and so I came." And they were handing the rifles around and they all began getting rifles, and a fellow came through and says, "Don't bother raising the windows, boys, you can shoot through the windows in case there is any shooting." When they got near Holly Grove they commenced turning down the lights.

MR. BELCHER: Who did?

MR. CALVIN: The brakeman. He was on the train. He commenced turning the lights low in our coach, so when the engineer came in front of Holly Grove he gave two short blasts from the whistle. And I was leaning out of the window that way [indicating] and they commenced streaming fire out of the baggage car— you know—flashes, reports, and cracks from the machine gun at a lot of tents and the train went along with a stream of fire which continued coming out of the Gatling gun all along, and in about 20 or 30 seconds there came a flash here and there from the tents—about four came from the tents altogether at about 100 feet apart. Each flash was about 100 feet apart. It would seem that way to me.

MR. BELCHER: Had you seen any shots fired from those tents prior or before the shots were fired from the train?

MR. CALVIN: No; I was leaning out of the window like that, and if I could have got in I wouldn't have been leaning out; but here was a big fellow next to me sitting on my neck, so I couldn't move back from the window, you see. They were all piled in the corners around the car. My head was down on the window looking out that way, and a man sitting on my neck that way, and I couldn't get in.

SENATOR KENYON: You say the shooting commenced as soon as the engineer blew the whistle?

MR. CALVIN: Yes, sir; I was leaning out of the window smoking, and at that a stream of firing commenced.

SENATOR KENYON: Was the whistle blown for a crossing?

MR. CALVIN: No.

SENATOR KENYON: Did you connect the whistle with any signal to commence shooting?

MR. CALVIN: I could not say why he blew the whistle unless it would be prearranged.

SENATOR MARTINE: But you are positive the shooting first began from the car ahead?

MR. CALVIN: From the baggage car.

SENATOR MARTINE: No doubt about that?

MR. CALVIN: No; I was in the first window next to the baggage car on the right-hand side.

(...)

MR. BELCHER: Did you see Quinn Morton after you had been up by Holly Grove?

MR. CALVIN: Yes.

MR. BELCHER: Where did you see him or what was said, if anything, by him?

MR. CALVIN: He came running from the rear end of the coach and wanted Howery to back the train up again until we could give them another round, he said.

MR. BELCHER: To whom did he say that?

MR. CALVIN: He talked to the sheriff.

MR. BELCHER: What did the sheriff say?

MR. CALVIN: I couldn't hear what he said. The sheriff seemed to say there were women and children in the tents, and he would not do it. That is what he seemed to say to him.

SENATOR MARTINE: This man, who in the name of heaven can he be, that would propose to go back and kill more? Is he an ordinary citizen?

MR. JACKSON: He will be before you, Senator.

SENATOR MARTINE: Well, God help us all, then.

MR. JACKSON: Now, I do request you, Senator—

SENATOR MARTINE: I cannot help it, sir.

(. . .)

SENATOR MARTINE: Who was by when this man Paul Morton—is that the name?

MR. JACKSON: Quinn Morton.

SENATOR MARTINE: Quinn Morton. Who heard the conversation besides yourself?

MR. CALVIN: There was no conversation to it, he just came running through the car hollering "Back the train up and we will give them another round."

SENATOR MARTINE: Do you recall the name of any man who was present?

MR. CALVIN: Yes.

SENATOR MARTINE: Was there any comment made afterwards by the sheriff or deputy sheriff as to that suggestion?

MR. CALVIN: No; I didn't hear them make any comment about it.

SENATOR MARTINE: You are sure about the assertion?

MR. CALVIN: Yes.

SENATOR MARTINE: "Let us back up and give them another round"?

MR. CALVIN: Yes.

(. . .)

MR. BELCHER: Did you have any trouble with the mine guards afterwards?

MR. CALVIN: I had trouble with the C. & O. men afterwards on the 4th of March in the Ruffner Hotel.

MR. BELCHER: What was the cause of the trouble?

MR. CALVIN: When I quit up there, I said I wouldn't like to work for the bunch of people like that, and I was downtown, and they sent for me to the hotel and told me George Lenz wanted to see me in the hotel. And I went up to the hotel and went to a room in the Hotel Ruffner, and all the C. & O. men were in there and they locked the door and asked me, "Didn't you say we were a lot of Hoosiers and you wouldn't work with a lot of crazy men springing rifles on people like that?" and I said, "If I did say it I will stick to it." So they slugged me, six or seven hit me, and cut me in the face and everything else.

SENATOR KENYON: Did you present that matter to the county attorney?

MR. CALVIN: No; I didn't bother about it. They just cut the skin off my face with their fists, and the boss of the gang, George Lenz and a fellow named Howery.

(. . .)

MR. BYRNE: Now, Mr. Calvin, you were on the train with Mr. Hill and several deputy-sheriffs who went up to Cabin Creek?

MR. CALVIN: Yes.

MR. BYRNE: I believe you stated that one of the cars was an armed car, armored?

MR. CALVIN: Yes.

MR. BYRNE: That it had a Gatling gun?

MR. CALVIN: A Gatling gun; yes, sir.

MR. BYRNE: Now, what kind of a car was that?

MR. CALVIN: A baggage car.

(. . .)

MR. CALVIN: The shooting came up so sudden that you wouldn't hear any order after it was started. The shooting was all from inside mostly, you know, and you couldn't hear very well.

THE CHAIRMAN: Did the sheriff see them preparing to shoot?

MR. CALVIN: Yes; he saw them getting the rifles there.

THE CHAIRMAN: He saw the preparations were being made to shoot?

MR. CALVIN: He saw the rifles being loaded, I guess.

THE CHAIRMAN: Did he tell them not to shoot?

MR. CALVIN: No.

THE CHAIRMAN: He seemed to be quiet and acquiesced about everything that was going on?

MR. CALVIN: Yes; everything was quiet.

THE CHAIRMAN: I mean did he seem to be quiet and agreeing to everything that was going on?

MR. CALVIN: He did not tell anyone not to shoot.

MR. MONNETT: The lights were turned out, you remember.

MR. CALVIN: But the loading was before the lights were turned down.

MR. JACKSON: I thought the witness said there were two lights turned down low and burning.

MR. CALVIN: They were turned down low; but they started to load the guns when they left the junction, and it is 3 or 4 miles up to where the shooting commenced, and the train was running slowly.

(...)

MR. CALVIN: The machine gun commenced to shoot as soon as the whistle blew two short blasts, and there came kind of a roar. It is different from the report of a rifle, and there was a continuous roar and flashes. I was in the first window next to the baggage car, on the right-hand side going up the creek.

MR. BYRNE: On the right-hand side going up the creek?

MR. CALVIN: Yes, leaning out the window.

MR. BYRNE: When the shooting was over, you say, the train stopped?

MR. CALVIN: No; the train kept on going gradually until it struck the switch at Mucklow. It didn't stop. When the shooting was over it kept gradually going through that way.

MR. BYRNE: You say that someone said, "Let us go back and give them another round"?

MR. CALVIN: Morton came running up to the end where the sheriff was and said, "Let us go back and give them another round."

MR. BYRNE: Did he say that to the sheriff?

MR. CALVIN: Yes.

MR. BYRNE: Did you hear him say that?

MR. CALVIN: I thought that was what was said; it was words to that effect. It might vary a little either way, you know.

MR. BYRNE: You thought that was what he said?

MR. CALVIN: Yes.

MR. BYRNE: Did you hear anyone else make that remark?

MR. CALVIN: There was lots of talk after it was all over.

MR. BYRNE: But I mean there was only one person who said, "Let us go back and give them another round"?

MR. CALVIN: Yes; there might have been a dozen persons say it, but I never heard but that one.

MR. BYRNE: And the sheriff, Mr. Hill, said, "No; we won't do that"?

MR. CALVIN: He said, "There are women and children in those tents; I am not going to do that." I thought that was what he said. It might vary a word or two either way, but I thought that was what he said. (. . .)

Testimony of Quinn Morton
to the U.S. Senate

Quinn Morton was the coal operator aboard the "Bull Moose Special." It was he who allegedly ordered the train to be backed up so that the miners could be exposed to more gunfire.

At the Senate hearings, Senator Martine of New Jersey expressed his outrage at the thought of men of wealth and power using machine guns on unsuspecting men, women, and children. As the reader will note, the exchange between the coal operator and the U.S. senator grew quite heated. Then, the record breaks off suddenly, the topic switches, and Senator Martine disappears from the panel of inquisitors.

MR. VINSON: You are Mr. Quinn Morton?

MR. MORTON: Yes, sir.

SENATOR KENYON: Are you interested as a stockholder and manager in coal companies, Mr. Morton, in Paint Creek?

MR. MORTON: I am general manager of the Imperial Colliery Co. of Burnwell and of the Christian Colliery at Mahan.

MR. VINSON: Those two?

MR. MORTON: Yes, sir.

MR. VINSON: How long have been interested up there in the coal business, Mr. Morton?

MR. MORTON: I have been interested with the Imperial Colliery Co. since 1906 and the other company since it was organized, something over two years ago (. . .)

SENATOR KENYON: Was there any firing from the coach you were in?

MR. MORTON: Yes.

SENATOR MARTINE: And who carried on the firing from the coach you were in?

MR. MORTON: I did for one, sir. I don't know about the others.

SENATOR MARTINE: You had been to the town a great many times before?

MR. MORTON: I had been through there on the train.

SENATOR MARTINE: You knew its general character. Did you know whether the town was inhabited that night?

MR. MORTON: Yes, sir; I knew the town was inhabited that night.

SENATOR MARTINE: You knew the town was inhabited that night?

MR. MORTON: Yes, sir; I could not help knowing it.

SENATOR MARTINE: At the time the fusillade was going on?

MR. MORTON: Yes, sir; I could see the flashes—

SENATOR MARTINE: You knew the general character of the inhabitants?

MR. MORTON: Senator, if you will let me finish my answer, please.

SENATOR MARTINE: I thought you did finish your answer.

MR. MORTON: I simply wanted to say I knew it was inhabited at that time from the number of shots I saw fired toward our train.

SENATOR MARTINE: How recently had you been there previous to the firing of the shots?

MR. MORTON: I passed through the day before on the train.

SENATOR MARTINE: You knew reasonably that it was an inhabited town. Now, I want to ask did you approve of the use of the machine gun through an inhabited village?

MR. MORTON: It was not a question that I could approve or disapprove. I had nothing to do with the machine gun and—

SENATOR MARTINE: No; but you were really in command, were you not?

MR. MORTON: No, sir; I was not.

SENATOR MARTINE: These men you were taking up were on your train?

MR. MORTON: It was not my train. I was not taking anybody up.

MR. VINSON: Now, if the Senator will pardon me—

MR. MORTON: No; let me defend myself.

MR. VINSON: I will defend you.

SENATOR MARTINE: I am not making any onslaught on you. I want to get the truth.

MR. VINSON: I say you keep repeating to this witness and saying "Your train," when he has repeatedly told you it was not his train and he had no control over that train and it is not fair to put that in this record.

SENATOR MARTINE: I do not want to be unfair, but it seemed to me the association was so utterly dovetailed in—

THE CHAIRMAN: Gentlemen, please stop this discussion. The committee will pass upon the question, but the hearing must be conducted orderly. The questions must be written down by the stenographer and we will pass upon whether they shall be answered.

SENATOR MARTINE: I want it distinctly understood when I say "your train" I do not mean necessarily that you owned the whole train or any part of it, but I only say "your train" in the same way that you ask me when I come to Washington or I say "my train came in at such an hour." I do not mean necessarily that I own it. So if you have construed my questioning in that way, Mr. Vinson, you have been groping in error.

MR. VINSON: Before we get away from that, here is just as good a place to fix this record right as any other. I would like to have Senator Martine state that when he uses that term, "your train," he does not mean it was owned by him.

THE CHAIRMAN: He has so stated.

SENATOR MARTINE: Now, I want to ask you, Mr. Morton—I ask you again, did you approve of the use of the machine gun?

MR. MORTON: I answered that question, Senator Martine, that I had no opportunity to approve or disapprove.

SENATOR MARTINE: But you have, in your own conscience and mind. Do you approve of the use of the machine gun?

MR. MORTON: I absolutely approved of undertaking to defend myself, and for others to defend themselves when they are attacked as we were attacked that night, sir.

SENATOR MARTINE: Suppose you had been attacked by a band of men who you knew lived in a house, would you deem yourself justified in poisoning the well?

MR. VINSON: I object to that sort of questioning.

SENATOR MARTINE: I have a right to ask that question. The question is insisted upon. I say in asking these questions I want to know whether this gentleman, a cultured gentleman and an educated gentleman, approves of the use of a machine gun in a populous village—do you or do you not, in your own conscience? Now, you have a right to say yes or no as to whether it should be.

(The question was repeated by the stenographer, as recorded above.)

MR. VINSON: I must say that I cannot think we are here to investigate what Mr. Morton has in his conscience.

SENATOR MARTINE: All right.

MR. MORTON: I am willing to make this statement.

THE CHAIRMAN: I understood Mr. Morton wanted to answer that.

MR. MORTON: I want to make a statement.

SENATOR KENYON: We are here to investigate the facts. Of course, some of the committee are not lawyers, and perhaps look at this in a little different way.

SENATOR MARTINE: I am frank to say I am not a lawyer.

MR. MORTON: May I make a statement in the record right here?

THE CHAIRMAN: Yes.

MR. MORTON: In this cross-examination by Senator Martine I feel that I have been done a very great injustice. Senator Martine, when this matter was brought up, and they had a man by the name of Calvin on the stand, got up in this room and condemned me absolutely and by his questioning seems to feel that I have been guilty of some great wrong, and I want to say in my opinion I believe my conscience is as clear today as yours is, sir, and because you are a Senator you have no right to condemn me.

SENATOR MARTINE: I do not want to compare my conscience at all with yours in the matter. Neither am I—I am only trying to get the truth in this matter. I do believe it is within my privileges to show the general condition that prevailed. That is the animus of this—

MR. MORTON: As judge and jury you ought not to convict me before I am tried.

SENATOR MARTINE: I am not convicting you at all. When you speak of my reference to you in the former testimony, I did rise in my place and say, "Is this man an American Citizen?" It seemed to me appalling, horrible.

THE CHAIRMAN: The subcommittee will come to order.

SENATOR MARTINE: Now, I am in order, Mr. Chairman.

THE CHAIRMAN: Senator, let me make a statement.

SENATOR MARTINE: Proceed.

THE CHAIRMAN: When there is a dispute about a question submitted, whether it is proper, in the future we will allow the stenographer to write the questions down and then if there is any objection the committee will hear it in the regular, legal way and proceed in a legal way.

SENATOR MARTINE: I am afraid that it will be impossible for me to come within your legal definition or scope and questions. I am not a lawyer. I cannot surround my terms, my phrases, my words, or my methods with your legal methods, and I do not deem, with all deference to my learned and very delightful colleague—I do not believe it is necessary. I do not believe the animus and purpose of the resolution that passed the Senate of the United States attempted any such thing. You may do as you please about striking this out. I want to ask, did you not—did you have a conversation with the sheriff regarding this firing, after the firing had gone on, Mr. Morton?

THE CHAIRMAN: That is a legitimate question. Mr. Morton will answer.

MR. MORTON: I do not recall having any specific conversation with the sheriff until the following morning. There was a great deal of talk and a great deal of excitement in the train.

SENATOR MARTINE: Now, you did, then, have a conversation? State that conversation with the sheriff.

MR. MORTON: I could not possibly do so.

SENATOR MARTINE: Can you state what he did regarding this particular matter?

MR. MORTON: On the train that night?

SENATOR MARTINE: Yes.

MR. MORTON: I could not, sir.

SENATOR MARTINE: Was there anyone that said, "Let's back up and give them another round"?

MR. MORTON: Not that I know of, sir. I didn't hear it.

SENATOR MARTINE: You were close enough by the sheriff to have heard had he said it?

MR. MORTON: Part of the time.

SENATOR MARTINE: Did you hear anybody else say that?

MR. MORTON: I did not, sir.

SENATOR MARTINE: With reference to where that conversation was held, where was one Lee Calvin?

MR. MORTON: I think he was in the coach there.

SENATOR MARTINE: How close was he to you?

MR. MORTON: I don't know, sir.

SENATOR MARTINE: Do you know whether at the end of the train or next to you?

MR. MORTON: If you will allow me to make an explanation there I think possibly this would clear up this understanding. This train was in utter darkness, except one lantern, and somebody had an electric flashlight in it. After this shooting occurred everybody in the coach mixed up and looked around to see if anybody was hurt. I think possibly everybody in the coach was talking more or less. It was only about a mile after the shooting occurred until we arrived at Mucklow. There could have been but little conversation of any kind, except just as would occur in the excitement going on at that time.

SENATOR MARTINE: Now, Mr. Morton, you are a gentleman of education and large interests and large influence and large prominence, financially and every way, in this community.

MR. MORTON: I am certainly in prominence at present.

SENATOR MARTINE: Well, every other way. I won't deny that you are. I want to ask whether you deem it a civilized method to use a machine gun on helpless women and children? You can do as you please about answering it. I would like an answer.

MR. MORTON: I don't care to go into this expression of my conscience in these matters or my opinion.

SENATOR KENYON: I don't think you are called upon to answer a question of that kind unless you want to.

MR. MORTON: I am tired of being browbeaten.

SENATOR MARTINE: I can stand the silence, and I think the public can, if you can.

(The record breaks off suddenly, the topic switches, and Senator Martine disappears from the panel of inquisitors.)

MR. VINSON: Where were we? We were up there when the strike was called, I believe, when this diversion took place. Mr. Morton, I believe you stated that you informed the representatives of the United Mine Workers of America at a time your negotiations were on that you could not pay this advanced scale which they demanded; is that true?

MR. MORTON: I did.

MR. VINSON: And you gave them the reason that you had a contract for taking out practically the whole of your output?
MR. MORTON: Explained it to them very fully.
MR. VINSON: Did you pay the same wages to your miners after the strike as you paid under the contract before the strike?
MR. MORTON: I did.
MR. VINSON: Have you got a statement prepared showing what your people, or some of them, earned by the day and by the month under that scale of wages. Just read it out, if you please, or we will file it as an exhibit. (. . .)

Although some details differ between the two accounts, this article, published in the next day's New York Times, *provides the complete story not told in the government transcripts.*

SENATOR IN A ROW WITH MINING MAN

Martine Withdraws from Conduct of Coal Strike Inquiry in Consequence

• • •

OPERATORS' STORY TOLD

• • •

Morton and Other Witnesses Say Miners Fired First upon the Armored Train

Charleston, W. Va., June 17—At a stormy session of the Senate Mine Strike Committee, at which a fist fight between Senator Martine of New Jersey and Quinn Morton, manager of the Paint Creek Operators' Association was narrowly averted, the coal operators of Paint and Cabin Creeks today presented their side of the controversy.

This afternoon, after an earnest conference, in which Senators Swanson, Kenyon, and Martine took part, Senator Kenyon assumed charge of the hearing and Senator Martine did not ask a single question, although he had been a persistent examiner during Mr. Morton's appearance this morning.

The excitement began with the opening of the morning session. Senator Martine was examining Dr. J.W. Ashby, physician for the Cabin Creek Consolidated Coal Company, as to sanitary conditions in the strike zone. Dr. Ashby said sanitary conditions were as "good as anywhere else around mines." The Senator contradicted this statement, and when he and the witness engaged in an argument, C.C. Watts of counsel for the operator, interfered.

"Mr. Chairman, I object to the Senator, who is supposed to be sitting as a fair judge," he shouted, "browbeating and bullying this witness. He should not take advantage of his position as a Senator of the United States."

Senator Martine leaped to his feet and shouted: "I am a Senator of the United States and I am exercising my prerogatives as a Senator. You gentleman with wealth and power at your command should provide sanitary conditions to protect the lives of these workingmen."

"West Virginia," interrupted Mr. Watts "does not need to go to the mosquito-ridden swamps of New Jersey to learn sanitation."

Both Senator Martine and Mr. Watts were arguing heatedly when Senator Kenyon interrupted.

"Either stop this or let's adjourn," he said, and Senator Swanson took command of the situation.

Senator Swanson defended the position of Senator Martine and reprimanded Mr. Watts.

Quinn Morton, who owns several mines on Cabin Creek, and who was charged by Lee Calvin, former mine guard, with participating in the attack on Holly Grove with the armored train, was examined at length as to negotiations which preceded the strike.

Senator Martine interrupted Mr. Morton's story of the negotiations to demand that he tell what he knew of the armored train attack upon the Holly Grove Camp. Mr. Morton described arranging for the trip with Sheriff Bonner Hill and buying thirty-one rifles in Charleston to arm the men on the train. Mr. Morton asserted that before the train reached Holly Grove the lights were turned down on the train because Sheriff Hill said the train was likely to be "shot up."

"Just as we got to Holly Grove," he said, "I heard two shots that seemed to come from the camp. One window in the car was broken, and a second later a general fusillade, both from the train and from the camp, was on. I shot, of course, just as everybody else did."

Here Senator Martine again clashed with the lawyers. Mr. Morton and Attorney Vinson remonstrated excitedly when Senator Martine demanded:

"In your conscience do you approve of the use of a machine gun to shoot up a village inhabited by defenseless women and children?"

As the lawyers argued over the question, Senator Martine shouted: "I thank God I am not a lawyer!"

"Senator Martine had already made an outrageous attack on me," said Mr. Morton, excitedly, "when Lee Calvin was on the stand. The Senator, without any proof, has by questions accused me of attacking women and children in their homes with a machine gun. This treatment is outrageous, and not even a United States Senator should be allowed to prejudge a case in this manner."

Senator Martine said that he had not prejudged the case, and again demanded of Mr. Morton whether there was any justification of the use of the machine gun. Mr. Morton declined to answer.

"Well, I can stand the silence and so can the people," said Senator Martine, "if you can."

Mr. Morton vigorously denied that he had ever urged that the train "back up and give them another round" after Holly Grove had been passed, as charged by Lee Calvin. Neither he nor Sheriff Hill had ever said anything of this sort, he said.

In response to questions from Senator Kenyon, the witness said that the Paint Creek Coal and Land Company, from which he and his associates held mining leases, was controlled by Charles Pratt of New York.

After questioning Mr. Morton as to his participation in the shooting up of Holly Grove, Senator Martine left the room, and returned just as the committee was prepared to take a recess for luncheon. He strode into the room, and without taking his seat resumed the questioning of Mr. Morton: He wanted to know whether Mr. Morton had expressed satisfaction at the effect of the firing on Holly Grove, but before he had developed his line of questioning, Senator Swanson, scenting trouble, adjourned the committee. Mr. Morton leaned back in the witness seat as Senator Martine, his hat and heavy walking stick in his hand, stood behind the press table, still asking questions.

"Well," remarked Mr. Morton, "we'll all go down and take a few drinks, and then we'll feel better."

The crowd had already begun to press toward the door, when it was arrested by a shout of Senator Martine.

Pushing his way through the little throng about the stenographers' table, Senator Martine shouted:

"You are a blackguard of the worst character to address such a remark to me!"

Out of the confusion that followed came the voice of Morton: "Did you not take three drinks with me in thirty minutes?"

With a bound Senator Martine covered the short distance that separated the two men.

"You have forfeited all right to consideration as a decent white man!" he shouted.

Senator Swanson hurried around the committee table and seized Senator Martine. Aided by Sergeant at Arms Higgins he hurried him from the room.

Peace in West Virginia

This story from the Literary Digest *(New York), May 10, 1913, discusses the conclusion of the Paint Creek–Cabin Creek strike. Most observers of the time, as well as historians of the period, generally praise West Virginia Governor Henry Hatfield's role in ending the bitter conflict by imposing a compromise settlement upon both industry and labor. But, as this article points out, there was an underlying discontent among the miners with the settlement—a discontent that exploded a few months later when they walked out again, renewing the strike. Unfortunately, this article does not discuss the second phase of the strike. But it should be noted that, with the U.S. Senate conducting its inquiry of the state government's actions during the first phase, the coal industry could not employ the violent strike-breaking methods it had before. Consequently, the coal companies capitulated and gave in to all the miners' demands. (A description of this aspect of the strike can be found in David Corbin's "Strike and Suppression in West Virginia," West Virginia History, January, 1973.)*

The reader might also note the media's portrayal, described here, of the Paint Creek–Cabin Creek strike at the most "bitter and protracted" labor conflict in American history.

The labor war of more than a year in West Virginia ends with what is generally taken by the press to be a nearly complete victory for the miners and something of a triumph, too, for Governor Hatfield. The open hostility engendered on both sides, the clashes between miners and guards, the repeated establishment of martial law with the consequent perplexing legal problems, and the appearance of such picturesque figures as Mother Jones, caused the *New York Sun* to refer to the strike in the West Virginia coal fields as "probably the most bitter and protracted industrial struggle of the kind in the history of the country." Governor Hatfield's intervention brought about an agreement between certain operators and their employees several weeks ago, as related in our issue of April 5. Elsewhere there was more obstinacy, and finally, according to one newspaper account, on April 25 at midnight, the Governor "issued what he termed an ultimatum, giving warning that 'this strife and dissension must cease within thirty-six hours.' The Governor's proposals were accepted a little more than twelve hours later."

Most of the miners have now returned to work, the State troops are being withdrawn from the coal fields, and normal conditions are being restored. "The strike is ended," declares Governor Hatfield in an official statement which reads in part:

> As Governor of West Virginia, I felt for the good of all that the dispute should be terminated. While I took no sides in the matter in so far as the contentions of the parties in interest were concerned, I took a decided position and suggested that certain concessions be made by both parties.
>
> I did not ask the coal operators to adopt something that was inimical to their interests or that will cast opprobrium upon or in any way handicap the industry in West Virginia. It was also foreign to me even to suggest or dictate how they should conduct their business, nor did I wish to conflict in any way by suggestion or otherwise with the rights and liberties of the laboring man.
>
> However, I felt it my duty as Chief Executive of the State to insist that the law be enforced in letter and in spirit.

The miner's demands, as stated by President White, of the United Mine Workers of America, were, besides better wages and hours, "the right to belong to a labor organization without discrimination; the semi-monthly pay day; the selection of checkweighmen to secure honest weights; to have their coal weighed, and that 2,000 pounds shall constitute a ton." And the Governor's recommendations, which were finally accepted, include most of the points in a proposition submitted to him by President White and published in the *United Mine Workers Journal*. To quote the Governor's statement of his terms of agreement:

> First—That the operators concede to the miners their right to select a checkweighman from among their number when a majority demands, as indicated and in keeping with sections 438–439 of the code, to determine, to the entire satisfaction of the employee, the exact weight of all coal mined by him and his co-workers.
>
> Second—That a nine-hour day be conceded to the miners by the operators. To be more fully understood as to what

constitutes a nine-hour day, I respectfully advised that it mean nine hours of actual service by the employee to the employer at the same scale of wages now paid.

Third—That no discrimination be made against any miner, and that if he elects he may be permitted to purchase the supplies for the maintenance of his family wherever it suits him best, as this was claimed by the operators who own and control commissaries to see that the prices of their merchandise are in keeping with the same prices made by independent or other stores throughout the Kanawha Valley.

Fourth—That the operators grant a semi-monthly pay.

It will be my pleasure to use all the means at my command to see that each and every proposition so acceded to is carried out in its fullness, and I will further endeavor in such cases where the law is not now explicit to have the same so amended as will secure in the future the carrying out of the suggestions I have made.

The West Virginia Correspondent of the socialist *New York Daily People* believes that the striking miners have been duped on one point, "that of no discrimination against union men." He says:

The discrimination clause in the settlement is of an equivocal nature. It was announced at the ending of the strike that there would be "no discrimination against the men." Just what that means and how it applies is proving a problem now.

The construction of this clause, according to other dispatches, has been left by the miners with Governor Hatfield, and, as the *Buffalo Express* sees it, "his firmness in dealing with both miners and operators would indicate that the trust is safely imposed."

The Federal investigation of conditions in the strike zone proposed by Senator Kern should not be killed off by this settlement, declares the *New York Globe*, for these reasons:

This West Virginia outbreak has been of such character, and on so extended a scale; it has cost so much in life, property, and business to a great State; it has indicated such a tensity of feeling between the miners and the operators, and that there is need for the community to know what it was about and on which side lay the merits. A settlement that merely sends the men back into the diggings, without assurance that the trouble may not break out again at any time, will not be satisfactory.

It is quite within the present demands of an exacting public sentiment toward these questions of industrial condition and human welfare that a thorough study should be made of such a situation. The whole nation is turning its thoughts to this great set of issues. It cannot think accurately or decide rightly until it knows the facts. Therefore, whether there is a present settlement or not, the inquiry ought to go ahead. If this course is taken, the chance of a future outbreak will be lessened.

(Correspondents in West Virginia write to inform us that the rifles and ammunition pictured in our issue of April 5 were not taken from the strikers, as claimed in the paper from which we had the illustration, but from the mine guards employed by the operators; and also that Judge Littlepage, whose ruling we quoted, is Judge of the Kanawha County Circuit Court, not of the United States Circuit Court, as the dispatches had it.)

MUNITIONS FROM THE STRIKE ZONE.
Note the coal company machine guns at front and the boxes of ammunition behind.
PHOTOGRAPHER UNKNOWN, COURTESY OF STATE ARCHIVES.

CHAPTER IV

CHAPTER IV
The Organizers

It was during the 1912 strike that an 82-year-old woman arrived on the scene in Cabin Creek, immediately making her mark on West Virginia and the American labor movement.

To her enemies, especially the coal operators, she was a vulgar, violent, and irresponsible agitator. But to those who followed her and witnessed her refusal to be intimidated by gunmen, machine guns, or incarceration, Mary Harris Jones was "Mother."

Born in 1830 in Ireland, Mother Jones became one of the most remarkable women in American history. In private, she was actually quiet and unassuming. But when promoting a cause—especially a fight on behalf of the poor, exploited, or oppressed—this gentle, little person became a fiercely combative foe. She became, in the words of a coal operator, the "most dangerous woman in America."

Upon being introduced to a college crowd as a "great humanitarian," Jones took the floor and exclaimed: "I'm not humanitarian; I'm a hellraiser!" And raise hell she did—all over the country on behalf of union workers, her "children."

But it was the coal miners who drew her particular attention, especially the miners of southern West Virginia. "Medieval West Virginia," she remarked, "with its tent colonies on the bleak hills! With its grim men and women. When I get to the other side, I shall tell God Almighty about West Virginia."

Mother Jones, as her critics charged, was often guilty of exaggerating the facts and she often distorted the truth to make a point. But she believed every word she spoke. To her, truth was not a photograph. It was something that lives and, above all, something that stirs.

Mary Harris Jones died in 1930. She had once promised the miners of southern West Virginia that she would not leave this world until she had seen them unionized, but she was three years off the mark. At the age of 100, her body had been used up by a thousand fights, trials, and tribulations.

Civil War in the West Virginia Coal Mines:
A Profile of Mother Jones
By Harold E. West

In his series on the Paint Creek–Cabin Creek strike, Baltimore Sun *reporter Harold E. West included a section on his conversations with Mother Jones. West's profile of her helps explain why this little woman was so hated and feared by coal companies, and so loved and respected by West Virginia miners and their families.*

The developments of the winter have been under the regime of a third governor, who came to the state house at a season when part of the commonwealth was under martial law. In March came the trials of a number of the strikers and their sympathizers—approximately fifty—by a military court on charges of inciting to riot, conspiracy to murder and conspiracy to destroy property. Among those in prison is Mother Jones, the "Stormy Petrel of Labor" who is always present in big labor disturbances, especially those of the miners and the railroad men. She has given the best part of her life to the cause of laboring men and they adore her.

This old woman, more than 80 years of age, was in the mines when I went there and I got to know her well. She passed the word along to the men that I was "all right" and reticent as they are to strangers, they told me their side of the case without reservation.

I have been with Mother Jones when she was compelled "to walk the creek," having been forbidden to go upon the footpaths that happened to be upon the property of the companies and denied even the privilege of walking along the railroad track although hundreds of miners and others were walking on it at the time. She was compelled to keep to the country road although it was in the bed of the creek and the water was over her ankles. I protested to the chief of the guards saying that no matter what her attitude might be, no matter how much she might be hated, that she was an old woman and common humanity would dictate that she be not ill treated. I was told that she was an old "she-devil" and that she would receive no "courtesies" there, that she was responsible for all the trouble that had occurred and that she would receive no consideration from the companies.

I was with her when she was denied "the privilege" of going up the footway to the house of one of the miners in order to get a cup of tea. It was then afternoon, she had walked several miles and was faint, having had nothing to eat since an early breakfast. But that did not shut her mouth. She made the speech she had arranged to make to the men who gathered to hear her although they had to line up on each side of the roadway to avoid "obstructing the highway," a highway that was almost impassable to a wheeled vehicle and on which there was no travel. And in that speech she counseled moderation, told the men to keep strictly within the law and to protect the company's property instead of doing anything to injure it.

I had several long talks with her. When she speaks to the miners she talks in their own vernacular and occasionally swears. She was a normal school teacher in her early days, and in her talks with me in the home of one of her friends in the "free town" of Eskdale, she used the language of the cultured women. And this is the old woman whom nearly all the operators in the non-union fields fear, and whose coming among their workers they dread more than the coming of a pestilence. They now have her safely in jail.

When I left the field the conflict was still on. It seemed likely to continue until one side or the other gave in. The presence of the military could only bring about a peace that is temporary. Having held out through the winter, the miners were preparing to hold out through the spring and summer and autumn if necessary, and the United Mine Workers of America were preparing to back them up with all the resources of the national organization.

Proceedings Held at Front Steps of the Capitol in Charleston, August 15, 1912

A Speech by Mother Jones

What follows is the major portion of a speech Mother Jones delivered to the Paint Creek–Cabin Creek strikers. Her words, taken down by a stenographer, describe a quest for justice, a desire for decency, and the dream for a better world this legendary labor leader shared with her listeners—the miners of southern West Virginia.

This, my friends, marks, in my estimation, the most remarkable move ever made in the State of Virginia. It is a day that will mark history in the long ages to come. What is it? It is an uprising of the oppressed against the master class.

From this day on, my friends, Virginia—West Virginia—shall march in the front of the Nation's States.

The womanhood of this State shall not be oppressed and beaten and abused by a lot of contemptible, damnable bloodhounds hired by the operators. They wouldn't keep their dog where they keep you fellows. You know that. They have a good place for their dogs and a salve to take care of them. The mine owners' wives will take the dogs up, and say, "I love you, dea-h" [trying to imitate by tone of voice.]

Now, my friends, the day for petting dogs is gone; the day for raising children to a nobler manhood and better womanhood is here. [Applause and cries of "Amen! Amen!"]

You have suffered; I know you have suffered. I was with you nearly three years in this State. I went to jail; went to the federal courts; but I never took any back water. I still unfurl the red flag of industrial freedom; no tyrant's face shall you know, and I call you today into that freedom—long perch on the bosom—[Interrupted by applause.]

I am back again to find you, my friends, in a state of industrial peonage—after 10 years' absence I find you in a state of industrial peonage.

The superintendent at Acme—I went up there, and they said we were unlawful—we had an unlawful mob along. Well, I will tell you the truth; we took a couple of guns because we knew we were going to meet some thugs, and by jiminy—[Interrupted by applause.]

We will prepare for the job, just like Lincoln and Washington did. We took lessons from them, and we are here to prepare for the job.

Now, brothers, not in all the history of the labor movement have I got such an inspiration as I have got from you here today. Your banners are history; they will go down to the future ages, to the children unborn, to tell them the slave his risen, children must be free.

The labor movement was not originated by man. The labor movement, my friends, was a command from God Almighty. He commanded the prophets thousands of years ago to go down and redeem the Israelites that were in bondage, and he organized the men into a union and went to work. And they said, "The masters have made us gather straw; they have been more cruel than they were before. What are we going to do?" The prophet said, "A voice from heaven has come to get you together." They got together and the prophet led them out of the land of bondage and robbery and plunder into the land of freedom. And when the army of pirates followed them the Dead Sea opened and swallowed them up, and for the first time the workers were free.

And so it is. That can well be applied to the State of West Virginia. When I left Cabin Creek 10 years ago to go to another terrific battle field every man on Cabin Creek was organized—every single miner. The mine owners and the miners were getting along harmoniously; they had an understanding and were carrying it out. But they had some traitors who made a deal with the mine owners and the organization was driven out of Cabin Creek. There were no better miners in the whole State of West Virginia than on Cabin Creek, and no better operators in those days. You got along together. They were trying to make it happy and comfortable for you, but the demon came and tore the organization to pieces and you are at war today.

I hope, my friends, that you and the mine owners will put aside the breach and get together before I leave the state. But I want to say, make no settlment until they sign up that every bloody murderer of a guard has got to go. [Loud applause.]

This is done, my friends, beneath the flag our fathers fought and bled for, and we don't intend to surrender our liberty. [Applause.]

I had been reading of the Titanic when she went down. Did you read of her? The big guns wanted to save themselves, and the fellows that were guiding below took up a club and said, "We will save our people." And then the papers came out and said those millionaires tried to save the women. O, Lord, why don't they give up their millions if they want to save the women and children? Why do they rob them of home; why do they rob millions of women to fill the hell holes of capitalism?

Here on the steps of the Capitol of West Virginia, I say that if the governor won't make them go then we will make them go. [Loud applause, and cries of "That we will," "Only one more day," "The guards have got to go."]

We have come to the chief executive, we have asked him, and he couldn't do anything. [Laughter.]

The prosecuting attorney is of the same type—another fellow belonging to the ruling class. [Applause and murmurings in the crowd.] Hush up there, hush up, hush up.

I want to tell you that the governor will get until tomorrow night, Friday night, to get rid of his bloodhounds, and if they are not gone, we will get rid of them. [Loud applause.]

Aye men, aye men, inside of this building, aye women, come with me and see the horrible pictures, see the horrible condition the ruling class has put these women in. Aye, they destroy women. Look at those little children, the rising generation, yes, look at the little ones.

I have worked, boys, I have worked with you for years. I have seen the suffering children, and in order to be convinced I went into the mines on the night shift and day shift and helped the poor wretches to load coal at times. We lay down at noon and we took our lunches and we talked our wrongs over, we gathered together at night and asked, "How will we remedy things?" We organized secretly, and after a while held public meetings. We got our people together in those organized states. Today the mine owners and the miners come together. They meet each other and shake hands, and have no more war in those States, and the workingmen are becoming more intelligent. And I am one of those my friends, I don't care about your woman suffrage and the temperance brigade or any other of your class associations, I want women of the coming day to discuss and find out the cause of child crucifixion, that is what I want to find out.

I have been in jail more than once, and I expect to go again. If you are too cowardly to fight, I will fight. You ought be ashamed of yourselves, actually to the Lord you ought, just to see one old woman who is not afraid of all the bloodhounds. How scared those villains are when one woman 80 years old, with her head gray, can come in and scare hell out of the whole bunch. [Laughter.] We didn't scare them? The mine owners run down the street like a mad dog today. They ask who started this thing. I started it, I did it, and I am not afraid to tell you if you are here, and I will start more before I leave West Virginia. I started this mass meeting today, I had these banners written, and don't accuse anybody else of the job. [Loud applause.]

It is freedom or death, and your children will be free. We are not going to leave a slave class to the coming generation, and I want to say to you that the next generation will not charge us for what we have done; they will charge and condemn us for what we have left undone. [Cries of "That is right."]

Now, my boys, guard rule and tyranny will have to go; there must be an end. I am going up Cabin Creek. I am going to hold meetings there. I am going to claim the right of an American citizen. I was on this earth before these operators were. I was in this country before these operators. I have been 74 years under this flag. I have got the right to talk. I have seen its onward march. I have seen the growth of oppression, and I want to say to you, my friends, violate the law; I will not kill anybody or starve anybody; but I will talk unsparingly of all the corporation bloodhounds we can bring to jail. [Laughter.]

I have no apologies to offer. I have seen your children murdered; I have seen you blown to death in the mines, and there was no redress.

I want you to listen a moment. I want the business men to listen. You business men are up against it. There is a great revolution going on in the industrial world. The Standard Oil Co. owns 86 great department stores in this country. The small business man is beginning to be eliminated. He has got to get down, he can't get up. It is like Carnegie said before the Tariff Commission in Washington, "Gentlemen, I am not bothered about tariff on steel rails." He says, "What concerns me and my class is the right to organize."

See the condition we are in today. There is a revolution. There is an editorial in one of the papers in your own State showing how little they have done for the workers, that the workers are awakening. The literature is being circulated among them. I myself have circulated millions and millions of pieces of literature in this country and awakened the miners. On the trains they say, "Oh, Mother, you gave us a book that woke us up." As long as you woke up right, it is all right. He says, "I have woke up right." Then, if you woke up right, you are my children.

O you men of wealth! O you preachers! You are going over to China and sending money over there for Jesus. For God's sake, keep it at home; we need it.

I want you to keep the peace until I tell you to move, and when I want you every one will come. [Loud applause.]

Now, be good. I don't tell you to go and work for Jesus. Work for yourselves; work for bread. That is the fight we have got. Work for bread. They own our bread.

This fight that you are in is the great industrial revolution that is permeating the heart of men over the world. They see behind the clouds the star that rose in Bethlehem nineteen hundred years ago, that is bringing the message of a better and noble civilization. We are facing the hour. We are in it, men, the new day; we are here facing that star that will free men and give to the Nation a nobler, grander, higher, truer, purer, better manhood. We are standing on the eve of that mighty hour when the motherhood of the Nation will rise, and instead of clubs or picture shows or excursions, she will devote her life to the training of the human mind, giving to the Nation great men and great women.

I see that hour. I see the star breaking your chains; your chains will be broken, men. You will have to suffer more and more, but it won't be long. There is an awakening among all the nations on the earth.

I know of the wrongs of humanity; I know of your aching backs; I know your swimming heads; I know your little children suffer; I know your wives, when I have gone in and found her dead and found the babe nursing at the dead breast, and found the little girl 11 years old taking care of three children. She said, "Mother, will you wake up, baby is hungry and crying?" When I laid my hand on mamma she breathed her last. And the child of 11 had to become a mother to the children.

Oh, men, have you any hearts? Oh, men do you feel? Oh, men, do you see the judgment day on the throne above, when you will be asked, "Where did you get your gold?" You stole it from these wretches. You murdered, you assassinated, you starved, you burned them to death, that you and your wives might have palaces, and that your wives might go to the seashore. Oh God, men, when I see the horrible picture, when I see the children with their hands off, when I took an army of babies and walked a hundred and thirty miles with a petition to the President of the United States, to pass a bill in Congress to keep these children from being murdered for profit. He had a secret service then all the way to the palace. And now they want to make a President of that man! What is the American Nation coming to?

Manhood, womanhood, can you stand for it? They put reforms in their platforms, but they will get no reform. He promised everything to labor. When we had the strike in Colorado he sent 200 guns to blow our brains out. I don't forget. You do, but I don't. And our women were kicked out like dogs at the point of the bayonet. That is America. They don't do it in Russia. Some women get up with $5 worth of paint on their cheeks and have toothbrushes for their dogs and say, "Oh, them horrible miners. Oh, that horrible old Mother Jones, that horrible old woman."

I am horrible, I admit, and I want to be to you blood-sucking pirates.

Now, be good, boys, Pass the hat around, some of these poor devils want a glass of beer. Get the hat. The mine owner robs them. Get a hat, you fellows of the band.

I want to tell you another thing. These little two by four clerks in the company stores, they sell you five beans for a nickel, sometimes three beans for a nickel. I want to tell you, be civil to those. Don't say anything.

Another thing I want you to do: I want you to go in regular parade, three or four together. The moving-picture man wants to get your picture to send over the country.

[Some one in the crowd asks what the collection is being taken for.]

The hat is for the miners who came up here broke, and they want to get a glass of beer. [Loud applause.]

And to pay their way back—and to get a glass of beer. I will give you $5. Get a move on and get something in it.

This day marks the forward march of the workers in the State of West Virginia. Slavery and oppression will gradually die. The National Government will get a record of this meeting. They will say, my friends, this was a peaceful, law-abiding meeting. They will see men of intelligence, that they are not out to destroy but to build. And instead of the horrible homes you have got, we will build on their ruins homes for you and your children to live in, and we will build them on the ruins of the dog kennels which they wouldn't keep their mules in. That will bring forth better ideas than the world has had. The day of oppression will be gone. I will be with you whether true or false. I will be with you at midnight or when the battle rages, when the last bullet ceases, but I will be in my joy, as an old saint said:

O, God of the mighty clan,
God grant that the woman who suffered for you,
Suffered not for a coward, but oh, for a man,
God grant that the woman who suffered for you,
Suffered not for a coward, but oh, for a fighting man.

MOTHER JONES IN MINGO COUNTY.
L-R: Charley Workman, Red Doyle, Mother Jones, Warren Hutchinson, Sid Hatfield, Andrew Wilson, Ezra Fry, and Dave Phillips. PHOTOGRAPHER UNKNOWN, COURTESY OF THE WEST VIRGINIA COLLECTION, WVU.

"Mother" Jones, Mild-Mannered, Talks Sociology
Incendiary Labor Leader Who Terrorized West Virginia Talks of Coming Industrial Peace, and Says She Is Neither Socialist nor Anarchist

Another interesting image of Mother Jones is offered by the following New York Times *interview, published June 1, 1913. Jones was well known for her fiery speaking style and calls for working-class militancy. But she surprised the unnamed journalist by being a reasonable and intelligent woman one would expect to find in a university. He marveled at this "hospitable" character who preferred peace to war, quoted Shakespeare instead of cursed, and preferred to discuss the sociology of mining communities rather than revolutionary theories.*

"I believe no more in thug-statesmanship than in thug-economics; either one will breed the other; they are brother. I am neither Socialist nor Anarchist; I decry them both, and, naturally, in decrying them, I must decry their causes.

"Note this: The well-fed man will never knock another down to steal his dinner. Note this, also: the violent employer and the violent employee both need curbing."

A white-haired old woman in a hotel room said these things and thus dazed me, for I had gone there with eyes ready for the blood-red flag.

Instead I got calm sociology, interspersed with humor which I shall not make an effort to transcribe because it would so lose in telling; I had expected much incendiary talk in uncouth English and found an educated woman, careful of her speech and sentiments. If she had a red flag with her she kept it in her satchel with her comb and brush and powder puff. She has a powder puff. That, too, astonished me.

During the morning not a labor leader came to see her, but among her visitors were three semi-famous writers for high-class periodicals, bent not on business, but wholly social calls; a woman author of importance; a widely celebrated woman student of the economic problems of the time.

Curiosity was not behind the visit of any one of these. All were a little more than friends, for all called her "mother" with affection. Indeed, the handsome, well-dressed, carefully spoken, hospitable, smiling, sympathetic, seventy-year-old woman who received them and myself was none other than that "Mother" Jones, widely heralded as the gray-haired virago of the West Virginia mines, the woman labor-leader who was held a captive in what was called the "bull-pen" on the theory that this was necessary for the safety of society.

I never saw her lead a strike; I have been told that she does so with force amounting to incendiarism. After two visits to her aggregating quite ten hours I should as much expect her to be violent as to see a matron at a charity ball spring into anarchistic action.

Which indicates that she is an extraordinary character. It is a fact that her name has held a State in terror, that the mine-owners declare her as their strongest foe, that within the year the State of Virginia has held her prisoner behind the shining steel of bayonets.

Only when we talked about the West Virginia situation did she show the slightest tendency to step down from her calmly judicial, somewhat scholarly attitude. She called some West Virginians capitalist rather mildly critical names; denounced the West Virginian industrial system as a definite infamy; told sad stories of its women and its children victims, but even as she told of fighting and her willingness to fight, in certain circumstances, she declared that fighting is unnecessary and that the men and bosses ought to get together for the common good, each make some concessions, and go on about their business like calm, co-operating, reasonable human beings.

Her Views on the Future

There obviously is a "Mother" Jones other than this extraordinary and wholly unexpected one whom I met at the Union Square Hotel; but as long as this one was then so definitely in evidence and based the arguments which she set forth on an experience in the midst of labor-turbulence undoubtedly unprecedented for a woman, what she says may be considered worth reading.

If she be, in truth, a Doctress Jekyll–Mrs. Hyde, she is a wonderful in her black silk, her carefully dressed, silvery hair, her silk stockings, and neat pumps, as Stevenson's male doublet is between the covers of his book.

"My husband died of yellow fever in the South," she said, "and the same disease made other widows by the tens of thousands. It is making no more widows, because we now have mastered it. The world is suffering, today, from an industrial yellow fever, not less fatal, but, I am certain, as preventable.

"We have applied to the economic disease which has distressed us all manner of remedies, all unintelligent. Students have delved widely, but wrongly in the main, in their search for causes. Each has devised his remedy; most remedies have failed because they did not touch the cause. Some remedies have succeeded; they got at the cause.

"I thoroughly believe that in the not far distant future an era of industrial peace is waiting; we shall overtake it. Real education is all we need to help us find it. . . .

"The equality which is the ideal of this country, of course, is nearer now than ever, and such situations as that which now exists in West Virginia are the exceptions which unquestionably prove the rule. That is the sort of medievalism which is as abhorrent to the intelligent employer as it is to the suffering miner. The employers suffer from it, too; they are as unhappy as their men are. But they do not understand. It is an extraordinary spectacle.

"I have as little patience with the workingman who cries that all employers are hard-hearted wretches as I have with the employer who declares all workingmen to be mere brutes who must be managed or ground into the dust. For the dynamiter among labormen I have as little sympathy as for the mill-owner who works children at his looms fourteen hours each day.

"Thousands of employers are feeling around for the way out of all this muddle; some of them are finding it and walking on it. If the workingmen were not as reasonable and progressive in most places the United States would be in poverty instead of riches. But, in order to be fair, we must remember this: The average employer has had a better chance than the average worker to learn economic wisdom. . . .

"I don't hate employers. What I hate is the cause of labor troubles. I hate no individual. There are those among the mine owners in West Virginia who deserve less hate than pity; they deserve more sympathy than I do, more sympathy than any of the striking miners do, for they are going to be beaten into doing right. The man forced into his righteousness is a sorry spectacle. . . .

"It's nip and tuck. The employers' injunctions are as dangerous to civilization as the strikers' shotguns. The striker becomes violent, and the employer chooses another kind of violence. They're perhaps equally at fault. But who began it? Consider what occurred.

"When forty-five or fifty miners were taken to the drum-head court which was established, attorneys for the miners got a District Court to issue an injunction restraining the drum-head court. The drum-head court, consisting of appointees of certain corporations, went to Charleston and induced the Judge to withdraw the injunction. Had he made it permanent instead, he would have been making history; but he did not. He missed the chance of being one of the greatest figures on the bench.

"Then fifty of us were tried by the drum-head court. I was held in the military prison, called the 'bull pen,' three months less five days. Others were detained three months and two weeks. We didn't suffer much; I was never really uncomfortable. But who gained anything?

"That's the point I'm trying to make. I am not railing against my imprisonment, but against the inefficiency of the system which so sillily imagined that to keep me there could do anybody any good. I accomplished absolutely nothing toward the solution of the trouble.

"To try to do that in that way was like an effort by a doctor who gives you a little morphine, when you ache, so that you won't feel the pain. The government of West Virginia gave a little morphine to the industrial situation. It did nothing toward the removal of the cause of the disorder which had brought about the ache.

"West Virginia shows the survival of conditions which existed elsewhere in the dark industrial ages of thirty years ago. It is very likely lucky for the country that I was locked up and that the others were locked up.

"It offered to the Nation an object lesson of what most regions have grown out of, and perhaps thus stimulated thought which may take all of us a little further toward enlightenment. The next twenty years will carry us along a constantly ascending path into conditions even more conspicuously better than those which rule today, than the West Virginia conditions are now worse than those which rule elsewhere.

"The people of this country must learn to choose their leaders—political, industrial, and social—not because they are good fellows but because they are intelligent students of great questions. No job is too small to put a thinker into. The voters at labor union elections and corporate elections of Directors, as well as voters at the polls in city, county, State, and National elections must try to find the men who understand. There are such men for every situation. When they get into the offices we will begin to hurry on the upward path. Politics, economics, and sociology should link arms.

"They are going to. Ten or fifteen years ago when someone spoke of the recall of Judges, the entire Nation rose in arms. Today it is a common issue, and in some States it is a fact. It will presently be fact in others, and then will follow other great advances as sensational, as bitterly opposed at first and as generally adopted after they have been threshed out and perfected. . . .

"I have said that I hate violence; I favor drama. We must wake the sleepers somehow, and where blindness can be healed by shock we must provide shock. Sometimes it hurts a little, but it helps the patient afterward, for, lo! it makes him see. The Coxey Army's march to Washington was a great joke, but it helped mightily to bring about good roads.

"And demonstrations are good things for labor in these learning days. They are good advertising, and the serious, progressive drama as well as comic opera needs advertising.

"I feel this: If labor would eliminate its violence and capital would eliminate injunctions, the battle would be practically over. We could then go sanely at arranging peace. Common sense, uninflamed, productive, could step in. But labor will be violent as long as capital swears out injunctions. Also, the first step toward peace must come from capital. It has more advantages. It must lead.

"The human being is most wonderful. We can do anything with him. If we would all agree to try to do the right thing with every human being over whom we are in power or over whom we have an influence!"

MOTHER JONES IN A RARE MOMENT OF REST.
PHOTOGRAPHER UNKNOWN, COURTESY OF THE WEST VIRGINIA COLLECTION, WVU.

Frank Keeney and Fred Mooney

While the Paint Creek–Cabin Creek strike established Mother Jones as a national labor leader, the bitter and protracted conflict also established a rank-and-file leadership among the West Virginia miners.

Frank Keeney and Fred Mooney were born in coal camps on Cabin Creek, and both were sons of miners. Their leadership during the 1912 strike and afterward helped usher in a new era for the miners of West Virginia.

It was Keeney and Mooney who led the miners back out on the second phase of the Paint Creek–Cabin Creek strike and turned the compromise into victory. In 1916, these two men led a revolt against UMWA District 17 officials, charging them with corruption and indifference to the problems of the rank-and-file miners. An investigation by the international union proved Keeney and Mooney correct, resulting in the dismissal of the officials. A new election was held and Keeney was elected president of District 17, with Mooney as his secretary-treasurer.

Before taking office in January 1917, Keeney said, "Brothers, if you give me your cooperation and your support, I don't think that you will ever have to regret it. You need never be ashamed of the trust reposed in me."

For his part, Mooney was an industrious, unassuming man. "He might have been a student under other circumstances," wrote journalist Winthrop Lane.

It was these two dynamic and charismatic leaders who guided the state's miners through the Mine Wars.

Frank Keeney's Words:

"I am a native West Virginian and there are others like me working in the mines here. We don't propose to get out of the way when a lot of capitalists from New York and London come down and tell us to get off the earth. They played that game on the American Indian. They gave him the end of a log to sit on and then pushed him off that. We don't propose to be pushed off."

"One day there will be no more gun men, no more tent colonies, because right now you people are going through what you are."

"Who are you, you dirty despised people who can't walk into Charleston because you'd give them a disease? That's what they say. It's no disgrace to dig coal. Coal makes civilization possible."

"Employers want to measure wages in cold dollars and cents, while miners insist that they be measured in human values. . . . Miners take the position that low wages deprive children of education, of good food, destroy self-respect, and drive men to degradation."

"Who made me a radical? I've seen the time when I didn't have the right to eat in this state. I've seen the time when I was refused a job. I've been served with eviction papers and thrown out of my house. I've seen women and children brutally treated in mining camps. I've seen hell turned loose."

"They didn't call me a radical when circular after circular went out from my office during the war, urging miners to waive their rights and produce all the coal they could!"

"If our organizers come back in pine boxes, neither heaven nor hell will be able to control the miners. Organize Logan County we will, and no one shall stop us."

"The only way you can get your rights [in this state] is with a high-powered rifle."

"They say we shall not organize West Virginia. They are mistaken. If Frank Keeney can't do it, someone will take his place who can. But West Virginia will be organized and it will be organized completely."

Said about Frank Keeney:

"Keeney is the embodiment of the union's spirit and purpose in West Virginia. . . . He is identified by the operators with all that they distrust in unionism. Nearly everything that the union has won in West Virginia has been won under his leadership." —Winthrop Lane, *Civil War in West Virginia*

"Keeney is a true leader of his people. He has the hypnotic influence of power. Even the passing of a union car with one of the union representatives in it brings a cry of 'Frank Keeney!' from the streets and the camps." —Edmund Wilson, *The American Jitters*

Fred Mooney's Words:

Much of the following quotation is from Struggle in the Coal Fields: The Autobiography of Fred Mooney *(J. W. Hess, ed., West Virginia University Library, 1967).*

"Someone plastered me with the name 'agitator' and it stuck. An agitator is man or woman to whom conventional environment has become monotonous, to whom the existing order of things holds no emotional appeal. They seek by agitation and education to bring about social change."

"These gunmen were unscrupulous and evicted miners from coal company houses without due process of law. They framed and jailed miners who would not agree with their terms. These gunmen cracked heads, maimed, and in many instances killed miners outright because they would not renounce the union."

"From these men of wealth who ground their employees into profits in order that they might fare sumptuously and clothe their offspring in purple and fine linen, state, county, and municipal workers took their orders. . . . Every dollar [they had] represented anguish, pain, misery, blighted hopes, crushed aspirations, stifled ideals. Viewing their activities from the proper angle, every dollar . . . represented the groans of overworked and underfed employees, the pitiful supplications of undernourished women, and the heart-rendering whines of starving babies."

"This is the spirit of fellowship, love and devotion that permeates the life of the union coal miner. He will give until it hurts, and then divide what is left with his fellow men."

"Decent treatment will always bring out the best qualities in the average working man. He responds to fair treatment and if there is any good in him, proper consideration for his joys, his sorrows, his woes, his successes and failures, will develop that good."

"The uprising of 1919 and 1921 have often been referred to in calumny by those who wished to camouflage the issue or throw a smoke screen around their own activities. . . . When the miners surrendered their arms to Brigadier General H.H. Bandholtz, and said to the grizzled veteran of many battles, 'General, we are not fighting our government,' it was similiar only to the signing of the Magna Carta by King John on the battlefield at Runnymede. Thus was established beyond question the fact that they were not in revolt against constituted authority but had taken to arms because they believed that there was no other way to correct the wrongs perpetuated upon them by a conspiracy between law and unlawful violence."

"Clean Coal the Keynote for an Early Victory"
A Speech by Frank Keeney

When President Woodrow Wilson declared World War I to be a "War for Democracy," coal miners believed him. It was logical for them to believe that such a war would bring democracy home to coal camps and company towns—as well to Europe.

Frank Keeney shared that hope. Addressing members of his union on Labor Day, 1918, Keeney speaks of "a new world" in the making. It would be a better, freer world. It was the first year of American involvement in the global war and, as is evident here, Keeney urged miners to dig the coal the country needed to win the war.

Unfortunately, the "War to End All Wars" did little for miners, who were forced to return to old, undemocratic ways of life and work. As a result, West Virginia miners launched a "war for democracy" of their own.

A new world is in the making, and the United States will play a most prominent part in the outcome, and organized labor will be one of the chief factors in the winning of a glorious victory, though it shall be won by the greatest human sacrifice in the world's history—a bloody conflict with the most venomous enemy that has ever faced humankind; but like all the great conflicts that have been waged for the preservation and protection of the human race, untold sacrifices, suffering and misery have been, and must be made that the principles and ideals of the world's Creator shall live, and the world war in which we are now engaged in order to make the whole civilized globe safe for democracy and humanity is no exception to the rule.

Right has always prevailed in the end, and it needs but follow that it will in this great conflict; that success will crown our efforts in sweeping from the face of the earth the feudalistic reign of the mad butcher of Berlin is self evident, but that bloody conflict may be terminated as speedily as possible and with the least human sacrifice it behooves every American subject to exert every energy to the extent of human endurance to hasten that day when world-wide democracy will prevail.

I consider it an honored privilege for the American workers to be in a position to render service to our government in any way possible that will bring about the speedy and successful termination of the conflict now raging fiercely "over there," and as a humble member of the United Mine Workers of America, the largest industrial organization of all time, which has unfalteringly furnished its quota for the trenches and responded to every call of our government and guaranteed to furnish all coal necessary to victoriously combat the Hun if given the opportunity, I wish to call the attention of the membership of our organization to still another duty which they owe our government, themselves and our posterity—the absolute necessity of producing CLEAN COAL.

To maintain our position and carry out the pledges of our organization to the fullest extent it is not only necessary to produce all the coal necessary but it is also our imperative duty to see that all the coal mined and loaded is free of dirt and impurities. Clean coal means greater efficiency; it means a greater output from our munitions factories in a given time and an increased production in every industry that is essential to the winning of the war and a speedier transportation service on our railroads. Clean coal when placed in the bunkers of our ships means their increased speed and efficiency and that our soldiers and sailors are guaranteed more safety on the high seas against the submarines of the vicious Huns; it means that our warships and transports will make swifter progress in carrying our boys to the assistance of those "over there," and food and munitions to supply the demand of our allies. Clean coal means the hastening of the new day for which every red-blooded American is striving. Clean coal will win the war.

On the other hand, every ton of dirty coal that is produced will retard the wheels of industry and weaken the efficiency of our great war machinery, endanger the lives of our boys on their voyage across the seas and will make our food and munition transports an easier prey to the hellish Huns and serve to prolong the war and increase the human sacrifice. Dirty coal is a weapon in the hands of Kaiser Bill, and I most earnestly appeal to every United Mine Worker to work every day possible and above all to produce clean coal, live strictly up to our contracts and our pledges to our government, and in doing this we are but doing our duty and loyally responding to the call of suffering humanity.

In this connection a great deal also depends upon the operator in order that the miner can successfully carry out his obligation to our government, he must co-operate, as without his co-operation the miner is handicapped and in this grave crisis it behooves every American to do his duty regardless of his station in life; there must be no laggards, no frivolous quibbling, and the operator must do his part if we are to be successful in meeting the demand for clean coal. We must stand shoulder to shoulder in this great battle for universal liberty and democracy that will reach to the four corners of the earth.

Thus far in the world conflict the great American labor movement has not been found wanting and it will remain thus unto the end, and I am satisfied that the United Mine Workers will be equal to the task of furnishing all the coal and *clean coal* that is necessary to usher in the new world with a vibrant, throbbing democracy that will establish the principles of the Fatherhood of God and the Brotherhood of Man.

FRED MOONEY AND FRANK KEENEY
COURTESY OF THE WEST VIRGINIA STATE ARCHIVES.

CHAPTER V

CHAPTER V
The Shootout:
The Matewan Massacre

When coal miners went on strike during World War II, an angry nation denounced then as ungrateful traitors. President Franklin Roosevelt offered to resign if United Mine Workers leader John L. Lewis would commit suicide.

Forgotten, however, was the national loyalty the union miners had shown during World War I. For the duration of the war, coal miners had set new production records to fuel America's industries and war machinery. They stayed on the job—even while the government tolerated the hateful conditions under which they were forced to live; company houses, dangerous working conditions, blacklists, and company thuggery. When those conditions continued after the war, the miners realized that, despite their sacrifices, the coal fields had not been made safe for democracy.

On May 19, 1920, the inevitable happened. On that drizzly spring afternoon, a group of Baldwin-Felts mine guards were preparing to leave the little town of Matewan, in Mingo County. They had just evicted striking miners from their company houses, leaving families and their furniture in the company road. The guards were now on their way back home to Bluefield.

As they walked toward the depot to catch the next train to Bluefield, the mine guards were stopped by Sid Hatfield, the town's 28-year-old chief of police. A former miner himself, Hatfield identified with the union men. He openly sided with their cause, and had protected them when they held meetings in town. Outraged by the callous and brutal treatment the striking miners and their families had received at the hands of the mine guards, Hatfield exploded into deadly fury that afternoon.

Testimony of Sid Hatfield
to the U.S. Senate

In testimony before the U.S. Senate, the Matewan police officer gave his version of what happened on that tragic, but historic day. Taken from the Senate hearings on Conditions in the West Virginia Coal Fields.

THE CHAIRMAN: Mr. Hatfield, where is your home?

MR. HATFIELD: In Matewan; I am living in Matewan, Mingo County.

THE CHAIRMAN: We want to ask about the time of this affair at Matewan. Were you holding any official position at that time?

MR. HATFIELD: I was chief of police at Matewan at that time.

THE CHAIRMAN: You were chief of police at Matewan?

MR. HATFIELD: Yes, sir; I was chief of police at Matewan.

THE CHAIRMAN: And how long had you been chief of police at Matewan?

MR. HATFIELD: Two years.

THE CHAIRMAN: Just what occasion, or what connection did that trouble at Matewan have with the strike. Had any strikes been called at that time?

MR. HATFIELD: No; it was not at that time.

THE CHAIRMAN: Did it grow out of these labor troubles?

MR. HATFIELD: Well, practically. That is the reason; the detectives were throwing out these people's furniture.

THE CHAIRMAN: What detectives were they?

MR. HATFIELD: Well, I don't remember the names. Albert Felts and Cunningham, the Baldwin-Felts detective agency.

THE CHAIRMAN: I wish you would speak a little louder. They were evicting the people and putting their furniture out on the highway?

MR. HATFIELD: Yes, sir.

THE CHAIRMAN: Now, what happened?

MR. HATFIELD: Well, me and the mayor of the town went up and asked them, did they have a right to do that, and Mr. Felts, the superintendent of the agency, said that he had. They told him that they had the right to do that, and had gotten it from the judge, Mr. Damron, who was judge at that time, and we asked them to show the authority, and they said they didn't have anything to show, they said two hours' notice was all they wanted. We told them they could not throw those people out unless they had papers from the court, to go according to law. They said two hours was all they wanted, and they went ahead and throwed the people out, and about 3:30 they came back to Matewan—

THE CHAIRMAN: I cannot understand you. You must speak louder.

MR. HATFIELD: About 3:30 they came back to Matewan and they had guns on their shoulders with high-powered rifles, and there were 12 or 13 of them, and they were in automobiles.

THE CHAIRMAN: How many automobiles were there?

MR. HATFIELD: Three.

THE CHAIRMAN: Three?

MR. HATFIELD: Three automobiles. The mayor issued a warrant for their arrest and gave it to me and told me to arrest them. I went up and told Mr. Felts—he was the boss of the gang—that I would have to arrest him. He said he would turn the compliment on me, that he had a warrant for me. I told him to read the warrant. He did not read the warrant to me but he told me what the charges were and he said he would have to take me to Bluefield. I told him that I would not go to Bluefield because I was chief of police, and I could not leave. He told me that he would have to take me anyway. I told him that if he would have to take me, I would have to go. We walked down the street to where the Pullman stops—

THE CHAIRMAN: To where the what?

MR. HATFIELD: To where the Pullman stop of 16, on the train, on the way to Bluefield. Someone went and told the mayor that the detectives had me arrested, and the mayor came out to see what the charges were, and he asked what the charges were, and he told Felts that he would give bond for me, that he could not afford to let me go to Bluefield.

Felts told him that he could not take any bond, and the mayor asked him for the warrant, and he gave the warrant to the mayor and the mayor read the warrant and said it was bogus, it was not legal, and then he shot the mayor. Then the shooting started in general.

THE CHAIRMAN: How many shots were fired?

MR. HATFIELD: Fifty or seventy-five.

THE CHAIRMAN: And how many men did you have with you?

MR. HATFIELD: Well, I did not have any men with me at the time they had me arrested. It was train time and a whole lot of people would meet the train.

THE CHAIRMAN: Did not the people come in to help you arrest them?

MR. HATFIELD: No, sir.

THE CHAIRMAN: Were you all alone?

MR. HATFIELD: I didn't ask for any help.

THE CHAIRMAN: How many people were killed there?

MR. HATFIELD: Ten, and four shot.

THE CHAIRMAN: Ten killed and four injured.

MR. HATFIELD: Yes, sir.

THE CHAIRMAN: Of the 10 killed how many were the Baldwin-Felts people?

MR. HATFIELD: Seven.

THE CHAIRMAN: And the other three were who?

MR. HATFIELD: Bob Mullins.

THE CHAIRMAN: One was the mayor?

MR. HATFIELD: Yes.

THE CHAIRMAN: Who were the other two?

MR. HATFIELD: Bob Mullins and Tod Pinsley.

THE CHAIRMAN: Were they citizens of the town?

MR. HATFIELD: Yes, sir.

THE CHAIRMAN: Did you know whether the Baldwin-Felts people had been employed in these labor troubles?

MR. HATFIELD: Mr. Smith, the superintendent of the Stone Mountain told us the Baldwin-Felts people were coming there.

THE CHAIRMAN: Are you a member of the United Mine Workers?

MR. HATFIELD: No, sir.

THE CHAIRMAN: Have you ever been a miner?

MR. HATFIELD: Yes, sir.

THE CHAIRMAN: Or a member of any of their organizations?

MR. HATFIELD: No, sir; nothing only the Odd Fellows and K.P. and Redmen.

THE CHAIRMAN: Were there any troubles after that at Matewan or in that immediate vicinity growing out of the labor situation?

MR. HATFIELD: Not that I remember of, right at the present.

THE CHAIRMAN: You were indicted yourself, Mr. Hatfield?

MR. HATFIELD: Yes, sir.

THE CHAIRMAN: And you have been tried?

MR. HATFIELD: Yes, sir; I was tried on one occasion.

THE CHAIRMAN: Were you acquitted?

MR. HATFIELD: Yes, sir.

THE CHAIRMAN: How many more cases are pending?

MR. HATFIELD: Six more, I believe.

THE CHAIRMAN: Six more growing out of that occurrence?

MR. HATFIELD: Yes, sir.

THE CHAIRMAN: Do you know anything yourself about any disorder in that county growing out of the situation there between the operators and the miners?

MR. HATFIELD: Well, I know there had been a lot of shooting down there in that community.

THE CHAIRMAN: A lot of shooting?

MR. HATFIELD: Yes, sir.

THE CHAIRMAN: Has there been effort to stop giving firearms? Can anybody get or buy any firearms they please in that county?

MR. HATFIELD: Not at the present; no, sir.

THE CHAIRMAN: They cannot get them at present?

MR. HATFIELD: No, sir.

THE CHAIRMAN: That is because it is under martial law, but before it went under martial law could anybody buy guns or bring them in or send them in?

MR. HATFIELD: Yes, sir.

THE CHAIRMAN: Or buy firearms?

MR. HATFIELD: You could sell guns before the present law—before the 19th of May.

THE CHAIRMAN: I suppose you could not make an estimate as to the number of firearms in that county?

MR. HATFIELD: No, sir; I couldn't do that.

SENATOR MCKELLAR: Let me see if I understand you. You say that on this particular day you were the marshal of that little town and the mayor directed you to arrest these seven or eight men who were there armed?

MR. HATFIELD: Thirteen men.

SENATOR MCKELLAR: Thirteen men?

MR. HATFIELD: Yes, sir.

SENATOR MCKELLAR: And the mayor had directed you to arrest them for what? What were they doing?

MR. HATFIELD: We had an ordinance for nobody to have no gun unless he is an officer.

SENATOR MCKELLAR: And these 13 men were there with guns?

MR. HATFIELD: Yes, sir.

SENATOR MCKELLAR: And in that way they were violating the town ordinance?

MR. HATFIELD: Yes, sir.

SENATOR MCKELLAR: Now, let me ask you, how did it happen that the mayor instructed you to arrest them?

MR. HATFIELD: I asked him for a warrant.

SENATOR MCKELLAR: You asked him for a warrant?

MR. HATFIELD: Yes, sir.

SENATOR MCKELLAR: You had seen the men there?

MR. HATFIELD: Yes, sir; they come through the town—through the back streets—in automobiles.

SENATOR MCKELLAR: When you first saw them, when you first talked with them, did they say anything about arresting you?

MR. HATFIELD: No, sir; not when I first talked with them.

SENATOR MCKELLAR: They did not say anything about arresting you until you attempted to arrest them?

MR. HATFIELD: No, sir.

SENATOR MCKELLAR: And then, as I understand you, they said, "Why, we have got a warrant for you"?

MR. HATFIELD: Yes, sir.

SENATOR MCKELLAR: Did they show the warrant?

MR. HATFIELD: They didn't show it to me.

SENATOR MCKELLAR: Did you ever see the warrant?

MR. HATFIELD: Yes, sir; here is a copy of it.

SENATOR MCKELLAR: I want to get at the facts. You say these 13 men attempted to serve this warrant on you and arrest you under this warrant?

MR. HATFIELD: Yes, sir.

SENATOR MCKELLAR: Were these 13 citizens of your county?

MR. HATFIELD: No, sir.

SENATOR MCKELLAR: None of them were citizens of your county?

MR. HATFIELD: None of them.

SENATOR MCKELLAR: Did they show any authority from the justice of the peace to arrest you?

MR. HATFIELD: That is all [indicating copy of warrant, Hatfield Exhibit 1].

SENATOR MCKELLAR: That is all?

MR. HATFIELD: That is all.

SENATOR MCKELLAR: And when they were in the act of arresting you the mayor came up, did you say?

MR. HATFIELD: Yes, sir.

SENATOR MCKELLAR: What did the mayor want and what did he say? Let us get the facts just as they were.

MR. HATFIELD: He asked Mr. Felts, who was the man over the gunmen, what the charge was against me. He told him for taking a prisoner from an officer.

SENATOR MCKELLAR: Taking a prisoner from an officer?

MR. HATFIELD: Yes, sir. He told him he would give bond. Felts told him he couldn't take any bond, you see.

SENATOR MCKELLAR: That he could not take any bond?

MR. HATFIELD: Yes, sir. He said he would take me to Bluefield. That is out of the county.

SENATOR MCKELLAR: That is out of the county?

MR. HATFIELD: Yes, sir.

SENATOR MCKELLAR: What were they going to take you out of the county for? Can they try a man for a misdemeanor outside of the county?

MR. HATFIELD: No, sir. He was going to take me to the headquarters of the Baldwin-Felts people in Bluefield. They couldn't try me out of the county.

SENATOR MCKELLAR: While they were saying they were going to arrest you under this warrant, the warrant of which this is a copy, you had been directed by the mayor to arrest them because of a violation of the city ordinance?

MR. HATFIELD: Yes, sir; and we had been informed that the justice of the peace at Williamson had issued a warrant for them for throwing these people out, in violation of the law, and the warrant was on the road to me then to serve on them.

SENATOR MCKELLAR: How did they happen to shoot the mayor?

MR. HATFIELD: When he told them the warrant was bogus and they got up an argument there.

SENATOR MCKELLAR: Who shot him?

MR. HATFIELD: Albert Felts.

SENATOR MCKELLAR: Was that the only provocation he had, because the mayor of the city told him that was a bogus warrant?

MR. HATFIELD: Well, there had been some argument about their throwing out the people, over them throwing them out, but that was what was said then he was shot.

SENATOR MCKELLAR: That was what was said when he was shot?

MR. HATFIELD: Yes, sir.

SENATOR MCKELLAR: Who did the rest of the shooting?

MR. HATFIELD: It was shooting in general then.

SENATOR MCKELLAR: The shooting became general then?

MR. HATFIELD: Yes, sir.

SENATOR MCKELLAR: It was a general fight?

MR. HATFIELD: Yes, sir.

SENATOR MCKELLAR: The mayor was the first man shot?

MR. HATFIELD: Yes, sir.

SENATOR MCKELLAR: And after that the shooting became general?

MR. HATFIELD: Yes, sir.

SENATOR MCKELLAR: And when the shooting was over seven on one side and three on the other had been killed?

MR. HATFIELD: Yes, sir.

SENATOR MCKELLAR: And four shot, four injured?

MR. HATFIELD: Yes, sir.

SENATOR MCKELLAR: The four have since gotten well?

MR. HATFIELD: Yes, sir.

MR. AVIS: Mr. Hatfield, you spoke about Mr. Felts shooting the mayor. How many shots did Albert Felts fire?

MR. HATFIELD: Well, I didn't have time to count them. If you had been there I don't think you could have counted them.

MR. AVIS: You say he shot more than once?

MR. HATFIELD: I couldn't say how many shots he shot.

MR. AVIS: When you were tried you were defended by the attorneys for the United Mine Workers of America, were you not?

MR. HATFIELD: Mr. Houston and Mr. Burkinshaw.

MR. AVIS: The United Mine Workers paid all of the expense of your defense, did they not?

MR. HATFIELD: I suppose they did.

MR. AVIS: Are you not under indictment for killing Anse Hatfield?

MR. HATFIELD: Yes, sir.

MR. AVIS: Are you not under indictment in McDowell County, an indictment returning this week, charging you with a conspiracy, in connection with others, to blow up the coal tipple at Mohawk?

MR. HATFIELD: That is the first I heard of it. . . .

MAYOR CABLE TESTERMAN
Taking Sid's side in the altercation with the Baldwin-Felts agents, Testerman was the first to fall in the shootout of May 19, 1920. PHOTOGRAPHER UNKNOWN, COURTESY OF JACK TESTERMAN.

SID HATFIELD
PHOTOGRAPHER UNKNOWN, COURTESY OF STATE ARCHIVES.

CHAPTER VI

CHAPTER VI
The Hit:
The Killing of Sid Hatfield
and Ed Chambers

Sid Hatfield did not return to the Senate hearings, but his widow, Jessie, did.

After the Matewan massacre and his subsequent acquittal, Sid became an overnight folk hero among the West Virginia miners. But that same notoriety made him a marked man among the Baldwin-Felts mine guards. He was to be killed at any cost.

On August 1, 1921, Hatfield was walking up the steep steps at the McDowell County Courthouse in Welch, West Virginia. He was accompanied by his wife Jessie, his former police officer and UMW member Ed Chambers, and Chambers's wife, Sallie. Hatfield had been called to Welch to answer charges that he had participated in the destruction of a non-union mine at Mohawk, on the Mingo-McDowell County line.

The foursome passed the first landing and Baldwin-Felts guards at the top of the steps opened fire. When the smoke cleared, Hatfield and Chambers lay dead. The following is testimony from Jessie Hatfield and Sallie Chambers, giving their account of what happened on that bloody day when the West Virginia miners lost a folk hero, and their movement gained two martyrs.

For his part, company shootist C.E. Lively contended he'd seen Hatfield reach for a gun, and killed him in self-defense. But there is every indication that Lively had acted to avenge the deaths of his friends, Albert and Lee Felts, the brother detectives of the Baldwin-Felts agency who had been shot down in Matewan more than a year before.

Testimony of Mrs. Sid Hatfield
to the U.S. Senate

The witness, having been first duly sworn, was examined by Mr. Frank P. Walsh, and testified as follows:

MR. FRANK P. WALSH: Please state your name to the committee, madam.

MRS. HATFIELD: Mrs. Sid Hatfield.

MR. FRANK P. WALSH: Where do you reside, Mrs. Hatfield?

MRS. HATFIELD: Matewan.

MR. FRANK P. WALSH: In what county is that?

MRS. HATFIELD: Mingo.

MR. FRANK P. WALSH: The state of West Virginia?

MRS. HATFIELD: Yes, sir.

MR. FRANK P. WALSH: And you are the widow of Sid Hatfield?

MRS. HATFIELD: Yes, sir.

MR. FRANK P. WALSH: And when did he depart this life?

MRS. HATFIELD: August the first.

MR. FRANK P. WALSH: Were you present at the time he lost his life?

MRS. HATFIELD: Yes, sir.

MR. FRANK P. WALSH: And your husband lost his life, I believe, in Welch?

MRS. HATFIELD: Yes.

MR. FRANK P. WALSH: The county seat of McDowell County?

MRS. HATFIELD: Yes, sir.

MR. FRANK P. WALSH: And where did you go from to that county seat upon the day in question?

MRS. HATFIELD: We went from Matewan to McDowell County.

MR. FRANK P. WALSH: From Matewan?

MRS. HATFIELD: Yes.

MR. FRANK P. WALSH: In Mingo County?

MRS. HATFIELD: Yes, sir.

MR. FRANK P. WALSH: And what time did you leave Matewan?

MRS. HATFIELD: About 5:15, I believe, in the morning.

MR. FRANK P. WALSH: In the morning?

MRS. HATFIELD: Yes.

MR. FRANK P. WALSH: And at what time did you arrive in Welch?

MRS. HATFIELD: A quarter to 9; between 8 and 9. I don't know just exactly; I couldn't say.

MR. FRANK P. WALSH: Briefly, what were you and your husband coming to Welch for?

MRS. HATFIELD: To appear before a court.

MR. FRANK P. WALSH: Were you subpoenaed as witnesses, or was your husband a defendant?

MRS. HATFIELD: He was a defendant.

MR. FRANK P. WALSH: And you were subpoenaed as a witness?

MRS. HATFIELD: No, sir; I was not. I didn't know whether I would be a witness or not.

MR. FRANK P. WALSH: You accompanied your husband?

MRS. HATFIELD: Yes, sir.

MR. FRANK P. WALSH: Now, did you see C.E. Lively at any time that morning before your reached Welch?

MRS. HATFIELD: Yes, sir.

MR. FRANK P. WALSH: Where did you see him?

MRS. HATFIELD: He got on the train at Yeager, and went through the car and spoke to us, and when we got off at Welch we went to the hotel, and it was too early in the morning to get a room, so we sent out for breakfast to the restaurant; so Mr. Lively was still on the track, and he went in the restaurant and ate breakfast at the same restaurant that we ate breakfast; so when we got back to the hotel we still could not get a room; so Mr. Van Fleet, a lawyer from Charleston, who had a room over in the annex in the same hotel, so he went over and said we could use his room until we could get a room later in the day; so we did that, and we was waiting for the 11:15—no, the 10 something—train to come in there to bring the witnesses, Mr. Hatfield's witnesses in on the next train. I don't know just what time, about 10:30, or something like that the train arrived in Welch. So Mr. Van Fleet had just left the room, and he said that when the train whistled that we could come over for the trial, so he had a change of venue, so that we all had to appear there, of course, but I don't guess they were going to try the case. So we were there in the hotel, and we could see Mr. Lively over on the courthouse lawn, and Mr. Kirkpatrick, the deputy sheriff, made the remark: "There is Mr. Lively," he said, "He is keeping pretty close track of us this morning, isn't he?" And Mr. Hatfield got up off the bed and looked out through the window, and we didn't say any more, and so when the train whistled we went over to the courthouse to the trial.

MR. FRANK P. WALSH: Was your husband armed or unarmed?

MRS. HATFIELD: He was unarmed.

MR. FRANK P. WALSH: How do you know?

MRS. HATFIELD: Because I took off his guns and put them in my traveling case.

MR. FRANK P. WALSH: Two revolvers?

MRS. HATFIELD: Yes.

MR. FRANK P. WALSH: And he started for the courthouse?

MRS. HATFIELD: Yes.

MR. FRANK P. WALSH: Was there any person else with Mr. Lively when you saw him on the train, or when you saw him on the courthouse lawn?

MRS. HATFIELD: Well, there were a good many men, but I don't know who they were.

MR. FRANK P. WALSH: Now, then, you proceeded with your husband to the courthouse?

MRS. HATFIELD: Yes.

MR. FRANK P. WALSH: And who, if anybody else, were with you?

MRS. HATFIELD: Mr. Ed Chambers and Mrs. Ed Chambers, and Mr. Kirkpatrick, a deputy sheriff.

MR. FRANK P. WALSH: Now, just describe what took place as you were going up the steps of the courthouse.

MRS. HATFIELD: As we were going up the steps, we went up this way, and we was coming up this side, and Mr. Hatfield threw his hands up and said, "Hello, boys," and a great number of shots were fired.

MR. FRANK P. WALSH: Shots were fired by whom?

MRS. HATFIELD: Detectives.

MR. FRANK P. WALSH: Who else did you recognize in the crowd besides Lively?

MRS. HATFIELD: Well, I don't know that.

MR. FRANK P. WALSH: Well, did you or did you not observe Lively shooting at your husband?

MRS. HATFIELD: No, sir; I did not.

MR. FRANK P. WALSH: What did you do when the firing began?

MRS. HATFIELD: I ran.

MR. FRANK P. WALSH: Ran where?

MRS. HATFIELD: I ran to the sheriff's office, because on the Monday before that they arrested Mr. Hatfield and taken him up there for bond, so I went up and went his bond, and Mr. Hatfield, Bill Hatfield, the high sheriff of that county, promised me that I would be protected and so would Mr. Hatfield, because we were afraid to come into that county, because they say they beat up people and drag them off the trains from Mingo, wouldn't let people come in off the trains from Mingo and all that kind of thing, and so I was afraid to come into that county, and so Mr. Hatfield said that he would guarantee protection to Mr. Hatfield and to me, and so then when we went back they treated us nice the first time, and I didn't feel afraid the next time, but when I got to the sheriff's office, after they had fired the shots at Mr. Hatfield, why I met a man with a big gun on him and he said that Mr. Hatfield wasn't in there.

MR. FRANK P. WALSH: That is, the high sheriff, Mr. Hatfield, wasn't in there?

MRS. HATFIELD: Yes.

MR. FRANK P. WALSH: How long did you remain inside of the courthouse?

MRS. HATFIELD: Well, I started out, and one of the detectives grabbed me, and he wouldn't let me go.

MR. FRANK P. WALSH: When did you finally get to your husband?

MRS. HATFIELD: They wouldn't let me.

MR. FRANK P. WALSH: When did you next see your husband?

MRS. HATFIELD: When I got home.

MR. FRANK P. WALSH: He was a corpse then?

MRS. HATFIELD: Yes.

MR. FRANK P. WALSH: That is all. Do you want to cross-examine this witness?

MR. VINSON: I don't think so.

JESSIE TESTERMAN HATFIELD AND SALLIE CHAMBERS
The widows of Sid Hatfield and Ed Chambers outside the U.S. Senate. The two women traveled to Washington in September, 1921, to testify before Senate hearings on coal fields violence. PHOTO BY HARRIS AND EWING, COURTESY OF THE WEST VIRGINIA AND REGIONAL HISTORY COLLECTION, WVU.

Testimony of Mrs. Ed Chambers to the U.S. Senate

MR. WALSH: How old a man was your husband, Mrs. Chambers?

MRS. CHAMBERS: He was 22 years old.

MR. WALSH: How old are you, if I may ask?

MRS. CHAMBERS: I am 24.

MR. WALSH: Please state now what took place as you were going up the steps of the courthouse; state it in your own way.

MRS. CHAMBERS: Well, as we went up the first flight of steps, just as we landed on the first landing, the other defendants and their witnesses, and probably some of Sid Hatfield's witnesses, were coming up the other flights of steps on the other side of the landing, and Sid kind of hesitated just a little bit when the boys were speaking to him and kind of waved his hand that way [illustrating] at them, and at that time the first shot was fired about three steps up the second flight of steps that led into the courthouse.

MR. WALSH: Who fired the shot?

MRS. CHAMBERS: Well, one of the detectives.

MR. WALSH: How many of them were there?

MRS. CHAMBERS: Well, I wouldn't say how many were there; there looked like there might have been 100 or maybe 200 there that day, and there were about 6 or 8 right on these steps shooting, while there were more at the top of the steps standing on the lawn.

MR. WALSH: Did they take aim at your husband and Mr. Hatfield?

MRS. CHAMBERS: They did. Lively put his arm across the front of me and shot my husband in the neck; right there was the first shot. I don't mean that that was the first shot that was fired, but that was the first time my husband was shot. Sid was shot first—Sid Hatfield.

MR. WALSH: How many times was your husband shot?

MRS. CHAMBERS: About 11 or 12 times.

MR. WALSH: And about how many times was Mr. Hatfield shot; how many shot entered his body?

MRS. CHAMBERS: I am unable to say; some said he had 9 and some said 11; so I am not sure how many.

MR. WALSH: You say Lively reached around your neck and fired a shot?

MRS. CHAMBERS: No; he was up on the step in front of me and kind of on this side, you see, and my husband was on this side of me [indicating], and kind of reached his arm across in front and shot my husband that way, you see, in the neck. My husband, he rolled back down the steps and I looked down this way and I seen him rolling down and blood gushing from his neck, and I just went back down the steps after him, you see, and they kept on shooting him, and when he fell he kind of fell on his side leaving his back up, you know, toward the steps and they were shooting him in the back all the time after he fell.

MR. WALSH: How many shots entered his back?

MRS. CHAMBERS: All the shots excepting these two; he was shot one time in the neck and the last shot that was fired, C.E. Lively shot him right behind the ear.

MR. WALSH: Just describe that, what was the position of your husband's body when Lively shot him behind the ear?

MRS. CHAMBERS: He was lying down kind of on his side at the time that he shot him the last time, and his head, of course, was turned up this way, kind of lying on his side, and he just reached down and put his gun just about that near his ear, and before he did that, though, I seen him coming down to do that, I said, "Oh, please, Mr. Lively, don't shoot at him anymore, you have killed him now."

MR. WALSH: Did you think he was dead and life gone, then?

MRS. CHAMBERS: No; life was not gone then, but you know I just said that because I knew he would die, so he just run down and stuck the gun about that near his head.

MR. WALSH: Did he have to reach down and put the gun behind his ear?

MRS. CHAMBERS: Yes; he done like that [indicating].

MR. WALSH: Where were you standing?

MRS. CHAMBERS: Right over my husband.

MR. WALSH: What did you do then?

MRS. CHAMBERS: I struck him with my umbrella, and he turned around to me and say, "Oh, don't you hit me with that umbrella again, you dirty devil, or I will shoot you," and he stuck his gun out, but he didn't shoot at me, so he went on down the steps and as he got around, he come around me somewhere else and got back up to the top of the steps, he didn't say anything to me as I met him that time; they had taken me away from my husband, and I went two or three steps up the steps and said, "Oh, no; I am going to stay with my husband," and as we got up at the top of the steps Lively was standing up there and he looked at me like he was so glad he had done that I couldn't resist the temptation I had to hit him again.

MR. WALSH: With what?

MRS. CHAMBERS: With my umbrella, and he made some more remarks and jerked my umbrella away from me and threw it over the bank, but before all that happened this Mr. Salter, the man that was shooting at Sid, and Prince and Buster Prince [George Pence], of course I didn't know the men's names at that time, but I recognized their faces, and I said to Mr. Salter, I said, "Oh, Mr. Salter, oh, what did you all do this for? We did not come up here for this." He said, "Well, that is all right, we didn't come down to Matewan on the 19th day for this either." So he followed me on up into the courthouse and they got hold of me, and told me, you know I was still rubbing my husband's hand and his face and feeling—

MR. WALSH: When was this?

MRS. CHAMBERS: That was before I attacked Lively the second time, and I was rubbing him and had hold of his hand, and I just begged for someone to come to me and no one did not come, but there was some men started to run up to me, you know, and those detectives would say, "Go back, stay back, we will take care of this," so those men had to stop, you see then.

SID HATFIELD'S TOMBSTONE

The mountains of West Virginia loom behind Hatfield's grave, which is on the Kentucky side of the river. Tombstone reads: "To the memory of Sid Hatfield, May 15, 1893–Aug. 1, 1921. Defender of the rights of working people. Gunned down by Felts detectives on the steps of the McDowell County courthouse in Welch, W. Va. during the great Mine Wars. We will never forget. His murder triggered the miners' rebellion at the battle of Blair Mountain." PHOTO BY MICHAEL KELLER.

The Labor Spy in West Virginia
By Winthrop D. Lane

While he was in West Virginia—following the Matewan shootings but before Hatfield's death—Winthrop D. Lane became fascinated with C.E. Lively and wrote this profile, based in part on Lively's testimony before the Senate investigating committee.

This interesting inside-outside look at one of the most notorious characters to haunt the southern West Virginia coal fields was published in the Survey (New York). *It appeared on October 29, 1921, just a few weeks after the labor spy killed an unarmed Sid Hatfield in Welch.*

Prominent in the headquarters of District 17 of the United Mine Workers of America, in Charleston, West Virginia, there is a photograph. This photograph shows the delegates who attended a convention of the union held in Williamson, county seat of Mingo County, in the latter part of June, 1920. The convention was in a sense a celebration of victory, because those who attended it believed that the union had at last broken into the unorganized stronghold of Mingo County; it was also a council for the future, held to discuss plans for securing better terms from the operators. Shoulder to shoulder with his fellow delegates and union members in this picture stands a man named C.E. Lively.

Three weeks ago Mr. Lively took the witness stand in Lewisburg, West Virginia, and swore that at the time the convention was held he was a secret operative of the Baldwin-Felts Detective Agency. He swore also that he was a member of one of the Mingo locals of the union and an accredited delegate to the convention. He had assisted, he declared, in the organizing of several locals in that county. He had been on intimate terms with union leaders and had gained their confidence. He had administered the "obligation," or oath, to new members of one local. He had opened a restaurant in the little town of Matewan, and his restaurant was situated directly underneath the meeting place of the union in that spot; in fact, the union was his landlord, and he paid his rent to it. His restaurant was known as a good "union" restaurant, and was a sort of hanging-out place for members of the union. He had befriended the union in small ways, he said, such as paying bills for it, for which he was later reimbursed by union officials. His life during all of this time was, in fact, a dual life. He was an active member of the union, on one hand, and a secret agent of Baldwin-Felts Detective Agency, on the other. Every day or so he mailed reports to his superior officers in the detective agency, at Bluefield, West Virginia, being careful to use addresses that would not allow his discovery and signing his reports with the mystic but significant symbol "No. 9."

Mr. Lively, whose testimony I heard, is a young man, thirty-four years of age, with a wife and five children. He spoke directly, and with a frankness that showed he considered his conduct entirely praise-worthy. He was not discomfited by a rather disagreeable cross-examination. Of medium size, stockily built, and with a smile that played pleasantly about his features, he showed unmistakable signs of a winning personality; it was easy to imagine him gaining the confidence of any group of workmen. The case in which he testified was that of a miner tried for having shot at the property of a coal company and having attempted, with other members of the union, to kill a guard at that place. Violence of this sort has marked the conflict between union and non-union forces in Mingo County for a year and a half. Both sides have taken part in a species of guerilla warfare. The main outlines of this warfare are familiar enough to readers of the daily papers.

Mr. Lively had, it happens, given testimony of a similar nature even more fully on another occasion. He had appeared before members of the Committee on Education and Labor of the United States Senate in Washington last July in connection with that committee's investigation of the West Virginia trouble. Extracts from that testimony are given here. They show the incredulity and even indignation with which some members of the committee heard his story.

After saying that, following service in other states, he had returned to West Virginia in January or February, 1920, just at the time when the miners of Mingo County were beginning to organize, Mr. Lively thus described, in answers to questions, some of his activities in Mingo County. The quotations are from the stenographer's official record:

MR. DAMRON [representing several coal operators in Mingo County, who were presenting testimony to the committee]: What, if anything, did you pose to the union miners at Matewan as?

MR. LIVELY: Just as an ordinary miner, and as belonging to the union, a member of the miners' union.

MR. DAMRON: At that place did you undertake to get into the confidence of the miners' union?

MR. LIVELY: Yes, sir.

MR. DAMRON: Did you get into their confidence?

MR. LIVELY: I think I did.

MR. DAMRON: In what way did you get into the confidence of the various local unions that were being organized in the county?

MR. LIVELY: By getting into the confidence of the organizers of these various local unions, making myself an active member.

MR. DAMRON: Did you assist in the organization of any of the locals in that county?

MR. LIVELY: Yes, sir.

MR. DAMRON: What locals?

MR. LIVELY: Mr. Lavender, who had charge, and Mr. Workman got me to assist in the organizing of War Eagle, Glen Alum and Mohawk. . . .

MR. DAMRON: Now, Mr. Lively, with what local did you affiliate?

MR. LIVELY: Stone Mountain local.

MR. DAMRON: Did you have membership in that local?

MR. LIVELY: Yes, sir, I deposited my card.

MR. DAMRON: And did you assist the miners and the organizers in organizing the various mines, in getting members to join?

MR. LIVELY: Only those three named.

MR. DAMRON: Would you make reports to your organization, which I believe was at Bluefield, is it not?

MR. LIVELY: Yes, sir.

MR. DAMRON: Of what information you would get from day to day?

MR. LIVELY: Well, I would make reports of what information I would get. I had no regular time to make reports. When I decided it was necessary I would make a report, so I would maybe make two or three reports, and sometimes go three or four days without making a report.

SENATOR MCKELLAR: How much were you getting for the work at this time, $75 a month [the amount Mr. Lively had testified he received when first going to work for the Baldwin-Felts Detective Agency]?
MR. LIVELY: Two hundred and twenty-five dollars and expenses.
SENATOR MCKELLAR: They had raised your salary?
MR. LIVELY: Yes, sir.

Mr. Lively's knowledge of conditions at Stone Mountain, where he was a member of the local, may have borne unexpected fruit. The Stone Mountain Coal Company was one of those that were active in discharging employees who joined the union. On May 19, 1920, thirteen Baldwin-Felts agents with guns came to evict employees of that company who had become union members. The result is well known. An altercation arising between the Baldwin-Felts men and persons gathered around the little station in Matewan, miners and citizens, a battle ensued in which ten people were killed, seven Baldwin-Felts men and three others. Mr. Lively was in Charleston that day, possibly with a view to avoiding the necessity of taking sides when the agents of the detective company went about their job. He returned in a day or two. A new task was then assigned to him. Mr. Damron asked, "And in addition to making investigations of matters connected with the organization of the union, did you take up the investigation of this killing?" to which Mr. Lively answered, "Yes, sir."

After Mr. Lively had testified that he had attended a convention of the union in Charleston some years ago, at the same time that he was an agent of the Baldwin-Felts concern, members of the committee took a hand in the questioning:

SENATOR MCKELLAR: What and when was that convention?
MR. LIVELY: It seems to me it was in May. It was in 1913.
SENATOR MCKELLAR: May, 1913?
MR. LIVELY: Yes.
SENATOR MCKELLAR: The convention of the United Mine Workers?
MR. LIVELY: Yes.
THE CHAIRMAN [SENATOR W.S. KENYON OF IOWA]: You were a delegate to that convention?

MR. LIVELY: Yes, sir.

THE CHAIRMAN: You were one of the Baldwin-Felts detectives at that time?

MR. LIVELY: Yes, sir.

THE CHAIRMAN: Did they know that at the convention when you were there as a delegate?

MR. LIVELY: No, sir.

THE CHAIRMAN: It was a part of your detective work to be a delegate?

MR. LIVELY: Yes, sir.

THE CHAIRMAN: And find out what was going on?

MR. LIVELY: Yes, sir.

THE CHAIRMAN: Your business was to make a report of the meeting to the Felts-Baldwin people?

MR. LIVELY: Yes, sir.

Mr. Lively then testified that he had worked in various states, mentioning Colorado, Missouri, Illinois, Oklahoma and Kansas.

THE CHAIRMAN: Did you work as a detective in those states?

MR. LIVELY: Yes, sir.

THE CHAIRMAN: Or as a miner?

MR. LIVELY: Well, both sometimes.

SENATOR MCKELLAR: Did you affiliate with the miners at the time, as if you were a member of their organization?

MR. LIVELY: Yes, sir.

SENATOR MCKELLAR: All the time?

MR. LIVELY: Yes, sir.

SENATOR MCKELLAR: And at the same time you were giving reports to the Felts-Baldwin agency?

MR. LIVELY: Yes, sir.

THE CHAIRMAN: Were your expenses paid by the miners when you went to the convention, or did the Felts-Baldwin agency pay your expenses?

MR. LIVELY: Well, the miners paid my expenses there to that Charleston convention, yes. I felt that it was necessary that I leave them pay them in order to keep off suspicion, or else they would wonder why I would not want them to pay them.

After some further testimony concerning expenses, this colloquy took place:

SENATOR MCKELLAR: If you had disclosed your connection with the detective agency do you suppose the miners would have let you in there at all?

MR. LIVELY: Let me in there?

SENATOR MCKELLAR: Yes.

MR. LIVELY: I think they would have turned me over to the undertaker.

SENATOR MCKELLAR: They would have turned you over to the undertaker—and you did not disclose to them or to anybody your dual capacity?

MR. LIVELY: No, sir.

SENATOR MCKELLAR: And you accepted money from the miners on the theory that you were aiding them in your business.

MR. LIVELY: I have. [Mr. Lively testified that the Western Federation of Miners had at one time paid him a salary.]

SENATOR MCKELLAR: And at the same time, while you were accepting money from the miners as their representative and employee, or as their representative, you were really, as you have just said, in truth and in fact, the paid agent of the company that you knew was opposed to the miners. That is true, is it not?

MR. LIVELY: Well, I was in the pay of the detective agency. . . .

SENATOR MCKELLAR: And did you think that was right? Now, while you are testifying, do you think that was the right action on your part?

MR. LIVELY: Yes.

SENATOR MCKELLAR: And you cannot see anything wrong in that action?

MR. LIVELY: I do not.

SENATOR MCKELLAR: And are those the views of your employers, the detective agency that employed you? Was it their idea and did they tell you that your action was right, that action on your part?

MR. LIVELY: I do not remember having talked with them anything along that line. . . .

SENATOR MCKELLAR: And did they approve of that conduct on your part?

MR. LIVELY: They never said anything against it.

It having developed later that Mr. Lively had been vice-president of a local in Colorado at the same time that he was agent of the Baldwin-Felts concern, Senator McKellar's opinion of the whole affair was thus expressed:

SENATOR MCKELLAR: And do you think that you would have been elected if they had known in whose employ you were?

MR. LIVELY: Been elected? I do not think I would have appeared before the committee at Washington.

MR. AVIS [representing the Williamson Coal Operators' Association]: He has that right. That is the method practiced by the Department of Justice.

SENATOR MCKELLAR: I certainly hope that it is not practiced by the Department of Justice. I would feel much more against the Department of Justice if I thought that.

MR. AVIS: I think it is practiced in every department at Washington.

SENATOR MCKELLAR: I do not believe it.

MR. VINSON [also representing the operators]: But the destruction of the Monte [Molly] McGuires [Maguires] in Pennsylvania was done exactly as this was done.

SENATOR MCKELLAR: I will say that it violates every idea of right that I ever had. I never would have believed that a thing like this would happen, and I am not surprised that you are having trouble down there in Mingo County.

The precise extent to which the use of under-cover men is resorted to in West Virginia, the number of men engaged in it and the exact value of their services to their employers, would be difficult to determine. W.E.E. Keopler, secretary of the Pocahontas Operators' Association, which embraces the two intensely non-union counties of Mercer and McDowell, told me that his association had a contract with the Baldwin-Felts Detective Agency, but declined on grounds of "policy" to tell me how many men the agency supplies. "I guess the number is large," he said, "because I know the bill is a pretty big one. You see, this is the home of the Baldwin-Felts agency. We're right on the home ground." Thomas L. Felts, partner of W.G. Baldwin in the agency, lives in Bluefield, Mercer County, and the agency maintains an office there.

George Bausewine, Jr., secretary of the Williamson Coal Operators' Association, embracing the operators of Mingo County, told me that

his association was enjoying the services of ten Baldwin-Felts opera-
tives. "We have retained the Baldwin-Felts Agency since March, 1918,"
he said. "We claim that we have a right to employ secret service men,
or detectives, to protect our interests. We want to know what our men
are doing, what they're talking about. We want to know whether the
union is being agitated." He said that the usual duty of a Baldwin-Felts
man was to work in the mines, under cover, and learn what was going
on. The individual operators had nothing to do with the selection of
the men, he said; that was left to the agency.

I talked with Thomas L. Felts. He said his agency supplied two
kinds of men to the operators. One of these is the guard or police officer, who is a private watchman and operates openly. The other is the
detective or secret service man of the Lively type. The secret service
man, said Mr. Felts, might be called upon to perform any kind of crime
detection. "And, of course," he added, "I'm frank to say that if someone
comes in and agitates around for the union, the secret service man
reports it to the company." He intimated that now that the non-union
operators were securing individual contacts with their employees—
the so-called "yellow dog" contracts—whereby the employee agrees to
have nothing to do with a labor organization during his employment
by the company, the use of secret service men might be reduced.

Mr. Felts said that, in his individual capacity, he also furnishes to
the county sheriffs in that region men who are sworn in as deputy sheriffs and become public officials. These men are pledged to serve the
whole community, yet their salaries are paid by the private operators.
"It works this way," said Mr. Felts. "A mine manager calls me up and
says, 'Mr. Felts,' or 'Tom,' 'I want a man to be deputized up here on my
property. Can you get me one?' So I get him one, and the man goes
up and the sheriff deputizes him." He thought that he had supplied
perhaps twenty men who had been deputized by the sheriffs of Mercer
and McDowell counties, but I suspect that the number is a larger one.

Mr. Felts estimated that from 250 to 300 men had been deputized in Mercer and McDowell counties in the spring of 1920, when
the union, gaining a foothold in Mingo County, adjoining McDowell,
threatened to extend its activities to the mines in those counties.

Mr. Felts is a respected resident of Bluefield. The business people
and other successful folk there regard him as one of their leading citizens. It was in the office of the Pocahontas Operators' Association that

I was introduced to him, and there I heard him entertain an audience of six or eight men—with stories of the exploits of his agency in serving the opponents of union labor. As we talked together for two hours or so afterward, he revealed an intense hostility to labor organizations and labor leaders in general. He seemed to regard a labor organization as necessarily "outlaw." A man who induced another man to join a union was apparently, in his eyes, a menace, to be watched as closely as one would watch a suspected thief. The United Mine Workers of America he singled out for special condemnation and referred to several of its officials by name as "bad ones" and "criminals." He apparently made little distinction, in regard to their desirability or value, between one union and another.

The miners of West Virginia regard the Baldwin-Felts Detective Agency as one of the most serious obstacles to the securing of what they deem their "rights." They look upon the practice of the operators in employing agents of that concern, as well as armed guards and deputy sheriffs, as a deliberate method of excluding the union from nonunion fields, and they assert that there can be no peace in the industrial struggle in that state until this kind of opposition is abandoned. Whether the miners are justified in this contention is, in my judgment, properly a matter for governmental inquiry. I do not think that the Senate Committee on Education and Labor, which has announced that it will resume its hearings on the West Virginia conflict on October 24, can perform any greater public service than to call Thomas L. Felts and some of the coal operators who employ his agency to the stand, and secure for public enlightenment all that can be learned of the activities of this agency and its relations to the industrial struggle now raging there. The nature of the contracts between it and the operators employing it, the number of men supplied, the kind of services rendered and the specific methods pursued by the so-called detectives in their task of espionage—all of these have a direct bearing, not only upon what is happening in West Virginia, but upon industrial strife and unrest throughout the nation.

CHAPTER VII

CHAPTER VII
Civil War:
The March on Logan

The Matewan Massacre had put southern West Virginia back on the national news media's map. Periodicals throughout the country began sending their top reporters into the area to ascertain and write about what was going on in southern West Virginia—why it was so different from the rest of the county.

Private Ownership of Public Officials
By Arthur Gleason

Arthur Gleason's 1920 "Private Ownership of Public Officials" is one of the best stories to appear about Logan County. It provides acute insight into what was going on in this unique, brutal region. The entire county was under total control of the coal companies, whose associations paid County Sheriff Don Chafin to keep the area union-free.

Gleason also proved remarkably prophetic about events in West Virginia. "The fight in Mingo [the Matewan Massacre]," he wrote, "is mild compared with that about to explode in Logan.... This section of the state is now a powder mine, ripe for blowing up." Just a year later, the area did explode with the miners' March on Logan and the ensuing Battle of Blair Mountain, an event that made the Matewan Massacre appear "mild" in comparison.

West Virginia has started in again on the organized killing which every few years breaks loose in the mining districts. On May 19, eleven men were shot to death in the town of Matewan, Mingo County. Seven of them were detectives, three were miners and one was an official. This skirmish is the first in the 1920 war between the coal operators of the State and the United Mine Workers of America. Mingo is one of the counties in the southwest of the State which has been held against organized labor by detectives, armed guards, and deputy sheriffs. With the beginning of May, the miners formed local unions, and brought in 2,000 members. As fast as the miners join the union, the coal companies are evicting them from the company-owned houses. I saw the typewritten notice of the Stone Mountain Coal Company on the window of the company-owned grocery store. It stated that the houses of the miners were owned by the company, and that the miners must leave the premises at once if they join the union. Ezra Frye, the local organizer, acting for the United Mine Workers, had leased land, and was erecting tents for the evicted families. He had ordered 300

tents on the first allotment. Matewan lies on the Tug Fork of the Big
Sandy River. It is run politically by the Hatfield clan, who for generations have had a feud with the McCoy clan. The economic struggle is
making a new alignment across the old feudist divisions. No stranger is
safe just now in these unorganized counties. We had a spy who trailed
us from Charleston to Matewan. In the town, we were kept under constant guard.

The Matewan killing is only the faint prelude to the war that will be
waged in attempting to unionize Mingo, McDowell, and Logan Counties. The stronghold of the operators' power is not Mingo, but Logan
County, and within a few weeks the center of disturbance will shift
to Logan.

"I shall not die till Logan County is organized," said Mother Jones to
me, and she is 90 years old. "George Washington said 'Join the union,'"
she added, "and Logan joins the union before I am 91."

There are 91,000 persons in West Virginia employed in and around
mines. Of these, 54,000 are organized in the United Mine Workers of
America. For the possession of the unorganized, 37,000, the coal operators and the union are engaged in the present bloody struggle. Of
these 37,000, 4,000 are in Mingo and 9,000 in Logan.

The fight in Mingo is mild compared with that about to explode in
Logan, which is under control of the coal companies. The best descrip-
tion recently written of Logan is that of Governor John Cornwell, on
November 7, 1919:

> Logan County is a political unit, self-governed, electing its
> own officers, who are not responsible to me for their official
> acts and over whom I have no direct control. Congress can
> only make public the facts. It has no power to remove a sher-
> iff or convict one who commits an assault. You know that can
> be done in Logan County only. I shall make public all the
> evidence.

In fulfillment of that promise, the Governor most courteously
turned over to me the full stenographic evidence of the unpublished
investigation into Logan County he has been conducting through three
officials. Its title is "Special Investigation by the State of West Virginia."

The coal operators maintain on their payrolls public officials who
preserve order, guard the company funds, and keep union men out of

the county. It is this exercise of public power under private pay which is one of the fundamental causes and is the most lively occasion of the bad blood between owners and workers. The operators pay directly to the sheriff $32,700 a year for this immunity from unionization. In addition, most of them pay the individual armed guard salary. These agents of the company are deputy sheriffs, appointed by the county court. The insider who operates this system is Don Chafin, county clerk, and running for sheriff. He belongs to the Hatfield clan, is an educated man, in early middle life, with a family. He is lord of Logan, controlling the deputy sheriffs.

C.W. Jones, treasurer of the Guyan Operators' Association (the Logan fields lie along the Guyan Valley), says: "The operators pay the sheriff of the county $2,725 a month, and the deputies look after their payrolls. If there is a fuss or anything like that, it is reported to the operator and the sheriff."

J.M. Vest, president and general manager of the Rum Creek Collieries Company, states:

At the present time we contribute a cent a ton to the funds of the Logan Coal Operators' Association for all purposes. Our income is approximately $100,000 a year. And out of that money perhaps $30,000 (exactly, $32,700) is contributed to the sheriff for police protection. And we have contributed largely to the Salvation Army Fund. In Logan County we have twenty-five deputy sheriffs and three constables. We have a population of a little over 60,000 scattered over an area of 400 square miles.

Pat Murphy, one of the deputy sheriffs, summed up the situation in his own style:

You don't have no idea how this worked. There is one-half a cent off of every ton of coal on Guyan River turned into the Association in Logan, where Don Chafin is boss. He owns and controls this association of deputies. It is turned into him, and he pays his deputies when pay day comes.

Actually, it is one-third of a cent on every ton which the consuming public of America pays to Don Chafin.

Logan County's potential coal is at least twenty million tons a year, but car shortage keeps it down to ten million tons. During the 1919 miners' strike, Logan and McDowell Counties worked a full production and broke the back of the strike. This is one of the reasons why the United Miners Workers are specializing on the district now. If Logan falls, West Virginia is organized.

Don Chafin has drawn heavily on the Chafin family for assistance, and finds it loyally rendered by Con, John and Wayne Chafin. John Chafin, deputy sheriff, says:

> The Amherst Coal Company and the Prockter [Proctor] Coal Company pay me $175 a month. I am on their payroll. If a man is fired I give him a notice.

Another alert deputy sheriff is Randolph M. Dial, who receives $120 a month from the sheriff and $50 a month from the Logan Mining Company. This private-and-public sheriff system is so thorough that when fifty-one union organizers came in on the Guyan Valley express on October 15, they went out on the same train on the same day. "Don't let your feet touch dirt in Logan County," said the deputies.

"I chartered an engine and two cabooses and forty-eight men," says President Vest (of the Rum Creek Company) in telling how he ran these organizers out of Logan. This train trailed the train of the union men, and once came up even with it on a parallel track.

There is only one incorporated town in Logan County, and that is the town of Logan, with a population of 3,500. Unidentified strangers are not wanted in Logan. The train that carries you the three hours from the city of Huntington into Guyan Valley is used by men who make it their business to find out yours. Deputies meet the train, as you pull into Logan—Dow Butcher, Buck White, Squire White, and Pat Murphy. You are sized up. This affectionate interest is directed for one purpose—to detect organizers and to invite them to go home. Commercial travelers, social workers, business and professional men pass in and out. Order is well kept; all the decencies are observed. Logan is a prosperous, busy little city. I stayed overnight, received welcome, and met a group of excellent sincere local folks, nurses, teachers, health experts, coal magnates. They are busy in every good work. They draw the line in this one matter alone: Logan County is not to be unionized. This led to an amusing mistake some time previous to my own visit. Mr. J.L. Heizer told me of it; it was his own experience in Logan. Mr. Heizer is chief clerk of the Department of Mines for the State of West Virginia. He is also Grand Chancellor of the Knights of Pythias for the State. He went to Logan to induct certain brethren. Mr. Heizer said on the train to Mr. Wayne Chafin that he had heard a lot about Don Chafin, and wanted to meet him. In the middle of the night, Mr. Heizer said,

> When I went to the hotel room, two men were standing at the door, and one of them stepped forward and said: "I understand you want to meet Dan Chafin?"
> I said "Yes."
> He said, "By God, you've met him now."
> A young man with me, E.R. Dalton of Huntington, tried to pacify Mr. Chafin, who stuck a gun into the stomach of Mr. Dalton and said, "Young man, you get to bed, and get there quick. I can kill both of you in this room."

Mr. Chafin then made a conscientious search of Mr. Heizer from top to toe. Somehow, the word "organizing" had got connected with Mr. Heizer's mission to Logan. Don Chafin was celebrating that particular evening, and failed to get the distinction clear in his mind between a fraternal order and a labor deputation. So, to carry out his firmly-held principles he invited Mr. Heizer out for a midnight ride, and clumped him one on the side of the head. Mr. Heizer returned to the Jefferson Hotel. Mr. Chafin then took over the management of the hotel for a few hours, relieved the clerk from duty and "shot up the place" with his revolver, but without injuring anybody. Since then, it has been explained to Mr. Chafin that Mr. Heizer is not a dangerous character. The Grand Chancellor returns soon for a further ceremony.

Mr. Chafin's control of the district reminded me of the way Timothy D. Sullivan used to rule south of Fourteenth Street in New York. His authority is that of a perfectly-oiled political machine with an abundance of funds, and a set of loyal adherents dependent on him for favors. As one of the colored miners, Luther Millis, puts it:

> Don Chafin says, "I want you to go up and get around among them men and find out who is tryin' to organize and report back to me."

Then he told the others, "Luther is goin' to come clean."

And Squire White says, "If you don't come clean, by God, we will kill you."

Don Chafin says, "Dead nigger if you don't."

I says, "I come clean, you let me go."

The attitude of the coal operators is best stated by George M. Jones, general manager of the Lundale Coal Company, Three Forks Coal Company, and the Amherst Fuel Company. Mr. Jones has installed admirable housing for his workers, and availed himself of modern improvements in sanitation, health devices, and recreational facilities. He says:

Our companies have contributed as a salary to the minister about 50 per cent. Our workers are 80 per cent American, 30 per cent black, and 50 per cent white. There have been some I.W.W.'s, Bolshevists, and these men have sown seeds of dissension, and we have picked these men out and discharged them. We have no police protection other than the protection we get through the sheriff's office, and three constables. We have three deputies at our operations—these men we pay ourselves. We pay them something; we don't pay their complete salary. We pay them for the work they do for us—guarding our payrolls from bank to mine's office, holding down speed limit of automobiles, collecting certain rents and accounts, preserving order and peace and the dignity of the community.

The principal point on this whole controversy is the question of the union or non-union in Logan. We oppose the unionization of the Guyan coal field. We are against the union and expect to do everything in our power to prevent its coming into our mines. We have never refused to meet any of our men at any time.

The leaders of the miners for this section of West Virginia—District 17 of the United Mine Workers—are C.F. Keeney and Fred Mooney. They are men in the middle thirties, and have been fighters for their crowded life-time. They are themselves miners, and carried a rifle in the Cabin Creek uprising of 1912. Mr. Keeney says: "If our organizers come back in boxes, neither heaven nor hell will be able to control the miners. Organize Logan County we will, and no one shall stop us."

The Miners of West Virginia are over 50,000 of them white American. They come of pioneer stock, and their people have lived in the state for generations. These mountaineers have grown up in the presence of implacable feuds. They are generous, hospitable, but clannish, suspicious of strangers, swift in action. Bred in this climate of warm friendships and enmities to the death, they are now stirred by the industrial fight. All their buried memories of night terror and sudden killings are awakened by the present struggle. They revert to their ancient way of settling trouble, and that is by private hillside and woodland warfare.

Today, wherever I have gone in southwest West Virginia, I find both sides armed. This section of the State is now a powder mine, ripe for blowing up.

Testimony of George Echols
to the U.S. Senate
Sunday, September 18, 1921

The March on Logan, which ended in early September, 1921, was covered by newspapers across the nation. For more than a week a stunned nation had read headlines like: "Troops are Ordered to West Virginia," "Martial Law Is Considered by Cabinet," "Fighting Now Raging on 20-Mile Front," and "Fighting Continues in Mountains as Federal Troops Reach Mingo."

Later that month, a Senate committee investigating the miners' march heard about conditions in Logan County from a number of miners and their family members. One by one, local people detailed the oppressive and exploitative industrial system prevailing in what the Washington Star *called the "Kingdom of Logan."*

One of the most interesting pieces of testimony came from miner George Echols, who pointed out that he had been "raised a slave."

"I felt just like we feel now," he said.

Echols detailed the miners' lack of basic American rights and privileges, how mine guards, state police and Don Chafin's deputies harassed the striking miners and why, in Logan County, miners felt that liberation from "King Coal" was a necessary fight.

Statement of George Echols (Colored), One of the Strikers

THE CHAIRMAN: What is your name?

MR. ECHOLS: George Echols.

THE CHAIRMAN: And you live in this tent here?

MR. ECHOLS: Yes, sir.

THE CHAIRMAN: How many are there around in these various tents?

MR. ECHOLS: I suppose there is something like—I could not tell you, and I have not an estimate of our men here.

THE CHAIRMAN: How long have you been here?

MR. ECHOLS: I have been here about five months now.

THE CHAIRMAN: Were you working in the mines?

MR. ECHOLS: I used to; yes, sir.

THE CHAIRMAN: And all these people in these tents, did they use to work in the mines?

MR. ECHOLS: Yes, sir; all of these are miners from the camps here.

THE CHAIRMAN: Where did you come from when you came to work here?

MR. ECHOLS: I came here from Columbus, Ohio. I have been here four years, very nearly five.

THE CHAIRMAN: You have been here nearly five years?

MR. ECHOLS: Yes, sir.

THE CHAIRMAN: And you were born in this country, were you?

MR. ECHOLS: Yes, sir.

THE CHAIRMAN: Where were you born?

MR. ECHOLS: I was born in eastern Virginia. I was born at Chatham, Virginia.

THE CHAIRMAN: And what is the trouble down here anyway?

MR. ECHOLS: I will tell you. The miners have asked the contractors or operators to give them an opportunity to weigh the coal, and they announced that they will not weigh it. They say that whenever we load a load of coal, then that is all that that amounts to, that it does not make any difference. We may load 2 tons to a car and they may say it is a ton and a half or two tons.

THE CHAIRMAN: Do they pay you by the ton?

MR. ECHOLS: They promised to pay us by the ton but they don't do it. They promised according to whatever the coal is to pay us by the ton, and we want them to put it on the scales. All they do is to say that [is] so and so much, and we have to take it. We feel we want to give and take, and we want them to measure it for us, that is, weigh it, and we are paid for whatever they like to pay us or feel like paying us, and they give it out at the office, they give us the balance. We pay them for the lights and the fuel and then the supplies, and whatever they say at the office they give us the balance. We always felt that we ought to have the coal weighed. I have loaded coal when I got $1.25 a car, and if we had the scales there I would get as much as $4 a car.

THE CHAIRMAN: Well, what seems to have been the trouble with you? Why are you not working?

MR. ECHOLS: Well, I think it is because I signed up with the union.

THE CHAIRMAN: And why did you quit?

MR. ECHOLS: I was discharged. I was vice president of the local, and many excuses, but if I am sitting in a church I try to do the thing as near right as I can according to the agreement. There is some things that we cannot stand for. I was raised a slave. My master and my mistress called me and I answered, and I know the time when I was a slave, and I felt just like we feel now. There have been several of the constabulary out this morning. There is a car there now that went down and whirled against a tent [indicating a car being whirled by another passing by the road]. You will notice it when you get down there. You can see those tents down there now. You can see the tents that are cut, too.

THE CHAIRMAN: Who cut your tents?

MR. ECHOLS: These men who we call the State constabulary, those men came out and they cut the tents. They came out here twice. They just rounded up the men and they shot from over across the other side [indicating] and they took this man here, and they dragged him into town.

THE CHAIRMAN: When was that?

MR. ECHOLS: That was in August or July. We have had quite a time trying to live here. They come in here, and they round them up, and they put as many as 67 men and turn them into town. They would come out here and walk up and down and talk at us in any way they want to. You know our right under the Constitution, that no man should be condemned or jailed until we have had a free and impartial trial. We claim to be citizens of the United States and we ask for the rights of citizenship; we claim to be loyal to our country, and we are loyal to our county, and all we ask is that we shall have our rights. We claim that we are citizens of the United States of America, according to the amendment to the Constitution. You know that that guarantees us free and equal rights and that is all we ask.

THE CHAIRMAN: Just what rights do you feel are getting away from you?

MR. ECHOLS: We are denied the right of anything to protect ourselves with. They will not let us have a gun. If we get together and are talking, we are ordered to scatter, and to move out. If we go out for a walk, two by two, we are ordered to scatter and to move out. If we go to town we have to go in such a way that we have to tell our wives good-by, for we know that we might not come back, and that we may be under lock and key. There has never been such a thing as these 300 men that come out here, there has never been anything like that, and when they came out here they would drive them like sheep, as they did before the Constitution prohibited slavery.

THE CHAIRMAN: Who do you mean did that?

MR. ECHOLS: Some of these gunmen. If you will go into town you will find them. They are called constabulary. In other words, when I first heard of them they were called the Baldwins. I know that they are very officious, and they take away from us our rights and privileges, and they would not allow me to speak as I am speaking to you now. I do not believe that those men think of citizenship at all. The United Workmen of America have privileges which are guaranteed by the United States, and we have rights to protect us, both the black and white, but they do not regard those rights at all. They take those privileges away from us. Now, we are asking you to give them back to us. Let us be free men. Let us stand equal. I do not mean that there is any prejudice against the colored people here.

THE CHAIRMAN: How many people are colored?

MR. ECHOLS: There are not so many colored here. I don't suppose that there are more than 150. I don't know. I have never taken an estimate of the men.

THE CHAIRMAN: And how are all these people around here living? Does the union support them?

MR. ECHOLS: Yes; the union supports them. The union supports some of these men that you see in tents and some others in houses.

THE CHAIRMAN: How does it happen that this particular tent here [indicating] is all slashed up and the other ones are not?

MR. ECHOLS: That was slashed by those men. These men came here and cut them.

THE CHAIRMAN: And what made them do that? What were you doing?

MR. ECHOLS: Why, I don't know, except that they were mad. Nobody didn't ask them to molest us. They just come in here and they slashed those tents.

The War in West Virginia

This September 17, 1921, story from the Independent *(New York), is a succinct, straight-forward account of the federal government's activities during the armed march and the extent of the violence that brought on the need for federal troops.*

On August 30 President Harding, after a conference with Secretary of War Weeks, Generals Pershing and Harbord, and a delegation of citizens from West Virginia, issued a proclamation calling upon the armed marchers, who took up arms again, saying the state constabulary had broken faith, to disperse and return to their homes by noon of September 1. This action was taken after Governor Morgan had acknowledged the inability of the state constabulary to deal adequately with the situation. At the same time instructions were issued to officers in charge of Camp Dix to have one regiment of infantry, comprising 1000 officers and men, in readiness for dispatch to the threatened territory.

Active hostilities occurred in the deaths of a deputy sheriff and a miner on August 31 at the boundary line of Boone and Logan counties. On the Logan side the defense against invasion was taken over by hastily organized volunteer bands consisting largely of clerks, business men, teachers, preachers and house-holders. Guerrilla warfare continued for several days, with no conspicuous loss of life, the rumors were afloat that over fifty of the miners had been killed. Airplanes, one of which fell to the ground with the death of four of the five occupants, were sent to reconnoiter the scene of hostilities and to drop printed copies of President Harding's proclamation. The "battle-line" was reported to extend for twenty-five miles along the boundaries of the two directly interested counties. Machine guns were in operation. Trains were commandeered by the miners and sent back of the lines to bring up more of the attacking force. A deputies' patrol was repulsed by the miners. General Bandholtz on September 3 telegraphed the War Department requesting that Federal troops be sent at once to Mingo County.

Affairs then on September 4 took a decided change for the better. Four hundred miners surrendered their arms and returned to their homes. All factions united in welcoming the coming of the Federal troops, and the establishment of law and order. Fighting ceased along the Boone-Logan County lines. Deputies captured by the miners were freed. The two thousand Federal troops had not been required to fire a single shot, and on September 5 Brigadier-General Bandholtz reported to Secretary Weeks that the situation was under control, and the miners' army entirely dispersed.

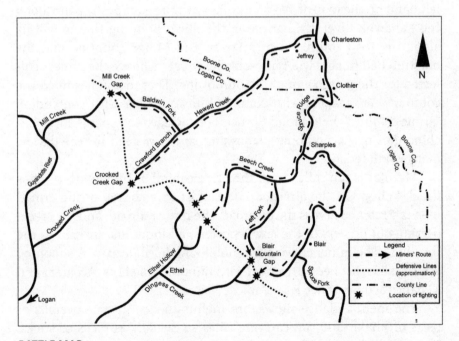

BATTLE MAP

The Battle of Blair Mountain was actually fought along an extended front, with Blair Mountain itself being only one point of conflict. In late August and early September angry miners tried to fight their way into the Guyandotte watershed above Logan, contesting major mountain crossing places from Blair Mountain to the northwestward.

Marching through West Virginia
By Heber Blankenhorn

Heber Blankenhorn's September 14, 1921, story in the Nation
*is a good depiction of the armed march. The reader can get a
sense of what happened during the march and during the military's effort to stop it, which included sending a mission of
bombing planes into the area.*

I

If—as the war correspondents used to begin—you will place your
left hand on the map of West Virginia, with the edge of the palm along
the Kanawha River at Charleston, the down-pointing thumb will lie
along the road southwest into Logan and Mingo counties, and the
outstretched fingers will represent the valleys whence the miners collected for the march along the thumb-line. That region has filled the
country's newspapers with communiqués, dealing with contending
"armies," "lines" held along Spruce Fork Ridge, entrenchments, ma-
chine-gun nests, bombing planes and so many dead for the day, so
many wounded.

Marmet is ten miles from the State capital at the mouth of Lens
Creek Valley. On the afternoon of August 22 a cordon of 100 armed
men is stretched across the dirt road, the mine railroad, and the creek,
barring out officers of the law, reporters, all inquirers. Inside lies the
"trouble." The miners have been mobilizing for four days. A snooping
airplane has just been driven off with hundreds of shots. Accident and
a chance acquaintance let me in.

The men, a glance shows, are mountaineers, in blue overalls or
parts of khaki uniform, carrying rifles as casually as picks or sticks.
They are typical. The whole village seems to be out, except the children,
women, and old men. They show the usual mining-town mixture of
cordiality and suspicion to strangers. But the mining-camp air of lone-
liness and lethargy is gone. Lens Creek Valley is electric and bustling.
They mention the towns they come from, dozens of names, in the New

River region, in Fayette County, in counties far to the north. All are union men, some railroaders. After a mile we reach camp. Hundreds are moving out of it toward Logan. Over half are youths, a quarter are Negroes, another quarter seem to be heads of families, sober looking sober speaking. Camp is being broken to a point four miles further on. Trucks of provisions, meat, groceries, canned goods move up past us.

"This time we're sure going through to Mingo," the boys say. "Them Baldwin-Feltses [company detectives] has got to go. They gotta stop shooting miners down there. Keeney turned us back the last time, him and that last Governor. Maybe Keeney was right that time. This new Governor got elected on a promise to take these Baldwin-Feltses out. If nobody else can budge them thugs, we're the boys that can. This time we go through with it."

"What started you?"

"This thing's been brewing a long while. Then two of our people gets shot down on the courthouse steps—you heard of Sid Hatfield and Ed Chambers? The Governor gives them a safe conduct; they leave their guns behind and get killed in front of their wives. It was a trap."

"But that was several weeks ago."

"Well, it takes a while for word to get 'round. Then they let his murderer, that Baldwin-Felts, Lively, out on bond—free—with a hundred miners in jail in Mingo on no charges at all—just martial law. Well, we heard from up the river that everybody was coming here. We knew what for. When we found lots had no guns we sent back to get them."

Bang! Bang-bang! from below the valley.

"That's a high-power," one remarks. "What are those damn fools wasting ammunition for? Maybe the airplane's come back. You know, several hundred service men was drilling this morning. After five minutes they was putting right smart amount of snap into it." We have forded the creek a dozen times, have passed through Hernshaw—a mean-looking mining village—we pass hundreds of men; then an auto with women passes us.

"See our Red Cross nurses?"

The women have nurses' white head-dresses, with big blue letters on the band over the brow, "U.M.W."

"They're wives of some of the boys. They've had experience nursing. They say they'll see us through."

A man says: "I got five children. I worked once in Logan. I thought this thing over a long time 'fore I started. Now I ain't going back." He thoughtfully weighs some long brass cartridges in his hand. Four others in the group do the same. The five kinds of heavy cartridges are all different, but each gun looks spotlessly well kept. One youngster in uniform even wears his overseas cap. "Does this look like Argonne?" "Them hills wasn't so steep."

At the upper camp are a thousand men in a group. Expressions of determination are frequent and profane. Explanations of the "army's" purpose do not agree. "We want the law." "We want justice." "We're going to drive out the mine guards." "Going to get our people out of jail." "A protest against the Governor's martial law in Mingo."

A pleasant man remarkable for a white collar is easing a pistol out of his belt. "What do you boys really think you can do?" He gives a short laugh. "Well, John Brown started something once at Harper's Ferry, didn't he?" Back in Charleston I was still wondering what to reply. But the "army" seemed too many-headed ever to march.

II

So much for the "inside." Outside, the Charleston newspapers displayed some perturbation over the miners at Marmet, who were "ravishing the country, robbing passers-by and threatening death to law officers." A "law and order league" to counteract the "crime wave" had just been organized. Governor E.F. Morgan had addressed it; "moonshine liquor, pistol-toting, and automobiles" were the three great evils responsible for West Virginia lawlessness, he said; the miners were at Marmet "for the sole purpose of terrorizing the government of the State."

Otherwise West Virginia was normal; the strike of miners in Mingo County was still on, in its fifteenth month. The heads of the union, C.F. Keeney, president, and Fred Mooney, secretary, of District 17, United Mine Workers, "had washed their hands" of the Marmet affair.

Next day "Mother" Jones, veteran organizer of the U.M.W., exhorted the miners to disband. She read what purported to be a telegram from President Harding promising that the Baldwin-Felts mine guards would go. The miners, through Keeney and Mooney, learned from the White House that no such telegram had been sent. That night the army, now swelled to 8,000, marched.

Coal mining in central West Virginia stopped. Miners with rifles, by the thousand, poured into Marmet, some riding on the tops of passenger trains. War maps with red and yellow pins appeared in Charleston shop windows, showing Spruce Fork Ridge on the border of Logan County as the "line" held by Sheriff Don Chafin with his deputies and mine guards, machine-guns, and two bombing planes. The Governor called for Federal troops. By Thursday night the "army" was strung out half across Boone County. They were marching in companies, in something like military order. At times they stopped to listen to speeches in which "deserters were cussed out"; or to listen to leaders on how to fight machine-guns—"lie down, watch where the bullets cut the trees, outflank 'em, and get the snipers." Stores in Peytona, Racine, and Madison were selling or loaning them all available stocks of food and guns. Women along the way set out food. Several doctors joined the army. Men who fell out had to leave their guns and cartridges behind.

At three o'clock Friday morning Brigadier General Bandholtz from Washington routed the Governor out of bed. At four he sent for Keeney and Mooney. He said curtly that the situation was in his hands and that he had "no concern with the merits of the controversy."

"What's the object of these miners?"

"To get the Baldwin-Felts detectives out."

"Do you think they will accomplish their object?"

"No."

"Can you stop them?"

"Probably."

"Will you try?"

At five o'clock Keeney and Mooney were pursuing the "army." By evening they were turning back the head of the column and ordering special trains, passenger and electric, to haul home. But some of the men were so dissatisfied that they commandeered a train that night, loaded it up with men and sped, headlight out, down the valley to Logan County. There they joined the union miners around Sharples, Blair, and Clothier, and found fighting.

General Bandholtz returned to Washington, first sending for Keeney and Mooney. He complimented them for their "efficient action." Then he read a statement for the press, holding them "responsible for the acts of the members of the society which they represent." Keeney hotly resented this. The general urged Keeney to use his influence to disarm the miners: "I've seen enough of shootings and hangings following insurrections. We don't want any more."

"Shooting and hanging don't scare me," retorted Keeney. "Taking guns away from miners is hardly my business. We have a constitutional right to bear arms—about the only right left to us. I've a high-power rifle, three pistols, and a thousand rounds of ammunition at home. I'd like to see anybody take away that gun—except smoking."

General William Mitchell also departed. He had flown in, wearing a pistol, four rows of ribbons, and two spurs (he is chief of the air service). "All this could be left to the air service," he said. "If I get orders I can move in the necessary forces in three hours."

"How would you handle masses of men under cover in gullies?"

"Gas," said the general. "Gas. You understand we wouldn't try to kill these people at first. We'd drop tear gas all over the place. If they refused to disperse then we'd open up, with artillery preparation and everything."

"What are you going to do about the other 'army' of deputies, etc., in Logan County?"

But those "were peaceful citizens defending their homes"; as for the machine-guns and bombing planes, "they belong to the sheriff, don't they?"

III

Such are the facts. They do not inspire confidence in the workings of government and law which the miners at Marmet so seriously affronted. For sanity, the actions of government and of the miners' army seem to be on a par.

The "trouble" in West Virginia is several years old. Its peculiarities are West Virginian but its bases are industrial and national. It has been marked by killings on both sides, by "investigations," by evils condemned, and nothing done.

It might be more sensible in dealing with West Virginia to begin by facing three facts. First, the present phase of civil war has lasted since 1919, its main features unchanged, with no attempt to change them hitherto by the Federal Government. An outbreak was bound to come. Second, the outbreak was rising of a considerable section of the people, not a mob of toughs. Estimates of the "army" ran from 10,000 to 14,000. Perhaps two or three times that number of people actively abetted or openly approved the march. Third, these people took the law into their own hands because they believe that *that is precisely what "the other side" has been doing for a long time.*

They believe that the coal operators have long supported private armies, chiefly Baldwin-Felts "detectives," who beat up or kill union miners; that lawless mine guards are frequently cloaked in county or State authority. They will tell you that on June 14, Flag Day, members of the State constabulary, aided by sheriff's deputies, assailed the Lick Creek tent colony. This camp contains part of the 10,179 men, women, and children of the Mingo strike who are still drawing relief from the union. The constabulary shot dead Alex Breedlove, a striker, then slashed many tents to pieces and destroyed the strikers' food supplies. It is public record that the recruits for the State constabulary were picked from lists provided by the coal operators. The law provides that the members must be residents of West Virginia and file a bond. No such bonds have been approved by the State Treasurer.

On July 8 the State constabulary shut up the union offices at Williamson, arrested twelve union officers and strikers there, and put them in jail under the martial law which Governor Morgan had declared in Mingo County. It is public record that this martial law was being enforced only against miners' assemblies, commercial and other associations being allowed to meet freely. Some of these officials have been fighting the union since 1912.

On August 1 came the killing of Sid Hatfield and Ed Chambers, on the steps of the courthouse in McDowell County, by Baldwin-Felts gunmen. The gunmen's leader, C.E. Lively, had been a spy inside the union for years, then served a year in prison in Colorado for killing a striker, then testified before the Senate committee in Washington last month; after being arrested for killing Hatfield he was released under bond. Hatfield and Chambers were members of the union; two other members, Collins and Kirkpatrick, who escaped the gunmen by running, were, with Mrs. Hatfield and Mrs. Chambers, to have told their stories at a mass meeting in Charleston on August 27. The authorities suppressed the meeting.

Thus 10,000 mountaineer miners have come to believe that certain persons have been taking the law pretty completely into their own hands. They retaliate in kind. It is hard to interest them in senatorial investigations. They may come to believe that the Federal as well as the State Government cloaks operators who take the law into their hands. Then they will talk even more of John Brown and Harper's Ferry.

The West Virginia state motto struck an ironic note among union miners. This 1921 cartoon from the United Mine Workers Journal *suggested mountaineers were anything but free.* DRAWN BY BUSHNELL, COURTESY UMW.

Fighting Unionism with Martial Law
By Arthur Warner

Arthur Warner's account, also from the Nation *(October 12, 1921), is interesting for its remarks and opinions that bear hauntingly upon current state and world conditions. Warner points out, for example, how the "home folks" in West Virginia resented outsiders' characterization of the industrial warfare in the state, a possible indication of historical misinformation, even at that time. He describes Mingo County as "West Virginia's Ireland."*

"A fine native population, goaded by many abuses and injustices . . . was driven . . . to mass violence in retaliation."

Warner also writes of the "system of terrorization" used to keep the miners subdued.

In writing of the visit of United States Senators Kenyon and Shortridge to Mingo and Logan Counties, West Virginia, the correspondent of a Huntington newspaper referred to the two men as a committee to inquire into "the industrial controversy said to exist in some coal fields." This phraseology sounds unduly cautious even for a newspaper which aims not to annoy the home folks with unpleasant truths. The home folks resent the words "civil war" as describing the situation, but they seem to forget that the phrase is that of their own Governor, who in proclaiming martial law in Mingo County on May 19, last, said that "a state of war, insurrection, and riot is and has been for some time, in existence" and "many lives and much property have been destroyed as a result thereof and riot and bloodshed is still rampant and pending." Since that time there has been a sympathetic march of several thousand more or less armed miners and others in the nearby county of Kanawha, which is still occupied by Federal Troops in consequence. The home folks would do well to worry less about the language applied to their State and more about the conditions that have occasioned it.

Mingo County is West Virginia's Ireland. A fine native population, goaded by many abuses and injustices and apparently hopeless of any other solution, was driven somewhere over a year ago to mass violence in retaliation. As in Ireland, mass violence was met with still greater force on the part of government but with no effort nor wish to remove the cause of trouble. The cause in Mingo is the objection of the coal operators to the unionization of their fields and the lengths to which they have gone to prevent it. For many years they have employed guards, authorized by the county to carry arms, who have manhandled and driven out of the coal fields union representatives or sympathizers found in or about the mines. These mine guards are commonly reputed to be Baldwin-Felts private detectives. This is an exaggeration of the fact. Most of the armed men about the mines are bona-fide workers in various capacities. The Baldwin-Felts men of whom there are probably several hundred in the non-union coal fields along the extreme southwestern border of West Virginia—Mercer, McDowell and Mingo counties—are mostly reserved for a higher realm of usefulness. They constitute a spy and surveillance service whose members move about getting and giving information; advising and assisting; resorting to assault and shooting when such methods suit them.

In spite of this system of terrorization maintained by the coal owners, a partial unionization was effected in the spring of 1920. Without waiting for further developments the mine owners soon began to discharge men as rapidly as they joined the union—a spy system furnished the information—and to dispossess them without notice from company-owned houses.

"I was let out of my job and put out of my house before I had time to eat another meal in it," an ex-service man now in the Lick Creek tent colony said to me. "I joined the union one morning in Williamson, and when I got back to the mine in the afternoon I was told to get my pay and get out of my house before supper."

Scores of similar cases are recounted. Finally the officers of the United Mine Workers asked for a conference with the operators and when this was refused they called all union men out of the mines of Mingo County. This was in July. Shortly thereafter a tragedy happened that was the beginning of the long trail of violence and disorder that ensued. A number of Baldwin-Felts men went to Matewan and ejected a group of striking miners and their families from company-owned houses. In this they had the support of a decision of the West Virginia courts, which have ruled that a company renting houses to its employees does not stand in the relation to them of land-lord and tenant but of master and servant, and may therefore dispossess without notice or legal process. After doing their work the Baldwin-Felts men encountered Sid Hatfield, Chief of Police of Matewan, friend of the miners, and crack shot. Without trying to untangle all that followed, it is enough to say that shooting began and did not end until seven Baldwin-Felts men, two union miners, and Mayor Testerman of Matewan lay dead. A reign of lawlessness and violence ensued in Mingo County in which both miners and coal companies participated. Federal troops went in twice in the autumn of 1920. The trouble culminated in May of the present year when what is known in Mingo as the Three-Day Battle took place along fifteen miles of the Tug River near Williamson. The Tug River at this point is the boundary between West Virginia and Kentucky. Many of the mines are in Kentucky, but the railway and the towns are in West Virginia. In West Virginia also are the striking miners, many of them living in tents—the only available habitations since their ejection from company houses.

The strikers say that the Three-Day Battle was begun by mine guards on the Kentucky side. The coal owners put the blame on the union miners. Who knows? The head of the State Police in Williamson says that for some time both sides had wished "to shoot it out." Doubtless he is right. Anyhow they did. It is estimated that 100,000 shots were exchanged across the river. Residents of the region feared to go out of doors; some in exposed positions had to take to their cellars. Passengers on Norfolk and Western trains went through the battle zone crouching on the floors of the cars while glass crashed overhead.

The Three-Day Battle brought martial law to Mingo County. The judge of the Circuit Court, the sheriff, and the prosecuting attorney united in asking for it. The circumstances justified the action; there is no reason to criticize it. There is reason to criticize the application of martial law which in practice has been directed only against the striking miners and toward the suppression of union activities. Under the terms of the proclamation of martial law public assemblies and parades are prohibited, except by permission, and nobody except officers in the law may carry or have firearms of any sort except "at their own homes or places of business." There is no pretense that the provision against public assemblies is enforced against anybody except union miners. Commercial and fraternal organizations assemble at will, the churches and motion-picture houses are open as usual, the Salvation Army conducts its customary parades and meetings. But the right of officers of the United Mine Workers to assemble even in their own headquarters in Williamson is denied. When residents of the Lick Creek tent colony of strikers near Williamson want to visit town they have to walk single file, with a lonesome space between. Two union miners cannot meet at a street corner without fear of arrest. Union propaganda and activity by word of mouth is effectively blocked by the provision against public assemblies; similar efforts through the printed word are prevented by a clause in the proclamation of martial law which says: "No publication, either newspaper, pamphlet, hand-bill, or otherwise, reflecting in any way upon the United States or the State of West Virginia or their officers, may be published, distributed, displayed, or circulated."

Arrests are made without warrants, but under the Governor's proclamation the civil courts remain in Mingo County to try persons charged with offenses against the laws. Such persons may obtain bail. Offenses against the proclamation of martial law are non-bailable and beyond the pale of the courts. In this realm Major Thomas B. Davis, acting Adjutant General of the State and commander of the militia in Mingo County, rules absolute and supreme. He is not only judge and jury; he is law-maker besides. He decides what are offenses against the governor's proclamation and how they shall be punished. He claps people into jail and lets them out as he pleases. Charges are regarded as superfluous and even the delay and bother of trial by courts martial have been dispensed with. Whatever else may be said against the system, it certainly cannot be condemned as enmeshed with red tape.

Remarkable as this regime sounds, it has no terrors for the average citizen of Mingo County. He scarcely realizes that it exists. It applies only to the union miner, and to him with its full rigor. At the Lick Creek tent colony I was told that in addition to the wholesale arrests made at the time of the Three-Day Battle there had been two "round-ups" since for no reason known to the miners. A score or more men had been locked up in Williamson without charges and after several days had been released without knowing the reason for their going in or their coming out.

"One time we were in for five days," said a man who spoke from experience. "For fifty-six hours of that time we were crowded in a room of the jail, with water covering the floor, and so closely packed together that we could not lie or even sit down."

Theoretically, martial law is maintained in Mingo County by a company of State militia about 100 strong. The body consists largely of very young men, many of them mere boys, who are called up only for temporary service and are without experience in police work. Practically, this work is mostly done by the State Police, a detachment of which has been in Mingo County for somewhat more than a year. The State Police has lately been reorganized, the pay of privates having been increased from $75 a month to $100, besides clothing, living, and transportation. Since July 15 it has been possible to recruit men from outside of the State. So far only ex-service men have been accepted. In all there are four companies, each about fifty strong. One entire company and the larger party of another are stationed in Mingo County. The members of the State Police are typical ex-service men of an excellent sort. They are not thugs or gunmen. Such faults as they have are due to their youth and inexperience and to the fact that they have carried over from the army a too military and super-legal conception of police duty—an attitude intensified by their service under martial law.

Captain J.R. Brockus, in charge of the company in Williamson, impresses one as straightforward and honest—a soldier trying to do his duty in a soldierly way. His industrial ideas, like his pay, have been drawn from the ruling classes, without suspicion or inquiry, and he makes no concealment of his hostility toward unionism. The fact that he has lost three men, all shot in the back, may have influenced his attitude. He told me that the United Mine Workers furnished arms to the strikers. When I asked for proof he cited, as one instance, that on May 15 some suitcases had been dropped at Merrimac from an early morning train. They fell into the hands of the police and were found to contain four high-power rifles and 1,000 cartridges, all wrapped in Charleston newspapers of the day before. (Charleston is the district headquarters of the United Mine Workers.) Fred Mooney, secretary-treasurer of the district organization, was seen to get off the same train that carried the rifles at Matewan, the first stop beyond Merrimac.

In addition to the regular force of State Police in Mingo County there are 800 "special police," sworn in and given permission to carry arms at the time of the disturbances last May. About 250 of these are residents of Williamson, recommended by a "citizens' committee." The rest are mine employees, admittedly appointed from lists sent in by the coal operators. These 800 "special police" are all in private employ and pay, subject only in the vaguest way to the control of the county or State.

The proclamation of martial law in Mingo County, as has been said, was justified last May. But quiet has ruled in the region for some weeks, and a military regime is not justified today, especially in its one-edged application to union miners only. Its perpetuation can only be regarded as an extra-legal method of fighting unionism, with the effect of deepening the unrest, bitterness, and sense of injustice felt by a large proportion of the producing classes of the county. Coal production in Mingo is some 50 per cent below normal and business is shot to pieces. The mine owners say that reduced production is due to low demand and not to the strike; but this sounds less plausible when one learns the neighboring county of Logan has produced more coal in 1921 than for the same period even in the banner war year of 1918.

Judge R.D. Bailey of the West Virginia Circuit Court, one of the three men who asked Governor Morgan for martial law in Mingo County, expressed the belief to me that if violence were to cease, public sentiment would compel the coal companies to accept unionism. Be this as it may, it is certain that normal civil relations and equality before the law is the first step toward even approximate equilibrium in Mingo County. With the withdrawal of martial law should too the cancellation of the pistol-carrying permits of all the 800 "special police" and, if necessary, an augmentation of the regular force to cover the field. All this is elementary and immediately essential. But of itself it will not insure industrial peace; it will bring only the kind of fighting under rules (no hitting below the belt and ten seconds to get up off the floor) that prevails in most other parts of the country. Industrial peace, or an approximation of it, can arrive only when the coal fields are worked as a community service and not as a means of private profit; only when it is recognized that the laborer has a legitimate voice in an industry dependent upon the sweat of his brow.

"Stand by the Miners of Mingo"
By the Communist Party of America

The March on Logan gained widespread national attention and thus invited a number of different views and interpretations. This is an account of the march offered by the Communist Party of America. It was part of a newsletter on the armed march that was reprinted in the Senate hearings record.

Fellow workers! Forty thousand miners in the Mingo region of West Virginia have for months been struggling for the right to live.

They have been fighting valiantly against greedy coal barons and hired thugs, gunmen, and spies.

The workers want a union to help them in their struggle against inhuman living conditions.

The capitalists and the corporation-owned county and State governments are doing all in their power to crush the miners and prevent their forming a union. This fight is a fight for the very right of existence. Driven on by the fierce oppression of the capitalists and their gunmen, thugs, and deputies, the nearby union members have arisen to the defense of their fellow workers of Mingo.

The march of the union men was a march against the bitter repression and a defiance to all enemies of unionism.

Now, the Federal Government is rushing to the aid of the coal barons.

Troops, airplanes, bombs, machine guns, and all the hellish devices of capitalist warfare have been rushed into Mingo.

These have supposedly been sent to save law and order, but they have actually been sent to crush the workers.

Workingmen and working women! Miners and their families have been cruelly evicted from their homes!

Miners have been murdered by the Baldwin-Felts detectives and gunmen in the pay of the corporations!

The State constabulary and deputy sheriffs have beaten and clubbed workers to death!

Strikers' leaders have been indicted, jailed, and murdered!

Their wives and children are being starved!

Fellow workers! You must come to the aid of your struggling brothers of West Virginia!

You must stand by the miners of Mingo. Their fight is your fight!

They are fighting against the vicious United States Steel Trust that owns the entire strike area.

They are fighting against a most tyrannical wage slavery.

Their defeat will be your disaster. It will mean the open shop— open slavery for the whole country.

Force the hands of your leaders! Force your union leaders into action. Make Gompers, Lewis and Co., who have been too long shirking the struggle, toe the mark or get out!

It is high time that they do something and stop betraying your interests.

You cannot afford to delay. Force your leaders to compel the Federal Government to disarm the murderous bandits—the Baldwin-Felts detective thugs. The gunmen must leave the strike area at once!

We must rise to the defense of our enslaved brothers.

We must everywhere organize meetings and demonstrations to help the Mingo miners financially and morally.

Let every union local and labor body force the Federal Government to compel the profit-hungry coal magnates to go into conference with the miners.

Our slogan must be, "Disarm the Baldwin-Felts spies, gunmen, and notorious guards!"

"Away with the deputy sheriffs and State constabulary hirelings of the greedy corporations!" All murdering of miners must be stopped at once!

Fellow workers! Act before it is too late! A defeat at Mingo will go a long way toward driving the whole American working class into lower wages, longer hours, and endless drudgery.

Don't rely on the Federal and State Governments to help you!

They won't give you a square deal. They are only brutal agents of the capitalist class.

The Federal, State, and county governments and their gunmen, thugs, spies, and white guards are fighting the battle of your exploiters and oppressor—the capitalists.

This capitalist dictatorship has already too often shown its ugly head for the workers to have any faith in it.

The miners' demand upon Harding for a conference has been met with bullets and gas bombs.

Only organized, united, country-wide working class action can stop the Governments committing outrages against the toiling masses.

Remember how the workers were massacred at Ludlow, Calumet, Mesabe Range, and McKees Rocks!

Workers! The Communist Party of America calls upon you to help your struggling brothers in the mines of West Virginia!

To your task! All as one in the name of working class solidarity!

Stand by the miners of Mingo!

Down with the hired murderers!

From your unions, mines, mills, and factories rally to the defense of your enslaved West Virginia brothers!

The miners must have their union!

Rally to their cause which is your cause!

The miners' fight for a union must be made the fight of all organized labor of all workers of America!

On with the struggle! On to victory!

Issued by the central executive committee.

Communist Party of America.

The Strike of the Coal Miners is Still On!

Help your brother to break the chains of industrial slavery!

Stay Away From West Virginia!

Present the solidarity of the working class to the machine guns and dum-dum bullets of the Coal Barons.

Men, women and children, who are fighting for human rights, need your moral and financial support!

Be not traitor to your cause!

Don't accept the job of your fellow worker, who is idle for advancing the interests of Labor!

WALTER W. SPOUSE

WEST VIRGINIA

Testimony of Col. Stanley H. Ford
to the U.S. Senate

U.S. forces were heavily involved in the armed march. Agents working for military intelligence, for example, were sent to the area to keep officials in Washington informed on this massive domestic uprising.

Once he received word that the armed march was actually under way, President Warren Harding sent in 2,000 U.S. Army troops under the command of Gen. Harry Bandholtz to put down the insurrection. Then Harding sent eleven bombing planes under the command of Gen. Billy Mitchell, in case they were needed.

This is a military account of the armed march.

The witness, having been first duly sworn by the chairman, testified as follows:

THE CHAIRMAN: Will you please state your name.

COL. FORD: Stanley H. Ford.

THE CHAIRMAN: And your rank?

COL. FORD: Colonel, War Department. General Staff, United States Army.

THE CHAIRMAN: Colonel, I want to interrogate you about this West Virginia situation, but do not want to ask you to give any information you do not desire to give. You understand that, do you?

COL. FORD: I understand.

THE CHAIRMAN: Were you sent or did you go to West Virginia at the time of this march?

COL. FORD: Yes, I went to West Virginia on two occasions.

THE CHAIRMAN: When was the first one?

COL. FORD: The first one was on August 26, remaining there two days.

THE CHAIRMAN: And the second one?

COL. FORD: The second occasion was on the 1st of September, remaining there 12 days.

THE CHAIRMAN: When was the order made for the sending of Federal troops into West Virginia?

COL. FORD: The request was made by Gen. Bandholtz, under the instructions of the War Department, on the evening of September 1, 1921.

THE CHAIRMAN: Do you remember when the order was issued by the War Department?

COL. FORD: We were not informed as to the exact time of the issuance of the order, but the understanding was that, upon the request of Gen. Bandholtz, two regiments of Infantry that were being held in readiness would be dispatched at once.

THE CHAIRMAN: That request came the 1st of September?

COL. FORD: That request came the 1st of September.

THE CHAIRMAN: You had charge of the actual work of getting the regiments in there didn't you?

COL. FORD: It was under Gen. Bandholtz, and I was his chief of staff.

THE CHAIRMAN: What regiment did you put in there?

COL. FORD: We put the entire Twenty-sixth Infantry from Camp Dix.

THE CHAIRMAN: How many men?

COL. FORD: Approximately 1,000 men. There were also portions of the Fortieth, Tenth, and a recruit detachment from Fifth Corps Area. Those latter detachments came from Columbus Barracks.

THE CHAIRMAN: How many troops altogether did you have there?

COL. FORD: Approximately 106 officers and 2,000 men.

THE CHAIRMAN: Have any of those troops been withdrawn?

COL. FORD: All troops have been withdrawn except what now constitutes the Fortieth Infantry and the Tenth Infantry, a total of about 400 men.

THE CHAIRMAN: Where are they located now?

COL. FORD: The last report we had was that they were located at Charleston and St. Albans.

THE CHAIRMAN: Have any orders been made public as to the time the troops will be removed from West Virginia?

COL. FORD: No, sir.

THE CHAIRMAN: When you were there on the 26th of August, you remained, I believe you said, a couple of days?

COL. FORD: Yes, sir.

THE CHAIRMAN: Where did you go and what did you find out about that situation?

COL. FORD: Gen. Bandholtz and I arrived in Charleston about 3 a.m. August 26 and went directly to the statehouse. We were met there by Maj. Thompson, a representative of the commanding general of the Fifth Corps Area, and Maj. Thompson oriented us on the situation. At the conclusion of the conference with him Gen. Bandholtz notified the governor of our presence and asked him if he would come to his office for a conference. He appeared about 4 a.m. and repeated to us substantially what had been included in a telegram to the Secretary of War concerning the situation in West Virginia.

THE CHAIRMAN: Had that march commenced at that time, the march at Marmet?

COL. FORD: That concerned particularly the march from Marmet. The governor was finally interrogated as to whether in his opinion he had exhausted all the means at his disposal for quieting the disturbance. He stated in no uncertain terms that he had done so, and therefore requested that the United States troops be dispatched to the scene of the trouble. He was then asked if he desired to be present when Gen. Bandholtz interrogated Mr. Keeney, Mr. Mooney, and Mr. Houston, the president, secretary-treasurer, and attorney, respectively, of District No. 17 of the United Mine Workers of America. The governor expressed himself as not desiring to be present, thinking perhaps it would be better for him to be absent.

At 4:55, as I recall, the three gentlemen of the United Mine Workers of America appeared before Gen. Bandholtz, and Gen. Bandholtz interrogated them at length concerning the situation, and their influence upon it. Concluding the conference, Mr. Keeney was asked if he thought that he could stop the march at that time. He stated that he could do so, he thought. Then on the suggestion of Gen. Bandholtz, Mr. Keeney, accompanied by Mr. Mooney, left in an automobile about 5:30 in the morning of the 26th for the scene of the trouble. They were furnished with a brief memorandum signed by Gen. Bandholtz stating their mission. They were requested to inform Gen. Bandholtz of the situation as they found it, and the disposition on the part of the marching miners to return to their homes as requested.

As I recall, about 11:30 the same morning, August 26th, the first message was received. It was from the vicinity of Racine, stating that the miners had then stopped there, and word had been sent to other places informing the marching miners that Mr. Keeney and Mr. Mooney were on their way, and to discontinue the march until their arrival. From that time on various reports were received during the rest of the day, indicating that the miners were returning. The concluding report was that they had voted to return and would do so, and requested the assistance of the authorities to provide rail transportation for miners coming out of the Coal River district. That request was called to the attention of the State authorities. Later on a similar request was received, stating that the cars had not arrived, and details of that character.

Gen. Bandholtz made the plan that night to visit the various places along the line of march early the next morning, to verify for himself the accuracy of the reports sent in by the officers of the United Mine Workers of America.

Gen. Bandholtz, accompanied by myself and Maj. Thompson, left early in the morning of the 27th of August, going a far as Marmet together, where we separated, sending Maj. Thompson in one direction and Gen. Bandholtz and I going in the direction of Racine. All along the road as far as Marmet and beyond we saw returning miners coming back in small groups. Upon arriving at Racine there were perhaps 150 armed miners there awaiting rail transportation.

Before we left, the train equipment sufficient for taking them out arrived and they were transported back.

All the indications were that the miners, so far as that particular march was concerned, were disposed to return, and every evidence was given that they had returned during the course of the day. Gen. Bandholtz then made his final report to the War Department, stating that in his opinion the troops that were being held in readiness—that is, the Federal troops—would not be required immediately, but they should be earmarked for the purpose, in case emergency arose. We left Charleston the night of the 27th.

THE CHAIRMAN: For Washington?

COL. FORD: For Washington.

THE CHAIRMAN: What happened after that?

COL. FORD: On the 29th of August word came to us officially that there was a recurrence of the trouble in West Virginia, and Gen. Bandholtz and I were directed to make our preparations to go at once. The governor of West Virginia had sent a telegram to the Secretary of War again requesting that Federal troops be sent to West Virginia. In addition to Gen. Bandholtz and myself there was designated for the detail an officer of the Judge Advocate General's Department, and an officer of the Militia Bureau to act as assistants. We selected the means that would take us or effect our arrival in Charleston at the earliest possible date.

The President had issued a proclamation requesting the armed miners in West Virginia to disperse and repair peaceably to their homes. Following that proclamation, Gen. Bandholtz received instructions to go to the scene of the trouble in West Virginia, examine into and report upon the extent to which the offending persons were complying with the President's request. In case compliance was not apparent, Gen. Bandholtz had instructions to report the extent to which noncompliance was evident, the number of offending persons, and the number of troops that should be sent to West Virginia to quiet the trouble.

In accordance with those instructions, Gen. Bandholtz and his staff arrived at Charleston, W. Va., at 11:30, September 1, 1921, one-half hour before the expiration of the time given in the proclamation of the President. The time limit therein given was stated as 12 o'clock noon, September 1. An immediate conference was requested with Gov. Morgan, and such conference was held. Also a conference was held with those officers of the United Mine Workers of America that we were able to return. As I recall, Mr. Philip Murray, the international vice president of the association, came before Gen. Bandholtz.

The conditions in West Virginia at that time could not be fully determined at Charleston, so Gen. Bandholtz directed me to visit the scene of the trouble and later make a report. I did so, accompanied on that trip by Maj. Thompson, and repaired by way of St. Albans to the Coal River district, visiting Madison, Clothier, Jefferys [Jeffrey], Sharpless [Sharples], and a number of towns that were reported to be occupied by armed miners. I was informed that Mr. Murray had gone down there to use his influence in stopping the march of the miners. I finally met him somewhere along the road and had a conference with him. The result of my trip in the Coal River Valley convinced me that the offending miners had not obeyed the President's proclamation, nor did they intend to do so. Accordingly, I returned to Charleston and so reported to Gen. Bandholtz who immediately dispatched a telegram to the War Department requesting that Federal troops be sent without delay.

Acting upon that request, Federal troops began to arrive on the evening of September 3. Upon arrival the troops were met by staff officers designated for the purpose to give information to the commanding officers as to their locations in West Virginia and duties that would be required of them. The disposition of the troops—that is to say, their actual location—had been arranged beforehand, and as fast as troops arrived they were placed and instructions given to take the necessary preventive measures against further disorder and to quiet any existing disorders.

Briefly, the troops were located in two districts—the district of the vicinity of Logan and the Coal River district. The troops in both of those districts worked in conjunction with each other and cooperated with each other to the extent that the patrols sent from either side met and exchanged information.

From the time of arrival of the Federal troops it became apparent that the disorder would cease and quiet would again be restored. There were some 1,300, as I recall, armed miners that were passed through the United States troops in the Coal River district. The other armed miners apparently, upon arrival of the United States troops, or upon information reaching them that they had arrived, repaired to their homes by way of various routes and trails through the mountains.

Inspection by staff officers, as well as by Gen. Bandholtz, and the reports from various commanding officers in the area, indicated that the miners were repairing to their homes as fast as was physically possible to do so.

On the 7th of September quiet had been restored to such an extent that a normal condition obtained, so that Gen. Bandholtz felt it proper to advise the War Department of his recommendation that the Twenty-sixth Infantry be returned to its station at Camp Dix. The War Department acted upon that advice, and accordingly orders were issued for the relief of the Twenty-sixth Infantry, as well as certain Air Service units and chemical war service units. Upon the departure of the Twenty-sixth Infantry the plan for the distribution of the remaining troops was made. This plan involved the withdrawal of the detachment at Charleston, and one farther east. The number of troops remaining for that purpose in the plan was about 400. No further relief has been effected, except those due to the discharge of men whose expiration of term of enlistment has arrived.

THE CHAIRMAN: Colonel, did you make any estimate, or can you give the committee any estimate, of the number of men in what has been termed here this invading army?

COL. FORD: Yes, sir. That was required by the instructions given by the War Department. I might say that it was only an estimate. It was humanly impossible to arrive at accurate figures. The various reports indicated the number to be from 7,000 to 10,000. In the War Department telegrams that were sent by Gen. Bandholtz the estimate was placed conservatively at 5,000.

THE CHAIRMAN: Was there any shooting after the Federal troops got in there?

COL. FORD: There was no shooting in the immediate vicinity of the Federal troops and none reported by the Federal troops.

THE CHAIRMAN: There was no shooting by the Federal troops?

COL. FORD: Absolutely none.

THE CHAIRMAN: Not a shot was fired?

COL. FORD: Not a shot was fired.

THE CHAIRMAN: And none of the Federal troops were injured?

COL. FORD: None of the Federal troops were injured.

THE CHAIRMAN: Colonel, from the time you left Charleston to come back to Washington, which I think you said was on the 27th—

COL. FORD: I left there the night of the 27th.

THE CHAIRMAN: Until the 29th, when you received dispatches from here that the situation had changed, what had occurred in the meantime there? Do you know anything that had occurred that had changed their minds or stirred them up again?

COL. FORD: This information that I give now came to Gen. Bandholtz in the form of various reports. Those reports indicated that shortly after the armed miners had repaired to their homes or were in the process of doing so, deputy sheriffs, the number undetermined, came over from Logan into the Coal River district for the purpose of serving warrants for the arrest of certain miners. The time chosen for the service was reported to be about midnight. In the process of the service, two miners were killed, it was reported. That service, according to the reports, was a signal for the miners to again seek their arms and again renew their purpose to march into Logan and into Mingo County. The fact remains that when we arrived at Charleston armed miners to the number given in the estimate were in the field, evidently for the purpose stated.

THE CHAIRMAN: When you arrived on the 1st of September?

COL. FORD: Yes, sir.

THE CHAIRMAN: What did you gather, Colonel, from your observation and from your reports, to be the object of that march?

COL. FORD: We gathered this and, of course, our conclusions were based upon reports, without detailed investigation that would vouch for its accuracy: It seems that in the month of May the governor had declared martial law in Mingo County. Following that there was considerable trouble in Mingo County and certain miners had been incarcerated. The miners so imprisoned were reported to be members of the union. I believe you are familiar with that portion of West Virginia which is unionized and with that which is not.

THE CHAIRMAN: Yes.

COL. FORD: It was also reported that efforts made on the part of union men to unionize certain nonunion mines in Mingo were met with resistance. This information was conveyed to the union miners in other parts of West Virginia, and as a remonstrance to the declaration of martial law by the governor in Mingo County, and the fact that the union men had been imprisoned there, the union miners armed themselves for the purpose of marching into Mingo County and releasing the miners that were imprisoned.

THE CHAIRMAN: You think that was the prime object of the march?

COL. FORD: Briefly, that is as it was reported to us.

THE CHAIRMAN: Are there any questions, Mr. Walsh?

MR. WALSH: Colonel, I saw quoted in some paper, and I have had a general here trying to quote it as nearly verbatim as possible, a telegram said to have been sent to the President by Gen. Bandholtz immediately before the troops went into West Virginia the second time, reading as follows:

> At my request, and aided by efforts of officers of the United Mine Workers of America, the miners were returning peaceably to their homes, but because of failure of State authorities to provide trains and the injudicious advance of State constabulary and State police upon village of Sharpless [Sharples], where two miners were killed, they are reassembling.

Do you recall that?

COL. FORD: I recall there was a telegram in substance that.

MR. WALSH: That is all; thank you.

THE CHAIRMAN: Are there any further questions?

MR. VINSON: None.

THE CHAIRMAN: You may be excused, Colonel. We thank you very much.

Jack Dalton vs. Bill Blizzard:
In These Two Leaders Are Personified Conflicting Ideals
By Boyden Sparkes

Boyden Sparkes was one of the most widely read war cor-respondents covering World War I. He gained fame and a large following for his reporting of General "Black Jack" Per-shing's campaign and the fighting in Europe. When warfare broke out in Logan, Sparkes was a logical choice to cover the fighting there.

While Sparkes spent more than a year on the European bat-tle fronts without getting so much as a scratch, he was in Logan County only a few days before being hit by gunfire. Here is one of his articles, appearing in Leslie's Weekly (New York), *on the miners' march on Logan.*

(Editor's Note—Mr. Sparkes, the author of this article, was sent down to the scene of hostilities in West Virginia as the staff corre-spondent of a New York newspaper. In the course of a thorough in-vestigation of the conflict, including interviews with the leaders on both sides, he exposed himself to rifle fire and came away with bullet wounds in the leg and scalp. He insists, however, on a strict neutrality of attitude, since both sides shot at him.)

In one of the old melodramas that toured the country before the movies came along to provide daily thrillers, the hero through clenched teeth would shout: "Now, then, Jack Dalton, gimme them papers!"

Then came the awful struggle on the edge of the precipice. So it was something of a surprise to discover that Jack Dalton is still cast in the role of villain in West Virginia's mine war, or at least that part of it which raged along the Logan-Boone County line until the Federal troops forced a temporary suspension of hostilities.

Jack Dalton is the principal owner of the largest nonunion coal op-eration in West Virginia. He is president of the Maine [Main] Island Creek Coal Co., which is operating about 27 mines on its 27,000 acres of Logan County coal land. It has other property in other counties.

It was with the intention of forcing the unionization of those mines that a red-badged army recently sought to invade Logan County from the neighboring and unionized county of Boone. To that mob, or army, if you would have it so, Jack Dalton represents "privilege" and "the interests" and "Wall Street," and yet he used to be a miner himself. His career, in fact, suggests one of Horatio Alger's boy heroes and is complete justification for those who argue that America offers every youth a chance to get to the top.

Bill Jones was the first man down there in the West Virginia hills to mention Dalton to me. Jones is the general superintendent of the Maine [Main] Island Creek Coal Co. I had gone with him to Omar, the center of their operations, to see for myself how nonunion miners are treated by their employers. All shooting had stopped two days before.

"You'll sleep in our president's house," said Jones, easing his six-shooter into a fresh position on the front of his khaki breeches. "He is in Huntington now, but the house is open." We mounted the steps of a large frame house with a pyramidal roof. On one side were the railroad tracks. Across the muddy street was the rambling Young Men's Civic Association, a clubhouse conducted by the company for their employees. Unlocking the door, Jones led the way through a deserted lower floor to a large bedroom upstairs. It was furnished in golden oak.

"Dalton's a great guy," said Jones. "He used to be a miner himself. Came up here with $10,000 and opened up this field. We're getting out 40,000,000 tons a year."

I went into the adjoining bathroom. It was as large as an ordinary apartment house living room. The tub was enormous, and there was a wonderful shower. Here was a miner's long-suppressed desire to be utterly clean and free from coal grime finally expressed in several thousand dollars' worth of plumbing. I used both baths and then crawled into the massive golden-oak bed with an armful of newspapers. Reaching up a foot or so I found a brass chain that controlled the lights . . .

I met (Dalton) the following day in Huntington, at the offices of the Maine [Main] Island Creek Coal Co., which occupy an entire floor of one of Huntington's all modern business buildings. He proved to be wide, stoop shouldered, clean shaven, and dark. He is big, and when he shakes hands you feel the power of muscles developed digging coal far back inside of a West Virginia mountain. Dalton was in the room where his board of directors meet. This is furnished in mahogany. Maps of his companies' properties hang on the wall. Half a dozen of his executives were there. Each of them told me something about depredations of union miners. They whispered tragically of nationalization; of the winter suffering of the Nation if ever the Guyan field is unionized and a general strike is called. Dalton merely listened. He puffed steadily at a black cigar, but sat impassive, sphinx-like.

One of his executives, when the boss was out of hearing, said: "He's a born trader. He'd rather trade than eat."

But I think that the important thing is that he used to be a miner, a nonunion miner, and that he is determined that his miners shall continue to be nonunion. When the unions are willing to use force to effect organization, Jack Dalton is willing to use force to prevent it.

His weapon—and weapon of the other coal operators in that field—is Sheriff Don Chafin and his deputies. And whatever you may think of the system, the coal operators pay their salaries, and the deputies make of Logan County a region utterly unhealthy for union organizers and agitators. Be sure, however, that Jack Dalton cares little what you think.

Chafin, whose mother was a Hatfield, a woman of the feudist clan, is called the king of Logan County. Yet, if there were no Chafin I believe that Dalton would have another king of the shrieval throne. Chafin is merely a convenient instrument, ready forged and tempered with Hatfield blood.

So much for Logan County, where each miner deals independently with his boss. Across the ridge in Boone County it is different. There collective bargaining is the method of dealing between miners and operators; and, it may be said, the operators there sing in a different key. Some of them openly supported the miners' army when it mobilized there in the Coal River Valley.

If there is a king in Boone County I should say it was Bill Blizzard. At least Blizzard was the dictator while the miners' army had a firing line that extended the full length of the Logan–Boone County line. Blizzard is a sub-district president of the United Mine Workers. His territory includes all of Boone County, and would include Logan if that county was organized.

Blizzard rose from the ranks in the coal mines to the leadership of his fellow miners. Ten years ago he worked in the mines of Cabin Creek and played an important part during the strike of 1912 and 1913. His work was recognized by the State Federation of Labor, and he was elected first assistant to Secretary James Pauley, State secretary. Two years ago he was elected president of subdistrict No. 1. I first saw him when the Federal troops entered Madison. The miners' army—the red-necks—then confronted along the serrated top of Spruce Fork ridge the hastily recruited defending army of Logan. That defending force was neither miners' nor an operators' army. It contained miners, operators, bank clerks, school-teachers, grocers, haberdashers, and any sort of man who could tote and fire a gun. A lot of them came from other West Virginia counties. They came because West Virginia had no National Guard nor any other force sufficient to cope with the miners' army but they were vastly outnumbered by their foes. That was why Gov. Morgan, of West Virginia, appealed for Federal troops.

The Coal River division, a section of the Chesapeake & Ohio, about 60 miles long, loading from St. Albans on the main line (15 miles west of Charleston, W. Va.) south across Boone into Logan County, for two weeks had been operated as the miners dictated, except for one train a day, that carrying the United States mails. Even on that the miners had exercised a strict supervision over the passengers. It had been the miners' main line of communication with the world outside the valley.

Up and down this valley foraging parties of armed miners had gone from store to store in the small towns purchasing entire stocks of supplies with receipts promising payment from the United Mine Workers' organization. They had even held drumhead court-martials.

Presumably as a sequel to one of these, a Coal River Valley undertaker was awakened at midnight one night by loud "hellos" and poundings on the front of his house. When he looked out through a raised second-story window a voice shouted: "Here's some work for you."

Something was dropped heavily on the undertaker's side porch. When he got downstairs he found the body of a foreign-born miner. There was five bullet holes in the jumper of the corpse. Later it was established that the man had refused to serve in the overalled army.

That was the way Pancho Villa kept reluctant peons in the field. It had been the way of military leaders since war began. It is the simple business of making a soldier fear the firing line less than the firing squad. I do not know that this was Blizzard's idea. But I do know that when Blizzard spoke, his overalled soldiers hastened to obey.

Order in Coal River Valley had been kept by armed patrols in overalls, distinguished by red bandanna handkerchiefs knotted about their necks or bits of red cloth tied in their sleeves. Seven moonshine stills were found hidden in the hollows of the hills and destroyed. Blizzard knew that he could keep his men in hand only so long as he could keep them sober.

It was through this region that Capt. John J. Wilson's command of 150 picked Regulars traveled by night to the scene of hostilities. The engine of the troop train pushed ahead of it three flat cars, two solider lookouts riding at the very front. Those extra cars were intended as a protection against obstructions on the track or explosive miners. The train ran along steadily at 20 miles an hour. Forty-five minutes ahead of it, although Capt. Wilson was then unaware of it, there traveled a commandeered train loaded with miners going to the front.

Two hours after the start from St. Albans the troop train entered Madison, unionized seat of Boone County, and with a normal population of 700. This night a number of its men were up on the Spruce Fork Ridge doing their best to kill other men who dwelt in the seat of Logan County. It was civil war; no less.

As the train slowed down the assistant prosecutor of Boone County swung aboard. His name was Hager, a lark, sharp-eyed little man, in a wrinkled suit of light summer "store" clothes. His knitted tie, almost thick enough to deserve the title of muffler, flopped over his shoulder.

"We're glad you're here," he said to the first soldier he saw. "A commandeered train went through here on the way to the fighting at Blair just 45 minutes ahead of you. It's been just terrible."

If Prosecutor Hager had been a woman, his state of mind might have been diagnosed as hysteria. His breath came convulsively.

The bugler sounded "assembly."

"Packs and guns," shouted a sergeant, "fall in."

Buckling on their heavy packs, each rolled as neatly and smoothly as a stove pipe, and running their fingers in a final pat over each stuffed pocket of their cartridge belts, the Regulars dropped to the cinder-covered right of way. There they waited, immobile, while half their slender number was selected for guard duty. Outposts with machine guns were sent up and down the tracks. Sentries were stationed at 5-yard intervals 50 yards up the hillsides from the train. As the last of these took his post, Blizzard appeared and accosted Capt. Wilson.

"William M. Blizzard, subdistrict president of the United Mine Workers," he introduced himself. He was young, wiry, dark-eyed, cordial, and convincing. He was short, almost undersized; Jack Dalton, physically, would make two Blizzards. Yet when both men were merely coal miners with numbered brass tags to identify them Blizzard probably loaded quite as much coal as Dalton.

The difference between them even then was mental. Where Dalton possessed the trading instinct, Blizzard was endowed—or accused, as you will—with the spirit of the zealot. When Blizzard takes sides on any question I can imagine that for him the other side is effaced.

Blizzard wore a weather-beaten, black-felt, narrow-brimmed hat, pulled low over his eyes. He did not wear overalls, but his suit appeared to have been slept in for a week. A necktie was knotted wrong side out against his soiled, white collar.

"Are you the general of the miners' army?" he was asked.

"What army?" countered Blizzard with a smile, and added: "I guess the boys'll listen to me all right. I just told the captain here that if he'll send a squad of his Regulars up the line with me I can get all our fellows out of the hills by daylight."

Blizzard launched into an account of a bombing raid made on Blair that day by what he described as a Baldwin-Felts airplane. With Blizzard all missiles launched by the defenders of Spruce Fork Ridge were from the guns of Baldwin-Felts detectives. Yet he must have known that this was not true. He must have known, too, that the men in that line facing his men had come from all over West Virginia at a call from Gov. Morgan. Blizzard must have known these things, because he had been moving at will between Charleston and the miners' camps in the Coal River Valley. But, even so, he persisted, and in speaking of his "foes" as "Baldwin-Felts thugs" or "Don Chafin's dogs," Blizzard, in fact, is an inveterate propagandist, with a propagandist's disregard of facts.

Capt. Wilson searched Blizzard and discovered he was carrying a pistol—"toting a short gun," as they expressed it in West Virginia.

The Army officer asked him if he had a permit, Blizzard produced one signed by the sheriff of Kanawha County. Charleston is in Kanawha. Capt. Wilson returned the gun.

"Does this mean you are going to allow only men with permits to keep their guns?" asked Blizzard. Capt. Wilson said that those were his orders.

"The men on the other side of the ridge will keep theirs?"

"If they have permits; yes."

Blizzard's eyes flashed. For a moment he ceased to be the diplomat. "Know what that means," he demanded. "Our boys'll be unarmed and those Baldwin-Felts thugs will just shoot 'em down whenever they please."

He thought a moment. Then he spoke to a man standing near. This individual trotted away to crank a flivver, and a few minutes later Blizzard was on his way up to the line. What he did when he arrived can only be surmised, but when the Regulars moved on up to Sharples at daybreak a few hours later, the miner fighters were coming out of the hills. Their guns had been hidden, probably far back in the black recesses of old coal mines. Their men getting out of the hills and back to their homes as quickly as flivvers could take them. But it was Blizzard who started them out.

FIVE ARMY AVIATORS FALL

Bombing Plane Crashes to Ground after Spin Near Poe, in Nicholas County

• • •

FATE OF AIRMEN NOT KNOWN
• • •

Machine Was on Way from Charleston to Langley Field, Va.,

When Storm Broke

This is one other story reported by the Baltimore Sun *as dramatic events unfolded in southern West Virginia.*

Charleston, W. Va., Sept. 8 (1921)—Five army flyers fell in a big bombing plane near Poe, Nicholas County, W. Va., late today. No word has been received at army headquarters here as to the fate of the men. They were Lieutenants Moek, pilot, and Fitzpatrick, observer, and three enlisted men.

Their machine was seen to go into a spin and crash to the ground by army flyers in two other bombers. One of the other machines flew low, located the scene of the accident and found the bomber in flames with its tail pointing upward. Several automobiles were observed in the vicinity. The exact place where the accident occurred is not known here. The flyers who witnessed the fall judge from their maps that it occurred near Poe.

Ran into Thunderstorms

The three planes started from the landing place here for a flight to Langley Field, Virginia. East of here they ran into a thunderstorm, and a few minutes later one machine fell. Another continued on and landed at Seebert, W. Va., about 100 miles east, while the third bomber returned and landed near here.

Army officers tonight were making every effort to find out what happened to the five missing men. They have enlisted the citizens near Poe to start out searching parties to find the burned plane.

The two planes that landed safely will resume their flight to Langley Field tomorrow.

Two Wrecked near Beckley

Beckley, W. Va., Sept. 8—Two Government airplanes of the DH-4-B type were wrecked near this city late today while attempting to land for gas and oil. One was commanded by Lieutenant Goodrich and carried Sergeant Dildipe as a passenger, the other by Lieutenant Liebhauser.

No one was injured.

The plane piloted by Lieutenant Goodrich crashed when it struck a small ditch extending across a field at Johnstown, near here, the landing gears and motor and part of the body of the machine being damaged.

Lieutenant Liebhauser's machine attempted a landing in a field near Haper and crashed. It immediately caught fire and was entirely destroyed.

Both airplanes were en route from Langley Field to Charleston.

CHAPTER VIII

CHAPTER VIII
Treason

As a result of the march on Logan, more than 550 coal miners were indicted for murder and treason against the government of West Virginia.

The coal companies, believing that no jury in a coal-producing county would dare convict the miners, arranged to have the trials of the leaders moved to Jefferson County, in the state's agricultural region. This meant the indicted union miners would be tried in the very same courthouse where John Brown had been convicted 63 years earlier for his abolitionist raid on Harper's Ferry. The national media covering the trials quickly picked up on the theme of union miners on trial for attempting to liberate the "industrial slaves" of southern West Virginia.

But there was another analogy. Just as the miners were on trial for their lives in Jefferson County, the entire American labor movement was on trial for its life. If laboring men and women could be tried and executed for attempting to abolish a brutal, anti-union regime (even in a state like West Virginia at that time), the entire labor movement could well have collapsed. Other employers could easily have adopted the anti-union tactics of the West Virginia coal operators. Consequently, the Charles Town trials received a great deal of attention across the United States. Thousands of reporters descended upon the peaceful, quiet village to cover the famous (or infamous) treason trials.

The following *Literary Digest* articles provide a sampling of editorials from newspapers throughout the country regarding the event. They make it clear how the tables were turned: it was not the miners who were on trial, but the state of West Virginia—and the state was found guilty.

West Virginia's Treason Trials

This first article in the Literary Digest *(New York) May 13, 1922, appeared while the trials were still in progress.*

Treason, an overt act of betrayal, treachery, or breach of allegiance of obedience toward the Government; levying war against the States, or giving their enemies aid and comfort. (Standard Dictionary)

Such is the most serious charge—the first to be brought since the Homestead, Pa., riots of thirty years ago—on which several hundred West Virginia United Mine Worker officials and miners are to be tried in the little red courthouse in Charles Town, W. Va., where John Brown was sentenced to die some sixty years ago for the same offense. The charge is not a Federal one, but is founded on an accusation of treason against the State of West Virginia. There are other charges against the miners, ranging from assault to conspiracy and murder—the outgrowth of the miners' march in August and September, 1921, from Marmet, Kanawha County, through Boone and Logan counties to Mingo, which the Governor of West Virginia had declared under martial law. There are twenty-four test cases, and more than five hundred to follow if convictions are obtained in these. "Nothing like it is recalled in history," writes Roy P. Roberts in the *Charleston Gazette* (W. Va.).

It is the contention of the State attorneys that the march of the miners last year, and the assistance given them by officials of the United Miners Workers, amounted to "levying war against the State"; murder, they say, was in the killing of three deputy sheriffs and mine guards. The district officers of the union, backed by the international organization of miners, are in charge of the defense. They hold that the uprising was in no sense an act of war either against the State or the people of West Virginia, but that it was a revolt against the acts of West Virginia coal operators in taking over the political power into their hands, and their suppression of free speech, free assemblage, and the liberties guaranteed American citizens by the Constitution.

The specific provisions in the indictment against the miners and their officials as summarized by Circuit Judge Woods, before whom the men are being tried, are as follows:

First—That the defendants, with their confederates, intended to invade Logan and Mingo counties, and by force, violence, murder and open warfare to deprive the people residing in said counties and members and citizens of the State of West Virginia of the protection afforded them by the laws of the State of West Virginia.

Second—To destroy and nullify by force of arms, violence, murder and open warfare, martial law in said Mingo County, and the military occupation in said county, which martial law had been duly proclaimed by the Governor of the State of West Virginia.

Third—To release from imprisonment persons who had been duly and legally arrested and incarcerated in the jails of Mingo County for violation of the law and violation of the martial law proclamation of the Governor.

Fourth—To take possession of the counties of Logan and Mingo in the said State and to prevent the execution of the laws of the said State in said counties and to deprive the people of said counties of the protection afforded by the laws of the said State.

Fifth—Especially to destroy and nullify martial law in said Mingo County, and to nullify the proclamation of the Chief Executive of the State.

Sixth—The release of prisoners duly held in jail in Mingo County as also stated in the first count.

Certainly, asserts the *New York Times,*

Such a demonstration of wild disorder and sedition could not be allowed to pass without action by the courts to vindicate the law. Examples must be made of the leaders of the mob and of those who conspired against the peace of the state. How shall insurrection be defended? How shall alleged wrongs be redressed by defying the police of the State? Can a labor organization be a law unto itself? What provocation and mitigation, if any, were there for such a rising, for such destruction of property, for such license and disorder and the taking of life?

"That armed march of miners was rebellion, and men convicted of rebellion deserve punishment," admits the *Newark News*, "but those who marched claimed the desire to liberate 'the slaves of the non-union coal regions' from a rule which has no place in free America." "Moreover," adds the *News*, "it may seriously be questioned whether the march ever would have started had there not been reasonable ground that the State Government was allied with the coal operators." "There was much violence in West Virginia," notes the Norfolk *Virginian Pilot*, "but no one believes that even the guiltiest of the guilty parties were guilty of intent to overthrow the State in the way that is suggested by the word 'treason.' Why, therefore, resort to such extraordinary prosecutions, when outraged law could be avenged far more simply—and less theatrically?" "When you charge treason," notes the *New York Evening Post*, "you must have an act so flagrant, so wanton, so menacing to the national existence as to convey in the very charge a sense of dreadful odium." Continues this paper:

Treason to a State is hard to conceive at best, and infinitely hard in the case of a State with the notorious recent history of West Virginia. It has been a State which had been derelict in exercising its duty to enforce order. It has left the maintenance of "order" to armed detectives in the employ of the mining companies or to deputy sheriffs, who too often have been in the pay of the operators. With so long a record of violence on both sides it is rather late in the day for West Virginia to awake to its injured dignity and invoke the charge of treason.

The West Virginia State code, points out the chief counsel for the miners and officials, prohibits the employment of deputy sheriffs by private persons.

The *New York Evening Mail* is another of many papers which "can not see on what grounds the miners are being prosecuted for treason." Says this paper:

> If the miners have been violent, let them be prosecuted for violence, and for violence let them be punished. If they have conspired together to commit a crime, let them be prosecuted for conspiracy, and for conspiracy let them be punished. Neither conspiracy nor violence is, however, treason.

"In bringing the charge of treason before the Court," maintains the *New York Evening World*, "the prosecution lays itself open to the suspicion that it is merely endeavoring to intensify the hostility of the two factions, and so win support for extreme measures against future efforts of the mine unions to exercise their rights. The very seriousness of the crime charged against the miners is an impeachment of the good faith of the prosecution."

Treason and Reason

The second Literary Digest *article (June 17, 1922) followed the acquittal of Bill Blizzard, the first UMW leader to be tried for treason and the alleged "Generalissimo" of the armed march.*

The name of William Blizzard, West Virginia miner, has been added to the few who have been tried in the United States for treason. Like most of the others, he was acquitted, yet, notes the *Washington Herald*, "there is plenty of reason to fear that if the case had been tried in Logan County he would have been found guilty and given the severest sentence possible on the treason charge." That any fair-minded jury must acquit the youthful official of the United Mine Workers of America was obvious from the first to the *Herald*, the *New York Times*, and other papers, and why the indictment for treason was brought is more than the *Times* can understand. "Attorneys for Blizzard," caustically observes the *New York Evening World*, "might have claimed that the crime charged was impossible, because no Government existed in West Virginia against which treason was possible." "In fact," agrees the *New York Herald*, "Government in West Virginia had broken down, and its power had passed in part to the mine operators." The leaders of the union miners who marched against Logan and Mingo counties last August, according to this paper, were manifestly trying to take the law into their own hands, "which the non-union coal operators, controlling the local government in the two counties, already had done." In the opinion of the conservative *New York Times*:

> Whatever their offenses, the union miners and their leaders were not trying to subvert the Government of West Virginia in whole or in part. Logan County can scarcely be said to have been under the rule of law or to have had a republican form of government. Private war was answered by private war. Some constitutional guaranties appear to have been suspended by conspiracy of non-union operators. If there was any "treason," it was on both sides; but there was no excuse for charging the leaders of the misguided invaders of Logan County with the highest of crimes.

Treason, however, is one of the most difficult crimes to prove. The offense, under the laws of West Virginia, must be established by an overt act, which must be testified to by two witnesses. Moreover, ruled the Judge at the Charles Town trial, since an indictment for treason had been brought in Logan County, only overt acts committed by Blizzard within that county could be regarded as evidence of guilt. It was the contention of the prosecution in the trial, which began late in April and lasted nearly five weeks, that several thousand West Virginia miners engaged in a demonstration against the non-union operators of Logan and Mingo counties; that they seized railway trains and automobiles, and waged a battle against State policemen, deputy sheriffs, and other State forces on Blair Mountain, and surrendered only to Federal troops. Blizzard, maintained the prosecution, was in touch with the miners during their advance into Logan County, and during the four days' battle of Blair Mountain. The prosecuting attorneys, reports George Wood, staff correspondent of the *New York Globe,* were not the Attorney General of the State, or the district attorney of the county in which the trial was held, or the district attorney of Logan County, in which the indictment was found, but attorneys for the coal operators.

The miner, on the other hand, had the backing of the United Mine Workers, with its retinue of lawyers. It was their contention that Blizzard did not go into Logan County with treasonable intent, but to induce the miners to abandon their march; that the gathering of miners was first of all to aid in forming a constitutional league for the purpose of restoring civil liberty in the State by political action. As for the battle of Blair Mountain, that was forced upon the marching miners by state police, according to the version of the defense lawyers.

"In large measure the State of West Virginia was on trial in the Blizzard case," remarks the *Duluth Herald,* "and the verdict of acquittal as to Blizzard was equivalent to a verdict of 'guilty' against the State." According to the *Herald*:

> The State Government was clearly in alliance with the employers against the strikers from the beginning. A State which allies itself unfairly with one class against another invites what, when it happens, it is likely to call "treason." The State has no business in any labor controversy except to preserve order; and it can not take sides with one or another, even under the guise of preserving order, without making itself at least in part guilty of what comes of it.

The *New York World*, too, blames the State Government:

The State of West Virginia is itself responsible for the abuse of power in Logan County. Because it has failed to interfere with the operators' government it is responsible for the disorders induced by that government. Whether or not William Blizzard was involved in the armed march, his action was assuredly not treason. It cannot be treason by any definition to rebel against a denial of constitutional guaranties.

But it is just as well that the case was tried, thinks the *Washington Herald*. Many editors believe that since Blizzard was acquitted the cases against the other miners will either be dropped or postponed until fall.

Meanwhile, the *New York Globe* notes—"the government of West Virginia will probably take measures to disassociate itself from the operators who so nearly succeeded in making themselves the State."

Nevertheless, maintains the *Baltimore Evening Sun*, "those who have talked to the coal operators of the West Virginia fields know that they have a case. They have a case in which doubtless some of the fundamental tenets of Americanism are involved."

CHAPTER IX

CHAPTER IX
James M. Cain:
Novelist and Journalist

This section is devoted to the work of James M. Cain, probably the most prestigious writer to report on the West Virginia Mine Wars. Cain was an important writer of many genres. He was a successful reporter, playwright, editor, and journalist. As a novelist, he made his fame and (limited) fortune with works such as *The Postman Always Rings Twice*, *Double Indemnity*, *Mildred Pierce*, and *The Root of His Evil*.

Cain's writing brought him numerous awards, including the Mystery Writers of America Grand Master Award, made him the subject of two book-length biographies, and even earned him comparisons to literary greats like Ernest Hemingway.

"Cain's power comes from his ability to show the fragility of order and common sense . . . [He is] one of the foremost storytellers in American popular literature, demonstrating from the outset of his career a mastery of place, set sense, and first person narrative," wrote one critic.

As a reporter, James M. Cain covered the West Virginia Mine Wars for the *Baltimore Sun* and several other important periodicals.

West Virginia: A Mine-Field Melodrama
By James M. Cain

In this piece, published in the Nation *(June 25, 1923), Cain
put his literary talent to work, describing conditions among the
miners in the exaggerated, melodramatic style of a novelist. The
"fragility of order and common sense" is well illustrated in this
account from the southern West Virginia coal fields.*

Rough mountains rise all about, beautiful in their bleak ugli-
ness. They are hard and barren, save for a scrubby, whiskery growth of
trees that only half conceal the hard rock beneath. Yet they have their
moods. On gray days they lie heavy and sullen, but on sunny mornings
they are dizzy with color: flat canvases painted in gaudy hues; here and
there tiny soft black pines showing against a cool, blue sky. At night,
if the moon shines through a haze, they hang far above you, dim outlines of smoke; you could throw a stone right through them. They are
gashed everywhere with water courses, roaring rivers, and bubbling
creeks. Along these you plod, a crawling midge, while ever the tower-
ing mountains shut you in. Now and then you top a ridge and look
about. Miles and miles of billowing peaks, miles and miles of color
softly melting into color. Bright yellows and reds give way to greens and
misty grays, until they all fade into faint lavender and horizon blue. . . .
A setting for a Nibelungen epic, revealing instead a sordid melodrama.

A melodrama where men carry pistols, often in leather holsters,
and wear big black felt hats of the kind affected by the late William
Frederick Cody. Where they give each other three-fingered hand-
shakes, and slips of paper pass from palm to palm. Where hoarsely
whispered plots are met by counterplots, and detective agencies flour-
ish. Where personal differences are settled by guns, and letters taken
from bodies designate persons by initials and numbers. Where murder, dynamiting, arson, and insurrection are the usual order of the day
and night. In brief, where life is a silly hodge-podge of two-gun heroes,
find-the-papers villains, and sweaty mysteries—a peanut-and-hisses
melodrama of coal.

For it is coal that has brought about this state of affairs. In West
Virginia it is the staff of life. The State is a huge layer cake, hacked

into grotesque slices by the elements; the slices are the mountains, the layers are rock, and the filling is coal. Coal, coal, coal. On one side of the creek, away up the slope, you see the blue-black streak; on the other side, the same distance up, you see the same streak. The seams run for miles, jumping across rivers and creeks, now broken by some convulsion an eternity ago, now tilted at crazy angles, but for the most part flat, thick, regular, and rich. Railroads, indispensable adjunct of mining, run beside every creek. A grimy structure of steel, a ribbon of shining rails right up the mountain side, a smudge of black dust, a monotonous grinding and clanking, and you are at a tipple. It is coal on which a third of the population depends directly for its living; it is coal on which probably another third depends indirectly. It is coal that has converted the State into one great pock-work of mines.

The coal development, however, is relatively recent. Only in the two closing decades of the last century was it of much importance; the richest fields of all are scarcely twenty years old. Before that, the State was a sort of wilderness, carved out of the backwoods of Virginia in the turmoil of the Civil War. Indigenous to it was a unique type of human being, the mountaineer. Here and there he survives today, and in spite of his baffling idiosyncrasies, is a most lovable person. If you have won his regard, he will take you into his home and seat you before his rude fireplace as the guest of honor. He will listen with respect to your discourse, and entertain you with homely comment of his own. He speaks a quaint language. It recalls an America that is fast passing, the America of the cross-roads schoolhouse and the cabin in the hills—with echoes of James Fenimore Cooper, and a forgotten generation of leather-shirted woodsmen. It uses "ary" and "nary," "cayn't" for "can't," "haynt" for "hasn't"; "done" and "done been" with verbs instead of "have" and "had"; it has odd words peculiar to itself: "swag" for a small marsh; and retains words long discarded in other parts of the world: "poke" for bag; a "panther" is still a "paynter." It is spoken with a plaintive drawl, gentle and unassertive. A language arresting and attractive, pathetically and insistently American. That, probably, is because this mountaineer who speaks it is one of the oldest and purest American types extant. He drifted westward with the migration of the eighteenth and nineteenth centuries, and finding habitable creek bottoms, loitered by the wayside, while his more energetic brethren pushed on to the Ohio River and the West. For a century he stayed here, and raised a few hogs, and corn for hominy, and carried on a small traffic in illicit whiskey. He was his own law, and his rifle was his last court of appeal. As time went on he and his kind interbred, the strain grew weaker and weaker, and he developed unusual ideas and customs. Personal grudges obsessed him. He nursed them for years, and prosecuted them with his rifle, until the outside world began to hear of strange feuds, such as the one between the Hatfields and the McCoys, that arose from trivial and incomprehensible causes. Whole families were exterminated in these feuds, and the rifle came forward with more and more sinister prominence in the West Virginia scheme of things.

About all this was the flavor of a queer, half-savage code, a *cavalleria montagnola* that was at least picturesque. Then came coal and the ever-advancing railroads. Mining companies bought the hillside cabin and dispossessed its lodger. The gaunt mountaineer, waiting for days, rifle on knees, eyes starry with hate, until his enemy should come up the creek bottom, was forced inevitably to enter the coal bank and toil for his living. Moreover, his new masters took leaves out of his own book and used them against him. They adopted the law of the rifle themselves. They hired armed gentry to watch him and police him and curtail his liberties. They told him where to go to church and where to send his children to school. They told him what he must take for his labor, how much he must pay for his food, and where he must buy it. Lastly, they told him what organizations he might join, and those that he must not join; prominent among the latter were labor unions. In vain he arose in his wrath. He oiled his rifle, but there was no dignity in it. He swore his vendettas against the mine guards, but the old heroic venom was gone. He killed his man, and it was a blowsy murder. He had brought all his former stage trappings, and they had become tawdry overnight. He was degraded, a serf: the Last of the Mohicans turned tourists' cook.

This was the condition of the mountaineer-miner when the United Mine Workers of America undertook to strike off his shackles. In this valiant enterprise the union was also strengthening its own position, for by the early years of the present century its pristine security in the Central Competitive Field was being threatened seriously by the growth on all sides of large non-union fields, and the largest of these was West Virginia. So it set about organizing the State. It was repulsed with medieval ferocity by the operators, who could make more money if they didn't have to pay the union scale. But it kept on, and eventually gained a membership of a few thousand. And to the occasional whisperings and shooting in the mine camp there was added a new and bigger kind of plotting. The union soon saw that the mine-guard system was the main bar to its organization; if the guards persistently ejected union organizers, there wasn't much hope of getting very far. So the mine guards quickly became anathema to all union miners; they were dubbed thugs, and took their places as permanent members of the cast, upstage, right, striding scowlishly about slapping their holsters while the trembling miner signed the open-shop agreement. . . . The first phase of the union's fight came to an end in 1912 and 1913, with strikes on Paint and Cabin Creeks, and three hundred guards imported by the companies, some of whom didn't get out alive. In all, nearly two score men lost their lives in those strikes, and people began to take gunplay and dynamiting for granted.

In 1918, the union, through a political deal, was allowed to organize the Fairmont field. By securing this territory and consolidating in the central part of the State, it pushed its membership to some fifty thousand. But ever the coal frontier receded past the horizon, and now southern West Virginia was mining enough coal to undermine the union power—to render any national strike largely ineffective. The southern part of the State was a big non-union stronghold, with the mine-guard system functioning perfectly. It embraced Mingo, Logan, McDowell, Raleigh, Mercer, and Wyoming counties. The union tackled Logan first—in 1919.

As usual, it met with armed resistance. Here was a mine-guard system, paid by coal operators, its main duty to eject union organizers. Its guards were invested with all the majesty of the law; they were deputy sheriffs on the county, duly sworn in under the Logan high sheriff, Don Chafin, who directed their activities and paid them out of a pool assessed against the operators. Mr. Chafin's deputies did their work thoroughly, and soon a wail drifted down the stage, over the Guyon Ridge: "They're a-murderin' the women an' children!" This is a very important line in the West Virginia libretto. It is always the cue for the big scene, of which more in a moment. So far as I know the deputies have never murdered any women or children, but art is art, and it is a good line. Why sacrifice it? Taking their cue, the union miners to the north assembled at a place called Marmet, within a dozen miles of Charleston, the State capital, and marched about a thousand strong on Logan. Then ensued the spectacle of the Governor of the State, John J. Cornwell, hoisting the gubernatorial robes aboard a wagon, beseeching the miners to go home, promising an investigation, and finally threatening troops. The miners went home, and their effort was abortive. But the West Virginian, a regular attendant at Western feature films and a diligent student of the Pluck and Luck series, had noted the possibilities of the scene.

So all energies were bent toward a successful staging of the great drama. The operators hired extra guards and howled defiance at the union. The union girded its loins, counted its money, and swore loudly that might should not conquer right. It sent its organizers into Mingo. A number of camps were organized. The union demanded recognition; the operators refused it. The union called its men out on strike; the operators evicted the strikers. As fast as the operators evicted them the union put them in tents. Guerrilla warfare broke out. There were massacres, ten men being killed in a battle at Matewan. The operators set spies to watch the miners and the miners pot-shotted the operators' witnesses. Plots were hatched by the dozen and card indices were needed to keep track of vendetta oaths. Federal troops were called in twice. The new Governor, E.F. Morgan, declared martial law, and the military commandant began clapping union men in jail. Finally, two sympathizers, Sid Hatfield and Ed Chambers, as the result of a quasi-official feud, were shot down at Welch, and this, with heavy mutterings and threatening sounding to the north, rang down the curtain on Act I—in August, 1921.

When Act II opened, two weeks later, union miners were assembling again at Marmet for another march. They gnashed their teeth and gritted they would redress their wrongs and stop further outrages. This time the plan was to march through Logan, kill Don Chafin on the way, continue to Mingo, liberate prisoners in its jail, nullify martial law, and proclaim liberty and justice once more in the land. For days they gathered and the press of the country screamed their purpose far and wide. Then they started, and as they swung down the road to Racine they sang:

Hang Don Chafin to the sour-apple tree,
Hang Don Chafin to the sour-apple tree,
Hang Don Chafin to the sour-apple tree,
As we go marching on!

They were halted once when their president addressed them at Madison. They threatened to hang him to a baseball grandstand, but they went home—at least, most of them did. Some of them stayed, commandeered a train and played with that—and waited. They didn't wait in vain. Down at Sharples, in Logan County, there came a clash between union miners and a party of Logan deputies and State police, coming, 250 strong, to serve warrants—at midnight (*sh! sh! sh!*). Two miners were killed. Then came the long-delayed cue that had been holding up the show: "They're a-murderin' the women an' children!" The miners reassembled, eight thousand strong. They flung out battle lines and donned red brassards. They gave out a password.

"Who's there?" whispered the sentries.

"I come creepin'," replied the miners, *misterioso*.

"Pass," said the sentries.

They drilled around the schoolhouse at Blair, while coal-company officials, powerless for the moment, snooped faithfully and took notes in memorandum books. Meanwhile the miners were bringing in truck-loads of food, rifles, machine-guns, and ammunition, and presently preparations were complete for the grand offensive.

On the other side of the ridge all was buzzing action too. Don Chafin issued a call for volunteers, and several thousand sprang forward ready to die for Logan County. He imported four airplanes. Then arrived a lord defender of the realm, appointed in this emergency by the Governor. He came, he saw, he took command. He addressed his troops and told them to advance not on these misguided miners, but to retreat not a single step. In the stilly night he had trenches dug. He filled the airplanes with bombs. All now being in readiness, both sides entered their positions and shot at each other for three days. The airplanes zoomed and dropped bombs on the rocks. The machine guns went *put, put, put*; the rifle fire never ceased. The noise was superb. On the fourth day a regiment of Federal troops came—and everybody else went home. It was the best second act that had ever been staged, and was marred by only one unpleasant event. Three men were killed. It is true they were killed in a purely accidental encounter between scouting parties, but the incident shows that great care must be exercised in the future if this march is to become a permanent institution in West Virginia, as it now promises to be. . . .

You rise in your seat. Stay. There is another act, the great courtroom scene.

Hardly had the last miner handed his gun in than the Logan County grand jury met in special session. It indicted whole pay rolls. It indicted for murder, conspiracy, and unlawful assembly. Then it rested, met in regular session, and indicted some more. It met yet again, and to the hundreds of indictments already found, it added a score or so for treason. And so, in a few months, after a change of venue had been granted, court opened to try these cases. The court sat in the same room at Charles Town where John Brown had been convicted of treason, and oddly enough, the first case called was a treason case. Defendants and witnesses appeared by the hundreds. State police paraded in front of the courthouse carrying big pistols, and a lieutenant of State police got arrested and locked in the town hoose-gow for getting saucy with the town constable. Witnesses told gory stories for a month. Lawyers orated. Foamy spittle flew hither and yon, and flecked the coats of the jury. The first treason defendant was acquitted, but in the next month two miners were convicted of murder. Then another treason trial; the defendant was convicted and sentenced to ten years. By now the pastoral community of Charles Town was so rent with the controversy that it was impossible to get a jury. The trials were removed, once to Berkeley Springs, and yet again to Lewisburg.

Thus life in West Virginia in this year 1923. In addition to the big show there are innumerable little shows. In all the coal counties the plots, the vendettas, the murders, and the trials go on incessantly. The Federal court at Charleston is a never-ending round of restraining orders, injunctions, and citations for contempt. The sterile conflict overshadows and paralyzes everything else. Before it, the State government is impotent. The State police, organized bona fide to enforce the law, are animated by no mature ideal than to posture as moving-picture editions of the Canadian Mounted, i.e., to wear pretty uniforms, carry pistols, and growl sidewise that they always get their man. They are now quite as detested as the mine guards; the miners call them the "Governor's Cossacks," and charge openly that they are on the side of the operators.

The bustling little inner-loop, outer-loop cities are but centers where gossip is exchanged and new plots hatched. Their weekly luncheon clubs are but debating societies devoted to denying the conflict. Their newspapers are degraded win-an-auto sheets whereof every other writer is in the pay of one side or the other. The activities of the State university, with its farmers' short courses and summer camps for girls, whatever their actual merit, seem innocuous and pointless while the banging of the guns echoes and reechoes. Culture is at a standstill; the only theaters are movies that show five-reel shooting features; there are no libraries, no concerts.

The conflict mars also what might stand forth as achievement. For in these mountains industry is organized on a gigantic scale. To see it is to get the feeling of it: the great iron machinery of coal and oil, the never-ending railroads and strings of black steel cars, groaning and creaking toward destination. A plume of smoke "down the holler" and a locomotive comes stealing around the bend. You are drawn close to these big inanimate things. The locomotive ceases to be a terrifying pile of steam jets and puffing, and becomes "she"; you lean affectionately against her as you swap talk with the engineer and spit familiarly on her wheels. There is crude outdoor poetry about it. Similarly to the north. Thousands of acres of orchards grow incredible quantities of apples, which are stored in warehouses redolent of fruity perfumes and shipped to far places of the earth. But this is all enchanting for what it suggests, not for what it is. Back of it all are always the scowling and muttering that spoil it.

Futile indeed seems the $50,000,000 road program that is to civilize the State. For ever recurs the question: Is the State civilizable? The answer is not apparent yet. Possibly it would be well to remember that this new West Virginia of great enterprises is still quite young. It may have a touch of industrial indigestion. Or its malady may be more grave. Give it a century or so. Then possibly it will shoot the pianist and call for a new score.

The Battle Ground of Coal
By James M. Cain

This piece by Cain appeared in the Atlantic Monthly, *October, 1922.*

I

As you leave the Ohio River at Kenova, and wind down the Norfolk and Western Railroad beside the Big Sandy and Tug rivers, you come into a section where there is being fought the bitterest and most unrelenting war in modern industrial history. The country furnishes a suitable setting. Rocky hills, small mountains, rise on each side. They are gashed by "creeks"; looking up these, you see that the wild region extends for miles back from the railroad. There is no soft, mellow outline about these hills. They are sharp and jagged; about their tops grows a stunted, scraggly forest. Their color is raw: glaring reds and yellows, hard, water-streaked grays. Here and there you see the blue-black ribbon of coal.

In this untamed section of West Virginia two tremendous forces have staked out a battleground. These are the United Mine Workers of America and the most powerful group of nonunion coal-operators in the country. It is a battle to the bitter end; neither side asks quarter, neither side gives it. It is a battle for enormous stakes, on which money is lavished; it is fought through the courts, though the press, with matching of sharp wits to secure public approval. But more than this, it is actually fought with deadly weapons on both sides; many lives have already been lost; many may yet be forfeited.

As the train carries you southeast-ward, you see some signs of it. You pass many coal mines, and some of these are closed down. At the stations, pairs of men in military uniform scrutinize all who alight. These are the West Virginia State Police; a strong force of them is on duty here, for bloodshed became so frequent that one of these counties, Mingo, was placed under martial law. You pass occasional clusters of tents—squalid, wretched places, where swarms of men, women, and children are quartered. Everywhere you are sensible of an atmosphere of tension, covert alertness, sinister suspicion. It is not by accident that these State policemen appear always in pairs.

If you get off the train at Williamson, county seat of Mingo, you will be at the fighting front. People there will tell you that this struggle has been going on for three years. They will tell you of the bloody day at Matewan, May 19, 1920, when ten men, including the mayor of the town, fell in a pistol battle that lasted less than a minute. They will tell you of guerrilla warfare that went on for months; how Federal troops had to be called in twice. They will tell you of the "three days' battle," which resulted, in May, 1921, in the declaration of martial law. Union partisans will tell you of the exercises on May 30 last, when the graves of a score of union fallen were decorated with all the ceremony accorded soldiers who have died for the flag. The operators will tell you of attacks from ambush: how their men have been shot down from behind; how witnesses for trials were mysteriously killed before they could testify. The atrocity list and quantity of propaganda give this war quite an orthodox flavor. It is very hard to sift out the truth.

II

Back in 1898, when the coal industry was quite as unsettled as it is now, the union and the big operators evolved a working plan to stabilize conditions and equalize opportunity. This was the conference in the Central Competitive Field, whereby a wage scale was arrived at for this region, and scale in all other union districts were computed by using this scale as a basis and making allowances for different operating conditions, freight rates, and so forth. This was in order to give all districts an equal chance at the market. Coal is probably the most fluid commodity sold: coal from one section competes with coal from another section remote from the first. It is not analogous to a trademarked article, for which an arbitrary price can be obtained by advertising campaigns and kindred methods. No amount of advertising can make coal of a given grade from one section outsell the same grade from another section at a higher price. This peculiarity of the coal market was the reason for the basic wage-scale arrangement which gave all districts as nearly equal chances as possible, and precluded the possibility that a miscalculated rate might put whole mining fields out of business altogether.

The plan worked fairly well for a time. Within a few years, however, it was discovered that large new areas of coal lands had been developed, and that most of these were being worked with nonunion labor. They had been left out of the original calculation, largely because the existence of such large virgin fields was not known until after the opening of the present century. Some of them were in Pennsylvania, but most, and by far the largest, were in southern West Virginia. Employing nonunion labor, they worked at a lower wage-scale than the union areas, and had become a formidable factor in the industry, for they were underselling union coal constantly. In the years just preceding the war, their effect on the market—and particularly the greater number of days their labor worked during the year—had become definitely noticeable. During the war, there was demand for everybody's coal, and there was no pinch then. The pinch came, however, in the year following the peace.

In 1919, there was a big strike, and the country saw that the nonunion mines had become a big factor in the industry. During the six weeks of that strike, the nonunion mines averaged about 4,000,000 tons of coal a week, and *the bulk of this came from southern West Virginia*. There was a demand for much more than 4,000,000 tons; but it was clear, too, that these fields were capable of much greater production, had transportation been available. The chaos incidental to government control of the railroads precluded an adequate car-supply, and so production was retarded; but the potential strength, the strategic position of these fields, had been demonstrated.

In 1919 even before the strike, the union had realized the necessity of getting into southern West Virginia. Early in that year, it began to send organizers into Logan County, one of the most important in the whole area. It encountered a stone wall. For when these fields were opened (which was only about twenty years ago), the operators there had determined that they were not going to be hampered by the union. In this determination they were doubtless reinforced by big subsidies of the United States Steel Corporation—the great antiunion capitalist group in this country—which had acquired large holdings in several of these counties. To keep out the union, they had developed a system of "mine guards," or "private detectives." The duty of these guards was, ostensibly, to protect property, but, in fact, to maintain an armed barrier to the union. The operators discharged all employees suspected of union leanings, and compelled all others to take oath that they would never join a labor organization. It was a rule of iron, backed by pistols and rifles, and it worked. The union had never obtained even a foothold in the big southern West Virginia field, including Logan, Mingo, McDowell, Wyoming, Raleigh, and Mercer counties.

It was this system the union met when it tried to organize Logan. In this county there was a slight variation. Back in 1912, Don Chafin, the legendary sheriff of Logan, had done away with the private-mine-guards system, but had substituted one of his own that was in all essential respects the same. The guards were sworn in as deputy sheriffs, but they were still paid out of an operators' pool, and their duties included ejection of union sympathizers. When the union entered Logan, its organizers were beaten, its members were discharged, evicted from their homes, and made to leave the county. Its meetings were broken up.

Finally, word came over the hills that women and children friendly to the union were being murdered. The report was not true, but a thousand or more union miners gathered at Lens Creek, about fifteen miles from Charleston, the state capital, and marched on Logan. They were halted by Governor John J. Cornwell and C. Frank Keeney, president of District 17, United Mine Workers. Governor Cornwell promised the men an investigation, and kept his word. A volume of startling testimony was compiled, and there was a wide demand that something be done. Governor Cornwell asked the legislature to act: so did the next governor, E.F. Morgan; but the legislature has done nothing, and the mine-guard system is still in effect.

And the union had failed to organize Logan. Next, in 1920, it struck at Mingo. It encountered the same obstacles here; but the resistance was not so effective, for Mingo is on the Kentucky border, and is easier of access than Logan. The union quickly got a foothold. Some of the county officers saw that its meetings were not disturbed, and locals were organized. The union demanded a wage conference with the operators, and, when they were refused, called their men out on strike.

Then the operators acted. They began to evict union miners from their homes (for in a coal camp the company owns homes, stores, churches, Y.M.C.A., and everything else). A party of Baldwin-Felts detectives went to Matewan, to evict miners, and the big shooting ensued. Evictions went on, however, and as fast as the miners' families were "set out," the union lodged them in tents. Within a short time there were some five thousand persons under canvas. They have been there ever since. The union feeds them, clothes them, and buries their dead. They sit by the Tug River, watching the coal trains pass on the railroad, flotsam cast up by the backwash of a mighty struggle, pathetically loyal to a cause of which they understand nothing.

"It's kinda slow-like," they will tell you, "and sometimes a fellow don't hardly know what to do to pass the time. Some of the boys fishes a little, and some of the women raises a few chickens and gardens around, on'y you cain't raise much on them mountains, like-a-that. But most of the time we jest set around and talk about when they're a-goin' to sign up."

Then came guerrilla warfare. Recall that these people, who were being evicted by thousands, were the same who had become such picturesque characters in popular fiction. For two centuries they had been frontiersmen; they had interbred and lived to themselves so much that there had come into being an atrophied race, a weaker strain of American stock. It was inevitable that they should furnish the labor for the mines. Nevertheless, although to the eye they seemed a singularly shiftless type of poor whites, they had high spirit of sort. They were capable of cherishing life-long feuds. In the prosecution of these they had a most peculiar code, and resorted quickly to the rifle, whether the enemy was a family inheritance or a federal revenue officer looking for moonshine stills. The evictions aroused their bitterest resentment, and in these circumstances atavism was predominant. Shooting and reprisals became the regular order of the day and night, whether union official or coal-operators sanctioned them or not.

Federal troops came and went, and came and went a second time. Their departure both times was the signal for renewed violence until, in May, 1921, Governor Morgan proclaimed martial law.

The state martial law commandant forthwith promulgated a set of regulations. The union was given so many days a week in which to visit its tent colonies. There were to be no meetings, and it was decreed that three or more union men gathered together would constitute a meeting. For violation of this fantastic order, scores of union men were jailed. The union fields to the north, as in 1919, were thrown into a state of seething indignation. Then Sid Hatfield and Ed Chambers, two union sympathizers, were shot dead by Baldwin-Felts detectives at Welch, in McDowell County (August 1, 1921). The volcano went into full eruption. The march of 1919 was reenacted, on a scale three times as large, and with the additional object of going through Logan to Mingo and liberating the prisoners in the jail there. The marchers were turned back once by Keeney. Two days later, however, two union miners were killed and three others wounded by Logan deputies and State Police.

The miners reassembled, and whereas, at first, they had numbered hundreds, they now numbered thousands. At Blair Mountain, in Logan County, the mob was met by a force gathered to defend Logan, and a three-day battle was fought. The operators hired four airplanes, and bombed the miners. Both sides used machine guns; both sides had a number of men killed. Civil war had broken out afresh. It did not stop until two thousand Federal troops were sent in on September 3.

This aroused the public again, but the thing was quickly forgotten, and, except for a Senatorial investigation, nothing was done. The union, moreover, now had Mingo on its hands. It was hampered by a set of regulations more effective than all the mine guards it had ever encountered. For, however they were intended, the martial law rules worked to preserve the status quo, and the status quo was precisely what the operators wanted. The tent colonies became a heavy drain on the treasury. The union has spent on them in the two years of their existence not less than $1,500,000 (the figure is probably over $2,000,000). The money is the smallest part of the tent-colony story however, these staggering figures suggest the iron determination of the union to get into these fields; suggest, too, the magnitude of the issues it thinks are at stake. At present, it is hanging on desperately, pouring out money there at the rate of $11,000 a week. At first it was $25,000.

III

What happened during the 1922 strikes makes it clear that it is a life-and-death matter for the union to get into these fields. There was probably never a strike when the union shutdown in its areas was so complete; union miners to the number of more than 600,000 walked out and stayed out. Yet the first week of the strike, with consumption averaging 8,000,000 tons a week, there were mined 3,784,000 tons. In the next few weeks the price began to climb; it soon became profitable for every little mine in the nonunion area to start up. Mile-long trains of coal gondolas began to groan and crawl around the bends in the Tug River, past the idle staring tent colonies; began to come out of the Winding Gulf, the great Pocahontas field. The weekly production rose. It passed the 4,000,000 mark, the 4,250,000 mark, the 4,500,000 mark.

Finally, by the end of June, it had passed the 5,000,000 mark, and the great mine-strike was hardly 40 per cent effective. It was fortunate for the miners, but quite fortuitous, that the strike of the railroad shopmen came on July 1. Again, transportation was a factor; the physical equipment of the carriers deteriorated so quickly that they could not supply coal cars, and production slumped sharply. It fell away below the 4,000,000 mark weekly, and, with reserve stocks already depleted, there was a crisis which brought the situation to a head and gave the miners an advantage they could not have secured otherwise. But the lesson was as plain as in 1919; the nonunion fields could practically break any strike henceforth, and the Gibraltar of the nonunion fields was southern West Virginia. These West Virginia fields mine more than a third of the tonnage for the whole country; and, leaving out of consideration the locally consumed output of small fields in the South and West, they produced much more than half the coal available for general distribution.

It would be a mistake, however, to consider the union's position only with reference to its effectiveness in time of strike. These fields are a menace to it in time of work as well. For the nonunion mines always have work, boom times or slack. If times are good, demand brisk, then all operators can sell their coal, the nonunion along with the rest. If times are bad and prices slump, then the union operator closes down, for there is a price below which he cannot afford to run his mine. The nonunion operator then gets the orders that might have gone to the union mine, for his costs are lower, and he can sell cheaper. The price that closes his mine is much lower than that which closes the union mine.

This is not theorizing. It is precisely what happens—what happened during the past year. In the union field of Allegany County, Maryland, for example, operators could not afford to run their mines. They offered the union miners work if they would take less pay. In view of the principle of 1898, the union held that this would be in violation of other contracts, and would not permit it. There was no strike, but there was no work; privation and suffering were widespread. Yet the operators who could not run their own mines, having contracts to fill, *bought coal in the nonunion fields of Connellsville and Somerset, Pennsylvania, and filled their contracts more cheaply than they could have done by mining the coal themselves.*

Most often, the way it works out is not so easy to trace as this. The union mine, unable to sell at the price offered, closes down and its men lose a day. The nonunion mine, able to sell at a lower price, can accept its orders. Its men do not lose a day.

All this can be checked up by a glance at government tabulations of the average number of working days to the year in union and nonunion fields. In 1916, the year just before the war, the average number of working days in three wholly-union states was: Ohio, 197; Indiana, 187; Illinois, 198. The average for three nonunion states was: Georgia, 280; New Mexico, 292; Alabama, 262. The partly union state of Pennsylvania averaged 259; the partly union state of West Virginia, 237. In 1920, which was another fairly typical year, the averages were as follows: (union) Ohio, 188; Indiana, 192; Illinois, 213; (nonunion) Georgia, 294; New Mexico, 302; Alabama, 247; (partly union) Pennsylvania, 244; West Virginia, 198.

Statistics for 1921, one of the worst years the industry ever knew, have not been completed. The tendency, however, may be traced by the current weekly bulletins issued by the Geological Survey for that year. These bulletins include an estimate as to the percentage of full-time production attained by miners in various districts. The reports are divided by fields, hence it is not necessary to examine partly union figures, as is the case when returns are made only by states.

For the week ending June 4, 1921, when the market had entered the second slump of the year, the percentage of full-time output was as follows: (union) Ohio, 25.5; Indiana, 34.8; Illinois, 37; (nonunion, in West Virginia) Winding Gulf field, 68.9; Pocahontas, 52.9; Logan, 55.6; Kenova-Thacker, 53; Tug River, 74.2. This relative activity continued, with the union fields gradually gaining ground, until October, when the peak for the year was reached. Percentages of full-time output for the week ending October 22 stood: (union) Ohio, 47.8; Indiana, 55.9; Illinois, 62.4; (nonunion in West Virginia) Winding Gulf, 65.5; Pocahontas, 63.7; Logan, 62.9, Kenova-Thacker, 44.3; Tug River, 55.1. From then to the end of the year, production in the union fields fell off sharply, as the market went into another slump, with the nonunion fields holding their own, now and then gaining a little. Nonunion mines supplied a large proportion of coal used last year, for the reason that they were the only ones which could afford to run. The union miner has come to such a pass that, even though paid at a reasonable rate, he is starving to death because he cannot get work. And the net result is that not only the union itself, but unionism as an idea, an economic scheme, is getting the blame for this condition. The union faces the most persistent fight against it that it has ever known—a fight no less in earnest because it usually appears under the guise of agitation for the open shop. The union is literally on the defensive for its very existence.

IV

From the foregoing, it would seem, indeed, that the nonunion fields are far more soundly organized than the union, and that the solution of the problem lies in putting the whole country on a nonunion basis. This is just what the operators are trying to prove. Not only the nonunion operators, but the union operators as well, distribute this sort of propaganda; newspaper offices are flooded with it. Yet it is clear that the argument of the operators is valid only in a superficial sense, even though present conditions lend it considerable plausibility. For obviously the prosperity of the nonunion fields prevails, not through any superiority of nonunionism per se, but from the artificial advantage they have on account of their lower wage-expense. One third of the industry, the nonunion, works at one level of costs; the other two thirds, the union, work at a higher level; and all slumps and reverses are born by the less fortunate two thirds. At the first sign of hard times, they are stranded high and dry, while the nonunion fields still feel the pulse of business—a bit slow, perhaps, but enough to sustain life.

It would be step back to the Dark Ages to put the whole country on a nonunion basis. No sooner would this be done than there would begin a cut-throat hammering of wages on the part of every operators' association in the country. It would be forced on them. If coal mined in Pennsylvania, with 70 cents a ton, say, as a wage basis, began seriously underselling coal from Indiana, which might have 75 cents as a basis,

Indiana operators would have to cut wages to survive. Pennsylvania, to retain its advantage, would cut wages in return; and so the thing would go on.

When you recall that coal from every big section competes with coal from every other big section, you can get an idea where this sort of thing would lead. The miner would be reduced almost to peonage, and the troubles of the industry would be multiplied a hundredfold.

Nor is the regional wage-agreement plan, recently advocated by the operators, much better. Indeed, this looks suspiciously like a move to divide the union against itself and thus pave the way for the end.

The trouble with this plan is that it allows independent agreements to be arrived at between operators and union representatives in a given section, whereby that section may enjoy a temporary prosperity comparable to that of the nonunion fields at present. Then the operators and union heads in another section will agree on an underselling scale, and this section will be prosperous while the first section will be stranded.

There is a point below which district presidents of the union would hardly dare go with this sort of thing; so the plan might work better than no union at all; but it is apparent that it holds unlimited possibilities for sharp dealing, and for disorganization of the business more serious than that which obtains at present. It should be borne in mind that subordinate union leaders, under pressure in their communities, are often willing to make clever bargains with the operators, and have to be restrained by international headquarters. But the trouble is that this kind of dealing, if carried on long, would inequitably bring the miner to a more degraded living than he has reached at present.

With these palpable defects in the nonunion and the regional-agreement schemes, there is one plan left—short of a big government corporation to run all coal mines—which promises some sort of solution. This is to put the whole country on a union basis, and give all operators an equal chance at the market, and all miners an equal chance at regular work.

There is probably no Federal agency that could compel this; it is questionable, indeed, whether it would be wise to try to accomplish it by government agencies. Yet it could be accomplished if there were sufficiently insistent public demand that the armed-guard system, by which the union is forcibly kept out of the nonunion fields, be abolished. With the public more and more inclined to think of coal as a national problem, a sort of public utility, it is less and less inclined to put up with the amazing medieval methods whereby the nonunion operators maintain their advantage. It is their declaration that they are opposed to unionism as a principle; that their labor does not want it; that they are splendidly isolated and intend to remain so. Their reason, in fact, is that under the nonunion system their coal mines have become gold mines; their object in keeping out the union is money, and nothing else. Their labor joins the union whenever it gets a chance. When it becomes more generally known that this sort of industrial feudalism is what is wrong with the coal business, more than any other single defect, then the public may voice a persistent demand that it be abolished.

V

In West Virginia, the union, all of a sudden, has a chance to profit by the greatest blow that has been dealt unionism in years, that is—the Coronado decision. This makes unions liable to suit, but it also gives them the right to sue. There is a law in West Virginia which prohibits private payment of deputy sheriffs. It carries no penalty, and has always been considered a dead letter. But it now becomes possible for the union to go into court as a plaintiff, and invoke the old bête noir of labor, the injunction proceedings, to prohibit such a system as is maintained in Logan County, and, on a lesser scale, in several other West Virginia counties. That is, it might ask the court to enjoin payment of deputies by the Logan sheriff, out of the operators' pool. It might also ask the court to enjoin mine guards from interference with union meetings and union organizers. Its attorneys, indeed, are considering such a step now. If it should succeed, and the union could get its organizers into southern West Virginia, then the unionizing of these fields would be virtually accomplished. And if this end could be attained peaceably, the long war in West Virginia might be ended, to the great advantage of the coal business all over the country.

CHAPTER X

CHAPTER X
Victory:
The UMWA Comes to Southern West Virginia

In early 1933, President Franklin D. Roosevelt signed the Industrial Recovery Act into law, at last giving American workers the right to join labor unions of their choice. For the union miner in southern West Virginia, Roosevelt's action meant that the federal government was finally on his side. With one stroke of the pen, the president had put the full force and power of the federal government behind the miner's hope and dream of a national union.

Overnight, mine workers flocked to the union. They came in such numbers that coal companies, as well as union officials, were caught completely off guard. Now, with the union in place, the iron grasp of the coal establishment was broken. The company town was abolished as a system for ruthless exploitation. Miners were "free at last." There would still be coal strikes—many of them bitter, some of them even violent—but the primary issues of the Mine Wars of 1912–1921 were settled. The Mine Wars were now over.

It is fitting to include two articles that celebrate the end of those wars. They tell about the union, the United Mine Workers of America, and its victory in southern West Virginia.

"Tidal Wave of Enthusiasm"

This first article is from the United Mine Workers Journal, *July 1, 1933, following passage of the National Industrial Recovery Act. It not only describes the miners' stampede into the union, but also captures the sense of excitement during those important, historic days.*

A wave of enthusiasm of mountainous proportions for the United Mine Workers of America is sweeping the coal areas of the United States and mine workers by the thousands are joining the United Mine Workers of America. So great has been the incoming of membership that it is almost impossible to keep track of it. The passage of the Industrial Recovery Act, which gives the miners—and all other workers as well—the legal right to belong to a trade union without jeopardizing their jobs, is the cause of the exodus from ranks of the unorganized to the shelter of the union. In hard-boiled anti-union states, where a trade unionist was even in danger of his life, in the old days, unions are flourishing and joyfully received by the people. The administration of the new law is now being worked out as to detail. President Lewis has been appointed as a member of the labor advisory board and will look after the interests of the miners. President Lewis has expressed the warmest admiration of the new law and the fact that the United Mine Workers can now organize without going into the courts and fighting injunctions by the dozens. It is a great day for organized labor over America!

Historic Convention Held

This United Mine Workers Journal *article, appearing August 1, 1933, describes a massive union meeting in Charleston, West Virginia, once the "citadel of the non-union bituminous coal industry." UMW officials anticipated about 1,000 miners at this most important event. To their delight, more than 2,500 showed up. Among those present were miners who had fought for years to see this day: the veterans of the Mine Wars of 1912–1921.*

It was a historic meeting in Charleston, W. Va., on June 23, when the very citadel of the non-union bituminous coal industry was stormed by 2,579 delegates, representing some 160,000 miners, members of the United Mine Workers in four southern states, and pledged their support to the National Industrial Recovery Act (NIRA) and to the union's efforts for the 40-hour week, and the demand for union recognition.

A dispatch to the *New York Times* gives an accounting of the meeting:

Hailed as the largest and most important union meeting, the dispatch says, ever held south of the Ohio River, delegates from Maryland, Virginia, northern and southern West Virginia and eastern Kentucky held an all-day meeting, voted full support to the officers of the international union and then disbanded to await the outcome of the hearings on the code for the soft-coal industry to be held by the recovery administration.

Whereas two months ago the United Mine Workers of America was confined to a skeleton organization, with the largest number in northern West Virginia, delegates reported that the union has 728 locals in four southern states with members in virtually every non-union coal camp in this territory.

Among those present at the convention were veterans of the 1921 pitched battles in Logan, Mingo and "Bloody McDowell" counties in this state. Many who took part in the "armed march" on Logan when troops of the regular army were called in to put down the revolt notified Mine Workers' officers that the hitherto solid non-union strongholds were practically 100 percent union.

From remote mountain camps of Hazard and Jenkins, Ky., about 165 miles as the crow flies and much more than that by road, several large delegations arrived by truck after riding all night. Others came from as far east as Cumberland, Md.; from the northern West Virginia fields around Fairmont and Morgantown and from the southern fields of eastern Kentucky to Tazewell, New River and the Pocahontas area.

As a result of the meeting, John L. Lewis, president of the United Mine Workers, will enter the hearings on the proposed coal codes in Washington two weeks hence and place upon the table the mandate to represent practically all the coal miners in the United States. Meetings north of the Ohio River have also delegated him to present the views of northern miners.

This demand will be bitterly contested by the non-union operators north and south, who are expected to formulate a code of their own.

The battle between the unions affiliated with the American Federation of Labor and the spokesmen of the open-shop and company unions, which will open during the hearings on the steel code, will be continued at the hearings on the coal code.

The meeting, arranged by Van A. Bittner, president, District 17, was called as the climax of union organization work in the south in the past two months.

Mr. Bittner told the delegates that the union would not cease its efforts until all operators had signed wage agreements and "until the flag of the United Mine Workers flies over every coal tipple in the south."

Union officials who expected as many as 1,000 or, at the best, 1,200 delegates at the convention, were enthusiastic upon receiving the report of the credentials committee. A statement that there were 150 delegates from Logan County, one of the strongest non-union centers in this state, was received with applause. The delegates cheered a telegram from President Lewis, who asserted that the meeting was a historic one and the most momentous in the history of the four coal states.

Mr. Bittner warned that the union would tolerate no "wildcat" strikes, as it was interested in solving the problems of the industry in a constructive manner, through co-operation with the coal operators.

"This is our day," he declared; "it is written in the stars that we shall survive. We shall follow a policy of co-operation in an intelligent way until wage agreements are written."

He said that the coal operators and the government might as well understand that so long as there was going to be any coal to dig it would be produced as the result of negotiations between the operators and the men who work in the mines.

"It is not a question as to whether the men will organize," he added. "They have organized. That is settled."

Mr. Bittner maintained that the operators by themselves could not solve the problems of the industry. He was confident that if they accepted the "constructive proposals of the United Mine Workers peace and happiness will reign."

Referring to the convention as a "new day and new deal," Mr. Bittner said that the day of the company-paid detective and deputy sheriff was over. He mentioned the signing of the Recovery Act by President Roosevelt with its guarantee of the right of collective bargaining as a historic act.

"With one stroke of the pen President Roosevelt wiped out the yellow-dog contract which you men had to sign in many cases to get a job," asserted Mr. Bittner.

"You men of McDowell, Logan, Mingo, the Winding Gulf and Kanawha fields, New River, Kentucky and Maryland—you are now free citizens of the United States and you enjoy every right the constitution and the laws give to citizens of the United States."

CHAPTER XI

CHAPTER XI
The History of *The Socialist and Labor Star*:
Huntington, W. Va. 1912–1915

The following essay on *The Socialist and Labor Star* was originally published by Appalachian Movement Press of Huntington, W. Va., in 1971. Appalachian Movement Press was a cooperative, radical press, and very much the product of the student New Left, especially influenced by the presence of Students for a Democratic Society (SDS) on the campus of Huntington's Marshall University. Besides contemporaneous analyses of the class structure of quasi-colonial West Virginia, the press also issued several pamphlets by poet and labor activist Don West, already then known for his regionalist radicalism.

Foreword by Danie Stewart

The United Mine Workers of America do not work without a contract. This is true in 1971, as a strike involving 100,000 miners enters its fourth week, and it was true in 1912–13 in the Paint Creek–Cabin Creek district in Kanawha County, West Virginia.

The current strike began with the old contract expiration, 30 September, but the leadership did not declare a strike until almost two weeks later, and only then under the prodding by rank and file forces who demanded that strike benefits be paid. The differences between the needs and values of the leadership of the U.M.W. of A. and its rank and file base has been a continuing focus since the Black Lung Strike and the Yablonski challenge—contract negotiations bring it into sharp relief. The rank and file of Cabin Creek knew the differences long ago.

Nor do the parallels between contemporary struggles and historical ones end with these, when grievances gave way to violence in the Paint–Cabin Creek strike, the U.S. Senate investigated. Their findings, contained in part in this paper, were clear enough, but as with contemporary investigations—whether of a ghetto or prison riot or a Consol #9 or Hyden mine massacre—the investigations produce reams of documentation of causal abuse and nothing in the way of action to alter the causes. The miners of Cabin Creek continued to struggle for their own relief, union leadership and Congressional inquiry notwithstanding.

But this is not a history of the Cabin Creek strike and the intrigues of conservative union leadership. It is the story of a once thriving socialist press in Huntington, West Virginia, that reported events of the strike from the rank and file viewpoint. *The Labor Star* treated the confrontation of forces and maneuvering of interests in the strike as a dramatic case in point for its basic critic of capitalist society. It was effective in using events of Cabin Creek to demonstrate the subordination of the political system to the economic system—and in developing a constituency to this view, both inside and outside the strike zone. And because it was effective—it was totally suppressed.

The socialists of *The Labor Star* were strongly allied with the trade union movement—both in Huntington and in the strike zone. They were themselves union men and women and they articulated the interest of working miners as no conservative U.M.W. could or would.

Appalachian Movement Press is proud to publish this well-researched and timely history. Although the paper was written to satisfy requirements for a graduate history course, it is printed without editing on our part. We believe the paper, in addition to telling an exciting chapter of Appalachian history, will be read and enjoyed by the general Appalachian audience whose history, culture, and contemporary struggles are our reason for being. We believe the paper could prove a valuable addition to the Appalachian studies programs increasingly available in regional schools. In addition, the history of *The Labor Star* demonstrates that radical history is not something one must set out to write—rather, events in working class struggle and the actions of state machinery define that history as radical.

One final note: the lessons drawn from history may elicit a number of responses for people currently engaged in actions for political change. One may be depressed and despair that nothing really changes despite countless struggles, or one may find a sense of solidarity and continuity of purpose. On reading this narrative of *The Labor Star*, I was reminded of the comment made fifty years ago by an imprisoned I.W.W. member: "The end in view is well worth striving for, but in the struggle itself lies the happiness of the fighter."

The Socialist and Labor Star:
The Harassment of Heresy
by David A. Corbin

Introduction

"Better heresy of doctrine than heresy of heart."
—John Greenleaf Whittier

The political heretic, innate in American history has persisted. Sometimes he has prevailed, but more often he has perished. He was with us yesterday, he is with us today, and he will be with us tomorrow. Society's safety valve against tyranny and despotism, the political deviant offers challenge and change and for his invaluable service his rewards are repression and abomination.

Society, like the human body, is resistive to change; it tends to reject and destroy that which is alien and foreign; it seeks to secure unto itself in the protective outer layers of orthodoxy and tradition. Confronted with the natural stabilizers of ignorance and fear, as well as the synthetic preservers of the status-quo, the political heretic is destined to a life of alienation. From the Alien and Sedition Acts through the eras of A. Mitchell Palmer and Joe McCarthy, the political deviant who dares challenge the existing institutions and cries out for change, has been victim of society's anathema and has generally suffered the consequences of its wrath.

True, even in a constitutional government, it is hazardous and precarious to permit absolute freedoms, but toleration of heresy serves to protect the citizenry, as much as repression serves to protect the government. More than granting civil liberties to involved individuals, or allowing criticism of governmental policy, the acceptance of social and political anomalies allows the people a more accurate if not sagacious attitude or alternative. Irresponsible repression serves only to promote dogmatism. It limits the public to available choices—the government's way and the wrong way.

This paper is a study of a political heretic, *The Socialist and Labor Star*, a socialist newspaper in Huntington, West Virginia, between the years 1912–1915. It is an attempt to focus on the ordeals and obstacles that it encountered as it sought to arouse the laboring class of West Virginia to improve their working environment and to demand the profit of their toil, the surplus value. During its three brief years of existence, it met with opposition from nearly all quarters of society; from the distant office of the West Virginia Chief Executive to the local rival newspapers, from the staunchest supporters of capitalism, to the staunchest proponents of socialism. Supporting and encouraging the exploited mines of Appalachia, *The Socialist and Labor Star* affronted the West Virginia state government, the United Mine Workers of America, and the Socialist Party of America. The paper encountered and suffered the wrath of their abomination, but it neither strayed from its goals nor surrendered its ideals. Never achieving the national accolades or the national notoriety of the major socialist publications, *The Socialist and Labor Star*'s efforts remain but a memory to those who published it, read it, and repressed it. The Huntington socialist journal stands as a forgotten monument in the history of American heresy and radicalism.

Background

"We should not forget that our tradition is one of protest and revolt, and it is stultifying to celebrate the rebels of the past . . . while we silence the rebels of the present."
—Henry Steel Commager, *Freedom, Loyalty, Dissent*

The Socialist and Labor Star began the turbulent path of heretical journalism in May, 1912.[1] The expressed purpose for its appearance was twofold: First, it was to "fill a glaring void in West Virginia journalism." It said:

Other newspapers are published in the interests of the capitalist class . . . and therefore taint and picture all news to discredit the working class. This paper, owned and controlled and published by the workers of West Virginia, is the avowed spokesman for the great majority who have been denied a fair hearing.[2]

Secondly, *The Star* was to uphold and safeguard the rights and interests of the working class. This extended beyond exposing the realities of a "capitalist society" to encouraging and supporting the laborers of West Virginia to demand the equal distribution of wealth. Consistent with its socialist foundations the newspaper theorized on the principle that labor produced all wealth and moralized on the goal that all wealth belonged to labor.

The Star was the chartered publication of the Socialist Printing Company, and the official "mouthpiece" of the Huntington Trades and Labor Assembly. The Socialist Printing Company was an incorporated commercial printing business. In addition to publishing the four-page weekly paper, the corporation printed and sold books, stationery and various materials for labor unions in the city.[3] Its main emphasis was, of course, the issuing and distributing of *The Star*.

Like most socialist publications, *The Star*'s inspiration and genius laid in the men and women who published it. In the opinion of the eminent American socialist, J. Louis Engdahl, these radical journals were more than "Marxian journals devoted to teaching the dismal science . . . they were the outpourings of the hearts and minds of those who saw in socialism the regeneration of the race." During its three brief years of existence, *The Star* was the "outpouring of the heart and mind" of its editor, Wyatt Hamilton Thompson.[4]

"Comrade Thompson," as his future friends would call him, was born in the small mining town of Mauldin, eighteen miles east of the West Virginia capital city, Charleston, in 1885. At the age of nine he went to work in the coal mines in the vicinity and in the same year joined the United Mine Workers.

After earning an apprenticeship in printing in Charleston, Thompson worked on various papers throughout the state, until his venture with *The Star*. As a journalist, he belonged to the International Typographical Union and the Huntington Typographical Union and served two terms as president with the latter. He was also a delegate to the Huntington Trades and Labor Assembly and the 1914 American Federation of Labor Convention. While editing *The Star* without pay, the socialist editor worked for a local daily newspaper.

Thompson's introduction into the world of socialism is relatively unknown. The nearest connection is drawn from his personal experiences in the exploration and tribulations of a mountain-state miner. For daring to express his radical philosophy through his paper, humiliation and imprisonment were often his rewards.[5]

Ralph Chaplin was another vivid individual who gave pulse and life to *The Star*. An experienced journalist and radical when he joined the staff, Chaplin had served on the publications board of the *International Socialist Review* and had fought with the Mexican revolutionaries. His role with the Huntington paper was a brief but vital one. He worked as a reporter and associate editor on *The Star* and "bootlegged" literature inside the martial law zone during the Paint–Cabin Creek strike. Several of the articles he wrote for the Huntington paper appeared in national socialist publications, as his name was becoming prominent in the radical movement. The experience he obtained and absorbed while working with the paper under the experienced editor Thompson was undoubtedly valuable when he later became editor of the official publication of the Industrial Workers of the World. As an artist, poet, pamphleteer, and editor, Chaplin was probably the most prolific writer of the I.W.W. As a "Wobbly" he rose to such prominence as to be labeled by Philip Foner as "the right hand man to William 'Big Bill' Haywood."[6]

The feminist side of *The Star* was presented by Mrs. Sarah Swann. As true virago, the "first lady" of the paper had been described as "worldly wise." Her habits included smoking, drinking with the men, inhaling "snuf" and complaining of the marriage bonds that confined her to womanhood. As a member of *The Star* she assisted in writing the weekly articles and later substituted as special correspondent to the *International Socialist Review* during the incarceration of Thompson.[7] It was under this philosophy, background and staff that *The Star* was published.

Paint Creek

"I don't think I have ever encountered such passionate love for freedom as I found in the hills of West Virginia."
—Ralph Chaplin

"God blessed West Virginia with a prolific hand; a topography grand to contemplate; a wealth unparalleled in coal, iron and ore—her hills fairly groan with undeveloped resources, and all of these at the very threshold of the great marts of trade and commerce of our country. Here, above all sections, should peace, plenty, and happiness reign supreme. On the

contrary, your committee found disorder, riot, bitterness, and bloodshed in their stead."
—Senator James E. Martine, United States Senate, September, 1914.

The account of *The Star* might have been the typical story of the hundreds of socialist journals that rose, flourished, and disintegrated during the first two decades of the twentieth century had it not been for a violent and protracted coal strike in the southwest mining districts of West Virginia—the Paint Creek–Cabin Creek strike of 1912–1913. This catastrophic clash of economic interests which resulted in personal and financial tragedy, played a dramatic and potent role in the life of *The Star*.[8]

The literary and historical accounts of this industrial conflict are prolific, and it is not the purpose of this paper to retell that story.[9] The subject of importance is the Paint Creek–Cabin Creek impact and relevance to the socialist paper, one hundred miles from the tent colonies and machine guns that symbolized the labor-management disputes on the Appalachian coal frontier.

The outbreak of the conflict was the reaction to a number of factors and conditions that had been imposed on the coal operators. The contributing causes as related by the United States Senate investigation of the strike included:

The failure of the operators in the district to renew their expiring contracts with the United Mine Workers; the determination of the coal operators under no circumstance to recognize the miners as an organization or union, and the equal determination of the miners to organize and form a union, a right as they claim guaranteed to them without discrimination by the laws of West Virginia; the employment by the operators of mine guards, many of whom were aggressive and arbitrary; mine guards in the employment of operators acting as deputy sheriffs and clothed with the authority of law; the failure of the civil authorities to attempt even to preserve peace and order at the beginning of the violence and permitting things to drift from bad to worse without vigorous interference and assertion and authority; discontent among the miners occasioned by no opportunity to purchase homes; no cemeteries except on company grounds; post offices located in the company stores; private roads only to the schools and stores; the disposition of the coal operators to keep strict espionage of all strangers who entered the district and to exercise their right of private ownership of this large district and to exclude from it all persons objectionable to them.[10]

These conditions were the multiplicand of two component factors that served to accentuate and strengthen the intensity of the hostility of the labor dispute. The first was the rapid growth of West Virginia as a coal-producing state. In thirty-two years (1880–1912), West Virginia had increased its coal production from two percent of the nation's total output (or 1,829,844 short tons) to 12.5 per cent (or 66,786,000 short tons).[11] The second was the contradictory dichotomy of needs and views over unionization. Due to the favorable conditions of West Virginia as a coal-producing state, the proximity to the Great Lakes coal markets, unusually thick veins, and the hilly topography that made the mining easier, and its rapid growth in production, West Virginia was a threat to the organized fields of the neighboring states. It was characterized as a "pistol pointed at the heart of the industrialized government in the coal industry." The operators, realizing that unionization meant not only parting with their absolute power as employers but also having their natural competitive advantages pared off in favor of the older fields, vehemently resisted.[12]

These conditions produced the bitter, violent, and destructive strike at Paint Creek–Cabin Creek, a strike so "intense and "fierce" to be described by the United States Senate as, "well-armed forces fighting for supremacy. Separate camps, organized, armed, and guarded, were established. There was much violence and some murders. Pitched battles were fought by the contending parties. Law and order disappeared, and life was insecure for both sides."[13]

During the first several months, the strike received little attention from *The Star*, but as the intensity of the conflict increased and news of the violence reached Cabell County, the Huntington socialists proceeded to become involved. A strike committee was organized, members of the paper's staff were selected to gather information and pictures of the conflict as well as to "bootleg" strike literature inside the martial law zone, and most important, to give encouragement and support to the striking miners through the columns of *The Star*.[14]

The strike was brought to a temporary stalemate in April, 1913, a scant year after its beginning. The newly inaugurated Governor Henry

D. Hatfield attempted to bring the conflict to an end by a proposed "compromised settlement." The terms of the settlement were: First, that the operators concede the miners their rights to select a check-weighman; second a nine-hour work day be conceded to the miners by the operators; third, that no discrimination be made against any miner; and fourth, that the operators grant a semi-monthly pay.[15]

This proposal was readily accepted by the coal operators and the officials of the United Mine Workers. The final procedure was to get the "rank and file" of the miners' union to ratify the "compromised agreement." This was accomplished by calling a miner's convention in which delegates from the striking miners accepted the terms. The strike was declared at an end on May 1, 1913.

Discontent was still rampant among the rank and file miners and opposition was reflected in the editorial position of *The Star*. Through the paper's articles and editorials and in letters to national socialist publications (*International Socialist Review*), *The Star*'s editors "severely criticized and exposed the 'strike settlement.'"

The position taken by Thompson was that Hatfield's proposal was an "unholy alliance among the coal operators, the officials of the United Mine Workers and the state's chief executive" to bring an aborted conclusion to the labor conflict. The terms of the proposal, argued the editor, had turned what could have been a "victory" for the miners into a "settlement."[16] Thompson alleged that after coal-operators and the state government had "failed to break the strike by barbaric and inhumane methods," they enlisted the officials of the United Mine Workers to deceive the rank and file of the union into accepting the terms of their "cooperative efforts." Having ignored the striking miners in drafting the settlement, the union officials proceeded to gain their ratification by coercion and deceit in the form of the delegate convention.

The alleged coercion took the form of Hatfield's notorious "36 hour demand"—where the Governor gave the delegates the choice between accepting his terms and the deportation of "the idle troublemakers" from the State of West Virginia.[17]

The deceit and fraud was the union officials "juggling" of the Governor's terms as well as those drawn up by the delegates, in such a way that when the delegates thought they were voting on their own proposals, they were actually voting on the Governor's.[18]

Thus, *The Star*'s opposition was twofold: it was opposed to the means used to gain acceptance of the settlement. The paper also opposed the results of the cooperative effort, the settlement itself.

Thompson insisted that the terms of the proposal offered "nothing tangible" in concessions for the miners, and what was conceded was already guaranteed by law. More important, the editor asserted that the basic demands for which the miners had gone on strike were not included. These cardinal points, according to Thompson, were "the elimination of the hated mine guard system," "the right to belong to a union," and the payment of wages based on adjacent organized districts.[19]

Therefore, the editors of *The Star*, feeling that the miners had been deceived and coerced to return to work under a settlement never actually accepted by the rank and file, and believing that the proposition would be detrimental "to their cause and against their best interests," severely criticized the proposed "settlement" and "the threatening manner" in which Hatfield attempted to force the acceptance, encouraged them to reject the settlement and carry the strike to a victory.[20] Because the reason for the strike had not been eliminated, *The Star* prophesied, "The strike on Kanawha is not settled."[21]

This prophecy was fulfilled six weeks later when the union's rank and file unanimously repudiated the settlement and "demanded of the United Mine Workers of America that the strike be declared still existent." As *The Star* had months earlier predicted, the anti-discrimination clause was not upheld by the operators as the mine guards continued their brutal assaults on those attempting to organize. A striking illustration of the fact that the operators had not recognized the union.[22]

The union officials found themselves in a position of being compelled to endorse a strike against the settlement they had forced upon the miners. They excused this reversal in attitude by laying the blame on the operators, who they said had not "acted in good faith."[23]

The renewed strike was of short duration as the operators finally agreed to the basic demand of the miners which was complete recognition of the union. In addition, the agreement included the Kanawha Scale, the guarantee of "no discrimination" and the eight-hour day. Jubilantly and unanimously the miners ratified the new agreement.[24]

With the basic demand of miners guaranteed, by a contract unanimously approved by the rank and file, *The Star* accepted and supported the new contract.[25] But, *The Star* had suffered the wrath of the interest groups it had exposed through its heretical columns.

Suppression

"What signifies a declaration that 'the Liberty of the Press' shall be inviolably preserved? What is the Liberty of the Press? Who can give it any definition which does not leave the utmost latitude for evasion? I hold it to be impracticable and from this I infer, that its security, whatever fine declarations may be inserted in any Constitution respecting it, must altogether depend on public opinion, and on the general spirit of the people and of the Government."
—Alexander Hamilton, *The Federalist* LXXXIV

The Star's position on the Paint Creek–Cabin Creek strike and Hatfield's proposed settlement, set in motion forces in the state capital that had a profound effect on the future of the socialist paper. In the early morning hours of May 9, 1913, the paper's presses were destroyed and confiscated and its editors incarcerated.

Events had taken place during the weeks preceding the suppression that made this attack appear imminent.

Two weeks prior to the raid on *The Star*, the socialist paper of Charleston was suppressed and its temporary editor Fred Merrick arrested and imprisoned. Merrick, the former editor of the Parkersburg *Social Rebel* and Pittsburgh *Justice*, both leftist journals, was substituting for the regular *Labor Argus* editor Charles E. Boswell who had been incarcerated by orders of Hatfield. Additionally, two associate editors were arrested and the plant's equipment was confiscated. The seizure of the printing materials was a simple procedure; the soldiers drove a wagon to the office of the plant and loaded the equipment on it and drove away.[26]

The spring rains of 1913 brought a disastrous Ohio River flood which resulted in a "trial" raid on the plant of *The Star*. Two companies of the militia were withdrawn from the Kanawha strike zone and were stationed in Huntington to "safeguard the city." During their occupation of the town, Thompson alleged: "They showed us what martial law in the Kanawha County had been. They confiscated whiskey and with their hides full of rot-gut, and their hands full of deadly weapons, they staggered about fighting both the citizens and each other, stealing everything that was not nailed down, and breaking into homes and carrying off what they wanted."[27]

226 GUN THUGS, REDNECKS, AND RADICALS

In reaction to *The Star*'s exposure of these alleged scandals the soldiers conspired to destroy its plant. The city's socialists were informed of the plot and prepared to repel the invasion. A wagonload of rifles and revolvers were brought in and type cases were moved around to barricade the doors and windows. When approximately 450 soldiers marched on the plant, they found "twenty determined looking men with Winchesters . . . therefore the gallant warriors decided to delay the attack."[28] The foray came several days later, in the dead of the night.

A mass meeting conducted by the Huntington Trades and Labor Assembly was held to "request the national government to institute an investigation in regard to the state of anarchy and military dictatorship . . . reigning in the commonwealth."[29] When the principle speaker, George W. Gillespie, a prominent state socialist and member of the state executive committee of the Socialist Party, began to address the crowd, bricks were hurled at the crowd by Baldwin-Felts detectives, the same agency that employed the mine guards in the strike zone. When a committee of socialists attempted to capture the "brick throwers" to eliminate the nuisance, the detectives turned and ran, shooting into the crowd as they fled seriously wounding one of the workers.[30]

A final guidepost illustrating that suppression was near was provided by the Huntington Socialists themselves. The issue immediately preceding the raid was important from two aspects. It was this issue that was used to fill the subscription of *The Argus*, which had been suppressed and was "bootlegged" into the strike zone. The edition was also a bitter and censorious assault on the chief executive and coal barons of West Virginia. The front page of the issue condemned Hatfield on three accounts: for the suppression of *The Argus*, for attempting to bribe a socialist Justice of the Peace in the strike district, and for ordering the arrest of socialist United Mine Worker's attorney Harold W. Houston. [31]

More vitriolic and increasingly bitter was the newspaper's major editorial, "Hatfield Has Gone Mad." The editor assailed the chief executive as having an "absolute disregard for the rights of others, inherited from a long line of outlaw ancestors."[32] The editorial proceeded to assert that, "Hatfield was irritated beyond measure by the fact that the people of West Virginia as a whole do not accept his dictatorial orders . . . and mad with knowledge of power secured for him by his sinister, ruthless masters through their legislative and judicial emissaries and drunk with the re-aroused half-savage instinctive desire for domination." The vilification concluded by stating that: "Hatfield has entered upon a course of brutal tyranny and oppression that has absolutely no precedent in American history."[33]

The paper also bitterly condemned the "proposed settlement" stating that the basic demands of the striking miners were not guaranteed in the Governor's proposition. *The Star* declared "the strike is not settled nor will it be settled right . . . be sure it contains something real tangible before accepting it."[34]

With the publication of this issue, Thompson realized that suppression and possible imprisonment was near. In an effort to delay the inevitable, the socialist editor fled to Kentucky once the paper had been distributed. From the hills of the bordering state, Thompson continued his onslaught on the West Virginia government by writing letters to other socialist papers and magazines. In a letter to the *International Socialist Review*, the socialist editor wrote, "We got out *The Star*, sending one to each of *The Argus* subscribers. Then I took a vacation with the emphasis on the vacate."[35]

The sojourn to Kentucky postponed the suppression but it did not prevent it. Warrants for the arrest of Thompson and four other officials of The Socialist Printing Company were issued May 5, three days after the release of the May 2 issue. The arrival of Thompson in Huntington late on the night of May 8, to help prepare the May 9 edition, "was the signal for the serving of the processes."[36]

Acting under orders issued by Hatfield, the military and civilian officials of Cabell County commenced their foray around two o'clock in the morning of May 9. The initial part of the raid was handled by the Cabell County Deputy Sheriff Frampton, who with warrants from the Governor arrested and incarcerated the officials of The Socialist Printing Company including editor Thompson.[37]

Two of the plant's officials were held in custody in jailer's residences at the instruction of the County Sheriff who claimed they were not responsible for what was published in the paper. They were placed in the County jail and held there until the next afternoon. At that time, the two men were turned over to the military authorities and were deported to Kanawha County.[38]

In the capital city, they were placed in custody of the civilian authorities again for incarceration in the Kanawha County Jail. Their confinement lasted for fourteen days, at which time they were released on the verbal order of Hatfield without a formal charge ever being brought against them.[39]

The confiscation and destruction of The Star's plant by the state militia promptly followed the arrests. The military authorities entered the plant by crawling through the transom over the front door and "mobbing" the sole guard of the plant. After gaining control of the building, the diligent representatives of "law and order" proceeded to destroy the "job work," type, printing plates, and other immovable objects. At this point, Deputy Sheriff Frampton, who accompanied the militia to the plant, protested against such "lawless action." The "midnight marauders" informed the Deputy Sheriff that they had "secret orders" from Hatfield to wreck the plant and proceeded about their business. Their execution took the form of smashing and breaking the "type forms" which had been completed for the next issue of The Star, confiscating the copies of the paper already printed, and scattering the type over the flooded streets of Huntington.[40]

After destroying The Star's facilities, the soldiers proceeded to demolish the departments in which The Socialist Printing Company did commercial job printing. A later edition of The Star stated, "Every job in this department including forms of several sets of By-Laws for local unions, which had not yet been printed, matters ready for delivery to local merchants were destroyed. All of the account books, letters, invoices, files, and copy in the office were confiscated and carried away."[41]

This ruthless act of suppression and destruction took place eighty miles from the martial law zone, and, as The Star and the Senate Investigating Committee pointed out, while the courts were still open.

Even the National Executive Investigating Committee, assigned to investigate the strike conditions, which was otherwise mild if not complimentary to the Hatfield Administration, vehemently denounced the act. Referring to the suppression as a "dastardly crime" the committee's report declared this was the "one act of his [Hatfield's] administration which stands out as utterly without warrant and subject to the severest censure."[42]

A different voice was presented by another Huntington newspaper, the Herald-Dispatch. Probably feeling that the confiscation was a part of the local cleanup campaign, then underway in the city, the Progressive Party press complimented the Administration's actions. Referring to The Star's articles as "treasonous" and its editors as "anarchist," the

"*Howling Dishpan*," (as *The Star* named it), asserted that the "action of the military authorities . . . created no surprise, it was a natural sequence following the course pursued by that publication during the past three months."[43]

Following the arrests and destruction of the plant, the military authorities ransacked the home of editor Thompson. With the editor safely incarcerated, the invaders met with only the mild opposition of Mary Thompson, the editor's wife, who was recovering from a protracted illness. They entered the house with neither warning nor warrant and proceeded to search and confiscate the editor's personal correspondence, books and files.[44]

Once more, the Deputy Sheriff protested to the solders against the searching of a private residence without a warrant only to be informed again that they had "secret orders" from the Governor. The invaders were primarily interested in obtaining *The Star*'s subscription book. Their efforts to secure it failed.[45]

The Governor's reasons for the suppression were generally to the effect that *The Star* was inciting riot and insurrection inside the strike zone. On the day of the attack the *Herald-Dispatch* reported that the charge lodged against the men were "inciting to riot in connection with the coal miner's strike and in sequel to the publication of articles in the local newspaper which it is alleged, tended to kindle bitterness between the strikers and the operators."[46]

These same reasons were maintained a year later when Colonel George S. Wallace defended the Governor's actions before the West Virginia Supreme Court of Appeals. Wallace maintained that Hatfield "had just cause to believe and did believe that the suppression of the issue of the Socialist paper in Huntington of the week of May 5, 1913, was necessary and proper in order to end the insurrection and riot and clash of arms then going on in the adjacent territory."[47]

To the supporters of *The Star*, the wanton acts of suppression and confiscation reaffirmed and supplemented their belief in the tyranny and despotism of the Hatfield Administration. They believed the general theme on which the Governor centered these actions was because of *The Star*'s criticism of the Administration's policies and the strike settlement.[48] In the first issue following the pillage, *The Star* asserted:

> Mr. Hatfield . . . has seen fit to order military confiscation of two Socialist newspapers that had the effrontery to disagree

with him in regard to the merits and demerits of the controversy on Paint and Cabin Creeks. In a manner unparalleled in American annals, he has ridden roughshod over blood-bought priceless liberties of American people.

Mr. Hatfield, you are dealing with American citizens, not Russian serfs, and the man doesn't live who can tell us what to think and what to say.

The settlement you proposed in the coal strike did not suit Comrade Thompson, and he thinking he was in a land where free expression and discussion is a cardinal principle, spoke up like a man and said so.

For this you send armed midnight marauders and destroyed our private property. And then you call us anarchists![49]

The suppression of *The Star* entailed both short range and long range consequences for the paper and its editors. The immediate consequences of the "midnight raid" were, in the overall perspective, small and insignificant. However, to the staff of The Socialist Printing Company and *The Star*, they were direct and frustrating tribulations. They were effects and consequences that never should have been. The major difficulty was primarily pecuniary. Until May 9, *The Star* had been financially stable, but following the suppression the paper stated, "As a result of the outrages perpetrated upon *The Star*, we find ourselves for the first time unable to meet pressing financial obligations."[50]

The long range consequences were more indirect, but nationally prominent and significant. The American Socialist Party was inspired to become involved in the West Virginia labor strife. Thompson wrote that as a result of confiscation "The National Socialist Organization was at last shocked into action and decided to send a committee into West Virginia."[51]

Moreover, the suppression had the effect of prompting the United States Senate to become involved. The Kern Resolution, calling for the second senatorial labor investigation in American history had been debated in the Senate for months. The resolution passed less than two weeks after the attack.[52]

Lastly, the West Virginia Supreme Court of Appeals, as a result of a suit filed by The Socialist Printing Company against the Governor for ordering the suppression, would deliver its third decision on martial law, a series of decisions that brought the State's high tribunal into national perspective.

In the Courts

"When Socialism first began to be talked about, the comfortable classes of the community were a good deal frightened. I suspect that this fear has influenced judicial action both here and in England."
—Oliver Wendell Holmes, *The Common Law and Collected Legal Papers*

The Star, being in extreme financial difficulty as a result of the "midnight raid," sought retribution from Governor Hatfield. The paper's publishers selected a committee to see the Chief Executive and request financial reimbursement for physical damages to the company's plant. Hatfield allegedly replied, "Go to Hell!"[53]

Based on their desperate need for finances and the Governor's refusal, The Socialist Printing Company, through its attorney Harold W. Houston, filed suit against the Governor and the military authorities who carried out his orders. The suit was entered in the Circuit Court of Cabell County, June 19, 1913, before Judge John T. Graham. It was styled "The Socialist Printing Company, a corporation, vs. Henry D. Hatfield, et al."[54]

The suit was filed as "an action of trespass" alleging that the Governor's forces had "combined and conspired together" to destroy the plant and printing office of The Socialist Printing Company. It requested $10,000 in reparations.[55]

The original suit was short-lived. On a technicality, the defendants, represented by Colonel George S. Wallace, had the case dismissed. In seeking redress, The Socialist Printing Company was required to guarantee payment to the persons it was suing, threefold the cost of the suit in the event the court found the defendants were not liable. Under this provision, the company was given sixty days in which to file a bond guaranteeing payment. There was, according to *The Star*, a misunderstanding concerning the dates and the bond was not filed until the expiration of sixty-four days. The defense attorney seized the opportunity offered by this technicality and had the case dismissed.[56]

The Socialist Printing Company filed suit once again and the case was re-entered into the Circuit Court. The defendants once again pleaded for dismissal on the case of "insufficient in law." This request was denied and Judge Graham docketed the case for February 9. *The Star*, commenting on the case, calmly mentioned that, "The Socialist Printing Company . . . awaits the outcome of the legal conflict with perfect confidence and serenity, in glaring contest to the actions of the defendants who have grasped, like a drowning man at a straw, at every subterfuge and technicality that could slave off the day of reckoning."[57]

The validity of this accusation was affirmed when the West Virginia Supreme Court of Appeals, on petition from Wallace and Attorney General A.A. Lilly, issued a "writ of prohibition" on the Circuit Court. The writ prohibited further proceedings in the lower court and ordered The Socialist Printing Company and Judge Graham to appear before the high court "to show cause, if they or either of them can," why a writ of prohibition should not be made permanent.[58]

By the time it issued the writ of prohibition, the State's high tribunal had achieved national notoriety. In two previous decisions dealing with martial law, the Supreme Court had upheld the legality of the actions of Governors Glasscock and Hatfield.[59] Both of the decisions upheld the Governor's use of martial law while the civil courts remained open, the suspension of habeas corpus and the issuing of prison sentences longer than the maximum prescribed by law.

Accusing the state government of flagrant violations on constitutional rights, important national magazines such as *Life, Collier's* and *Everybody* vehemently castigated the Hatfield Administration and the Court's decisions. One such condemnation was from *Current Opinion* which accused the court of having "falsified facts and falsified law openly, defiantly, and arbitrarily." The judgments of the courts, it wrote, were "the boldest assertions of autocratic power ever recorded in the United States."[60]

Additionally, the report of the Senate Investigation Committee also censured the Supreme Court's rulings on martial law. The Committee asserted: "The court deemed itself bound alone by orders of the Governor, and in no respect bound to observe the Constitution of the United States or the Constitution . . . of the State of West Virginia. . . .

They acted under the claim that all the provisions of the Constitution both State and National . . . were suspended and for the time inoperative by reason of the existence of martial law."[61]

The Court's dictum in Hatfield v. Graham was consistent with the two earlier decisions.

Basing their "Petitions" on the Court's previous decisions, Wallace and Lilly asserted that the facts in *The Star*'s suit were accurate and not refutable. They declared that,

> The pure questions involved . . . are whether the court has jurisdiction to try this kind of a case against the Governor of the state and his subordinate officers for the discharge of an official duty imposed upon him by the condition and the laws and in the discharge of which there is no abuse of discretion. . . . The suppression was necessary and proper to end the insurrection and riot in the strike district. . . . The Governor was acting by the authority of the constitution and laws. . . . Therefore it is submitted that the courts have no right to interfere by suit with his political acts in that behalf.[62]

Wallace then supported and concluded this contention on the theory of the "separation of powers." He asserted that the Chief-Executive was responsible only to the Senate and the people by right of impeachment and not the judiciary, therefore a write of prohibition was "necessary for an adequate and speedy remedy for the illegal action underway" in the Circuit Court of Cabell County.[63]

The Socialist Printing Company was again represented by its attorney Harold W. Houston. In his "Return," the socialist attorney advanced the constitutional issues involved in the case and reasserted the original charge that the suppression represented a conspiracy to destroy the printing plant and "in pursuance of said unlawful combination and conspiracy, injured, mutilated and carried away 'property totaling several thousands of dollars, eighty miles outside the martial law zone.'" Denying that *The Star* was a threat to the strike area, Houston declared that the paper "severely criticized" the proposed settlement "as it believed it had a lawful and legal right to do."

Houston further alleged that the Governor acted in "excess of his constitutional authority and executive power" when he denied to *The*

Star "Due Process of law," "the rights of citizens to be secure . . . against unreasonable search and seizure" and "equal protection of the law."[64]

The socialist attorney concluded his "Return" by stating that "a writ of prohibition would be to further extend the denial of the equal protection of the laws" as guaranteed by the Constitution of West Virginia and the United States. A "Writ of Error," he argued, was the only proper remedy if the case involved judicial injustice.[65]

The West Virginia Supreme Court of Appeals decided in favor of the petitioners and awarded the "writ of prohibition." In a four to one decision, the High Tribunal declared that "the only questions presented to this court are questions of law relating to the power of the Governor and the jurisdiction of the court and to inquire into and pass upon the legality of his official act."[66]

In applying the standards of war as the criteria for military action in times of industrial strife, the Supreme Court ruled:

1. Constitutional Law:
The office of governor is political and the discretion vested in the chief executive by the Constitution and laws of the state respecting his official duties is not subject to control or review by the Courts. His proclamations, warrants and orders made in the discharge of his official duties are as much due process of law as the judgment of a court.

2. States—Acts of Governor and Liability:
The governor cannot be held to answer in the courts in an action for damages resulting from the carrying out his lawful orders or warrants issued in good faith in discharge of his official duties.

3. War—Governor, Power, Martial Law:
By virtue of the authority invested in the governor by the Constitution and laws of the state, he has authority as Commander-in-Chief of the military forces, pending the existence of martial law covering any portion of the State's territory, to cause to be arrested and imprisoned, until peace is restored, any person who he had good reason to believe is aiding or encouraging disorder and rioting; and he may also temporarily suppress any newspaper published in the State, having a

circulation in the martial zone and containing articles which he has reason to believe will encourage the continuation of the disorder therein."[67]

To *The Star*, the decision was "another nail into the lid of the coffin" that encased freedom and liberty. The editor wrote, "it has interred the last remains of the respect the citizens of this State once had for their courts." Further it has "fertilized the growing contempt in which every honest man holds the bunch of ex-corporation lawyers who have made the term 'justice' a mockery, and 'constitutional rights' a tragic farce."[68]

Referring to the Court's ruling that the acts of the Governor were not subject to review or control by the judiciary, *The Star* vehemently declared:

> "Under this infamous decision the Governor of West Virginia can declare martial law around your home, murder you in cold blood, ravish your wife or daughters, appropriate or destroy your personal belongings, and still not be answerable to the laws of the land. The court has placed the crown of absolute and irresponsible authority upon him by declaring that the is above all law and that he is answerable to no power on earth for his actions—no matter how vile and venal they might become."[69]

The Star appropriately editorialized the Supreme Court had seen fit to clothe Governor Hatfield with the arbitrary powers of a monarch of the fourteenth century and averred, "we are at the mercy of the whims of the individual who happens to fill the chair of the chief executive, and are not protected by the established principles of constitutional law."[70]

Charles Fairman, in a study of martial law in the United States, *The Law of Martial Rule*, agreed with the editorials and position of the Huntington socialist journal. The constitutional historian, in a more sophisticated and rational presentation, concurred wholeheartedly and maintained that, "Short of impeachment, there is, according to this view, apparently no limitation on the governor but his conscience."[71]

In writing on the Hatfield v. Graham decision, Fairman concluded, "In holding that the governor himself should fix the limits to his own powers the Supreme Court of West Virginia is believed to have fallen into error—the decision of the dissenting Judge Ira Robinson is preferred." Robinson, who had been the sole dissenter in the two earlier decisions, said in opposition:

> The unsound principle established by this decision permits a Governor to deal with private rights and private property as he pleases. He has only to answer that he does so officially, and an action, though alleging facts showing that his act is wholly without his political province, will be prohibited. Such a view is wholly un-American, and inconsistent with constitutional government. Reason and authority condemn it, and the administration of even-handed justice cries out against it.[72]

The Star and Mr. Socialist

"Since there can be no talk of an independent ideology being developed by the masses of the workers in the process of their movement, then the only choice is; either bourgeois or Socialist ideology."
—V.I. Lenin, *What Is to Be Done?*

"How many a dispute could have been deflated into a single paragraph if the disputants had dared to define their terms."
—Aristotle

"Socialist Committee Exonerates Hatfield of Many Accusations" read the emblazoned headlines of the local rival *Herald-Dispatch*, June 4, 1913. However, referring to the same subject, several days later, the headlines of *The Star* declared "Socialist Failed as Investigator."[73]

This inverted dichotomy of opinion was the result of an investigation of the Paint Creek strike conducted under the directions of the American Socialist Party. The failure of the national party to become involved in the Paint Creek–Cabin Creek strike had caused considerable criticism of the national office. Typical in content, but probably the most influential was the letter from the Secretary of the

West Virginia Socialist Party, Harold Houston. It read, "West Virginians are disgusted with the paralytic apathy of the National Organization. It seems totally oblivious of the epochal struggle now on here." Pointing to the flagrant violation of constitutional rights and the suppression of the socialist presses Houston asked, "What have you to say about it?"[74]

The National Executive Committee responded by assigning an investigating committee composed of three prominent American socialists, Eugene V. Debs, Victor L. Berger, and Adolph Germer. Debs, who was commonly known as "Mr. Socialist" for his efforts to bring the cooperative commonwealth to the United States, was quite ill and involved in a family feud when he was designated by the party to go to West Virginia.[75]

Victor Berger was a conservative socialist from Wisconsin who had been elected to Congress by establishing a strong socialist party machine in Milwaukee. The Wisconsin State Party protested to the National Executive Committee for appointing him, claiming they could not "spare him." Germer was a national officer in the United Mine Workers of America and a member of the Socialist National Executive Committee.[76]

The committee was assigned a dual role. First, they were to obtain in an "authorative way," the facts of the labor situation and present them in the form of a report to the party members and to gain an audience with the President and "request him to take such action as he may think proper" to secure to the aggrieved party members and to the unionists the rights and the protection to which they are entitled under the Constitution and the laws.[77]

Second, the committee was instructed to work in harmony with the officials of the United Mine Workers and to promote the cooperation between that union and the Socialist Party in compiling their report. During the Executive Committee's discussion on the West Virginia labor conflict, the proposal was made to send as many organizers as possible to the state. This suggestion was vetoed in fear that the agitators "might not be able to work in harmony with the United Mine Workers." The controversy was settled by instructing the committee to cooperate with the union officials, a decision that led to the headlines "Socialist Committee Exonerates Hatfield."[78]

The committee arrived in Charleston on May 19, 1913 and began their investigation the next day. Their research brought them into contact with the striking miners, state socialists, the incarcerated Thompson, and most importantly Governor Henry D. Hatfield and the officials of the United Mine Workers. Debs interviewed the Chief Executive on May 23, after Hatfield refused to meet with the entire committee.

Immediately following his conversation with Hatfield, local newspapers published articles claiming Debs endorsed the Governor's policies. "Mr. Socialist" was quoted as saying that Hatfield "had a difficult problem on hand, but we believe and are convinced that conditions are improving."[79]

The state socialist locals and presses, convinced that the press interviews were a "capitalist conspiracy" ignored them at first. However, as the reports increased and became more consistent, both the *Wheeling Majority* and *The Star* telegrammed Debs regarding the accuracy and validity of the statements. To both papers the socialist leader replied, "Absolutely false. You will receive authentic report soon."[80]

When the investigating committee's report was made public two weeks later, *The Star* declared, "Socialists Failed as Investigators." While briefly castigating the coal operators and former Governor Glasscock, the report was generally favorable to Hatfield. The report read, "We freely admit having given Governor Hatfield the credit he is justly entitled to . . . we insist that he shall not be held accountable for the crimes committed under the administration of his servile predecessor."[81]

The following issue of *The Star* vehemently castigated the Investigating Committee's Report. Thompson labeled it "a weak mass of misstatements . . . and a sickening eulogy of Dictator Hatfield." Referring to Debs as a "sentimentalist," Berger a "compromising vote hunter," and Germer as an "official of the U.M.W.," the socialist editor claimed the selection of the committee was unfortunate. Debs and other members of the committee were accused of being misinformed and misled into endorsing the Hatfield Administration by the union officials who had accompanied the committee members from the time of their arrival in West Virginia to their departure. They were the same officials who had been instrumental in working out the proposed settlement with the Chief Executive.

Thompson refused to publish the report in his paper because he said, "We have never, and never will, devote any of our space to whitewashing a cheap tool of the capitalist class—not even when the whitewash is mixed by members of our own party." Thompson's retort initiated a bitter and protracted feud and dialogue between *The Star* and "Mr. Socialist."[82]

In his first reply to *The Star*'s editor, Debs briefly requested that the paper print the report and let the people "judge for themselves."[83] Thompson replied that Debs' letter "reached me just as we are preparing to go to press with the abbreviated issue of the paper. . . . Consequently we cannot go thoroughly into a defense of our last week's article." He did proceed to point out "a few of the more glaring misstatements," which he claimed were "inexcusable and very hurtful to the cause of the struggling worker in the State." The editor concluded that the report served only to exempt Hatfield and the U.M.W. officials of the accusations from the West Virginia socialists for their role in threatening, imprisoning, and coercing the rank and file miners into returning to work.[84]

The following week brought another invidious reply from Debs. "Mr. Socialist" wrote to Thompson again insisting that the report be published along with *The Star*'s attacks. Debs claimed:

> A thousand times I have had the experience of a capitalist paper denouncing a speech I had made without allowing its readers to see a word of it. I was neither surprised nor offended. I expected nothing better from the capitalist papers. But I do expect different treatment from a socialist paper. I would not change a single word of the report. . . . There are those who are assailing our committee's report today who in less than six months will wish they could retract their words.[85]

Although Debs claimed he would "not change a single word" of the report, his next correspondence with *The Star*'s editor read to the contrary:

> I should have made the exception heretofore noted in reference to the administration under which Mother Jones, John Brown, C.H. Boswell and other comrades sixty-four in total were tried by the military commission. . . . This error of dates for which I alone am responsible I frankly confess.[86]

In exonerating Hatfield, the Investigating Committee reported "It was under the administration of Glasscock and not Hatfield . . .

that the military commission was created; Mother Jones . . . et al. were court-martialed and convicted."[87]

In an earlier issue, *The Star* had demonstrated the fallacy of this statement. Hatfield was inaugurated on March 4, and the courts martial were the following week. The Kanawha County Circuit Court had issued a writ forbidding the enforcement of these "drum-head" courts. When the County Sheriff attempted to serve the court order, the Provost Marshall, under orders from the Governor, "forcibly prevented him from performing his civil duty."[88]

Taking advantage of Debs' confession, Thompson commented:

> Now that Comrade Debs has begun to compare the report with the FACTS in the case we may hope that he will ultimately apologize for the outrage he perpetrated upon our feelings when he devoted three-fifths of the report to 'exculpating' Hatfield of acts no one had ever charged him with and in denying for him the things we had charged him with.[89]

The feud between *The Star* and "Mr. Socialist" soon achieved national prominence. Major socialist publications including the *Appeal to Reason, New York Call* and the *International Socialist Review* began to publish letters from Debs and Thompson and commented on the controversy.

The *International Socialist Review* was one of the first to speak out on the Debs–Thompson conflict. In an editorial the periodical cited "a very few of the opinions" it had received criticizing the committee's report. Their citations were followed by headlines and editorials of "capitalist papers that praised the investigation and used the report . . . to discredit Socialist and union opponents of Hatfield." The editorial concluded with a condemnation of the "U.M.W. compromising officials," Hatfield, and the Investigating Committee and explained, "it is the rank and file of the U.M.W. who have found it necessary to fight and expose the Governor as well as their own officers."[90]

National attention focused on the feud when Debs publicly claimed that the Industrial Workers of the World was responsible for the opposition to Hatfield and the committee's report. Using the "Wobbly-Scapegoat" tactic that he used in similar situations, Debs evaded the validity and accuracy of *The Star*'s attack and claimed that the West Virginia socialists opposed the Governor's settlement "because a contract had been signed," this he wrote was the true "animus" of its critics and assailants.[91]

Claiming he was an "industrial unionist, but not an industrial bummereyite," Debs wrote, "the whole trouble is that some Chicago I.W.W.-ites, in spirit at least, are seeking to disrupt and drive out the United Mine Workers to make room for the I.W.W. and its program of sabotage and strike at the ballot box with an ax." Having distorted and misrepresented the issues and facts involved, "Mr. Socialist" proceeded with one of his customary tirades against the industrial organization:

> The I.W.W.-ists have never done one particle of organizing, or attempting to, in the dangerous districts of West Virginia. The United Mine Workers have been on the job for years. . . . The United Mine Workers is steadily evolving into a thoroughly industrial union . . . but never in a thousand years will the efforts of these disrupters unionize the miners of West Virginia.[92]

Thompson immediately answered this unfair and irrational charge. In his reply, the socialist editor brought the "real issues" into perspective and the true reasons *The Star* vilified and assailed the proposed settlement and report. The accusations were generally the same as in the earlier denouncements; the report exonerated a Governor who had threatened and coerced the miners into returning to work and the state administration's flagrant violation of the constitutional rights of the involved citizens. Next, the socialist editor repudiated Debs' charge that the opposition was based on "Wobbly philosophy."

Thompson wrote:

> Speaking for myself, I will say that I have never seen a real live I.W.W.-ite . . . I have heard of this new species from the capitalist press and I note that the capitalists are very hostile toward it. I consider that a good recommendation for a labor organization, and will certainly not speak slightingly of it. As for the I.W.W. being responsible for the attack of the Mine Worker's officials, who deliberately attempted to betray the Kanawha strikers, I think Comrade Debs' fear was father to the thought.[93]

Several interesting factors should be discussed at this point. First, there is some question as to the accuracy of Thompson's statement, "I have never seen a real live I.W.W.-ite." Ralph Chaplin had belonged to the organization before coming to West Virginia, but during the time he was with *The Star*, he was not an official member. He did speak about the "one-big union" idea to fellow workers on the staff, but he admitted he was able to convert only one person.[94]

Secondly, Thompson used the line of reasoning that Debs later used in upholding the I.W.W. "The I.W.W.," Debs said four years later, "is anathema wherever capitalism wields the lash and drains the vein of its exploited victims. It is a wonderful compliment!" At the time of this article, the entire radical movement was in the process of being emasculated of its leaders and energy by the war administration of Woodrow Wilson, and Debs continuously spoke of the need for solidarity. In the years 1912–1914, the Socialist Party was at its height, and the future erroneously forecasted the advent of the cooperative commonwealth. "Mr. Socialist" was in a position to denounce the deviants from his proposed "Sound Socialist Tactics."[95]

Debs' contention that the West Virginia socialists were "Wobbly oriented" and were opposed to Hatfield, the proposed settlement, and the report "because a contract had been signed" is seconded by the eminent historian James Wienstein in *The Decline of Socialism in America*.[96] The author of this paper does not accept this conclusion. Thompson never proposed "to strike at the ballot box with an ax," but favored quite the contrary. Through his editorials he continuously encouraged the people of Huntington to join the Socialist Party and to vote the Socialist ticket, which he said represented the "political expression of the working class." Thompson himself ran for the office of county clerk in 1914 and supported the Socialist candidate for Congress from the Fifth Congressional District.[97]

Evidence does reveal that Thompson was opposed to the Hatfield proposal and the report because it would turn a "victory into a settlement" and because the rank and file never accepted it. The miners proved Thompson's assessment correct when they went on strike again in June, 1913. *The Star*'s editor favored the second contract, which to him represented a "victory."

Based on the available and examined evidence, this writer agrees with the position of *The Star* in condemning the Investigating Committee's Report for exculpating the Governor and the United Mine Worker officials' contract which the rank and file never accepted.

Conclusions can be affirmed that:

The committee was impelled to whitewash Hatfield because the officials of the U.M.W. of A. had endorsed Hatfield's conduct and the Paint–Cabin Creek "settlement." . . . If the Socialist Committee condemned Hatfield, it would lead to condemnation and exposure of the "settlement" and the treachery of the officials of the U.M.W. of A.[98]

Debs supported this assertion when he concluded the committee's report by writing, "At the close of our labors we rejoiced to see the better understanding that existed between the U.M.W. and the Socialist Party, which we sought in every way to encourage and promote."[99]

A Calm Amid the Tempest

"The war against capitalism is not a rosewater affair. . . . It is rather of the storm and tempest order. . . . All kinds of attacks must be expected, and all kinds of wounds will be inflicted. . . . You will be assailed within and without, spat upon by the very ones that you are doing your best to serve, and at certain crucial moments find yourself isolated, absolutely alone as if to compel surrender, but in those moments, if you have the nerve, you become supreme."
—Ferdinand Lassalle

"Raise our scarlet banner high,
Beneath its folds we'll live and die,
Though cowards flinch and traitors sneer,
We'll keep the red flag flying here."

(Old Socialist Song)

The next few years saw The Star's growth, continued attacks on the "capitalist system" that hated it so much, and a final effort to make it a stronger, healthier and wider-read newspaper.

The Star grew into what it termed "a plant that excels the majority of capitalist newspapers in the state." The value of the plant had increased threefold and it boasted of modern machinery with the "latest improved linotypes on the market, operated by electric power."[100] The staff of the paper increased from the six original founders to over twenty dedicated socialists, all of whom worked on the paper without pay. The paper's circulation, although the majority of the subscribers were in Huntington, included persons residing in distant states and territories of the United States.[101]

As the paper grew, so did the ambitions and aspirations of the publishers. The directors of The Socialist Printing Company, feeling they could gain "the respect and confidence of the citizens of the State," attempted to make *The Star* a daily paper. Their intention for the paper was to continue "championing the interests of the working class" and to "present a bright, newsy paper that will keep our readers informed as to what is happening the world over in every walk of life."[102]

In an editorial noting the second anniversary of its birth, *The Star* announced: "We start this third year of our existence with the same fervor and enthusiasm that marked the first issue of the paper and we bring to it the accumulated experiences of two years of the battle." That would be the last year of *The Star*.[103]

With an "earnest desire for the emancipation of the working class," *The Star* continued its acid and caustic tirades against the capitalist system and its offspring. All areas of the corporate economy were touched by the socialist columns.

Constant victims of the paper's literary assaults were "national capitalist policies" including American intervention in Mexico, the national government's attitude toward the European war which *The Star* claimed would eventually involve the United States, and the hypocritical doctrines of the established churches.

Having never learned the lessons of repression, *The Star* continued in its editorial forays on the state government, as personified by Henry D. Hatfield. In the first issue, following the suppression, the newspaper again castigated the Chief Executive and the coal operators for their role in the Paint Creek–Cabin Creek strikes, and the vilification never ceased. The paper never forgave or forgot the Governor's acts of aggression, and constantly reprimanded him for it.[104]

The city of Huntington was also a constant target of *The Star*'s attacks. One of the major and most successful local efforts was the paper's exposure of the "filthy and corrupt" conditions of the West Virginia Asylum located in Huntington. Calling attention to the degenerate environment of the institution, the socialist journal aroused enough interest and concern in the affair to cause a gubernatorial investigation, ordered by its old nemesis, Governor Hatfield.[105]

As *The Star* grew and its assault on the establishment continued, it remained the victim of abuses from the organs of that system. Never reaching the sequel of the "midnight raid" of May 9, they were nonetheless frustrating and troublesome; they vividly illustrated the difficulties of a political heretic in American society.

The local conservative presses were particularly prolific in their assailment of the local socialist paper. The *Herald-Dispatch*, the Progressive party "paper" of 1912, maintained a moratorium on *The Star* during its first year of publication. The *Herald-Dispatch* broke its silence to compliment the Governor's suppression during the strike and thereafter proceeded to denounce and vilify *The Star* at all available opportunities. When the opportunities did not prevail, it created them. A typical attempt to discredit *The Star* is found in an article published by the "progressive" paper, which told of a man's assault on a widowed waitress in Logan, West Virginia. The article concluded that the man "is a stockholder of *The Socialist Star*, it is stated." Thompson, quite concerned about the invidious implication retorted:

> The cowardly thugs and character assassins who distorted and doctored it [the article cited above] so that his paper could not be held financially responsible, knew it was a lie. . . . These are the tricky phrases of the filthy, slimy capitalist newspapers, their cowardly method of putting their own villainous slanders into the mouths of fictitious parties.[106]

The rival Democratic newspaper, the *Huntington Advertiser*, was not mute. In one instance, three men were arrested for "illegally trespassing" ("hopping") a Chesapeake and Ohio Railway freight train. The fact that two of the men had never been in Huntington before was obviously irrelevant to the *Huntington Advertiser* as it wrote that all the men were employed by *The Star* and had been on a "secret mission in the mountains."[107]

Another source of journalistic opposition came from the newspaper published by the local union of the United Mine Workers, *The Miners Herald*. Writing under the philosophy that "any paper or organization that tries to antagonize labor and capital and the employee against the employer, is an enemy to both and generally injures the party whose cause it espouses," the union press constantly and vehemently attacked *The Star* and its editor.[108] Its assaults were of a wide variety, ranging from accusations against Thompson for not contributing as much to charity as did its own editor, to the direct implication that the editors of *Labor Argus* and *The Star* were employed by the "Baldwin-Felts" detective agency to destroy the United Mine Workers union.[109]

A significant accusation was made by the union paper when it delivered a vituperative condemnation of Thompson. Claiming that Thompson was "an ex-something or other" and a "complete failure in everything he has undertaken." *The Miners Herald* declared that he possessed neither a "union card" nor a "skill" to obtain one. The socialist editor immediately repudiated the attack by illustrating its fallacies, the fact that he belonged to the miners' union, and currently belonged to the Typographical Union. The refutation was followed by a resolution from the Huntington Trades and Labor Assembly denouncing *The Miners Herald*, and its editor. As a result of this feud, several miners drafted resolutions denouncing *The Miners Herald*. One local union writing: "Resolved, that this local accepts the *Labor Argus* and *The Labor Star* as the official organs of the working class in this district."[110]

A massive array of obstacles was always provided by the city of Huntington. From having their mailing privileges denied to various judicial battles with institutions it had exposed, the city provided constant turmoil and confusion for the socialist publishers.[111]

The most dramatic and flamboyant assault on *The Star* following the pillage of May, 1913, was an afternoon raid on the plant in February, 1914. This time the paper was charged with circulating "lewd, lascivious, obscene matter through the U.S. Mail." The violations of puritanistic decency occurred in an editorial where *The Star* exposed a "drunken debauchery" held by the upper echelon of Huntington society at the Frederick Hotel on New Year's Eve. In the process of describing the affair, the socialist journal referred to certain portions of the female anatomy which were decorated for the celebration.[112] For this alleged violation, members of the local Huntington police force, the United States Deputy Marshall and his assistants and the Post Office inspectors were instituted to "secure the plant" and arrest editor Thompson and business manager Edwin Firth.

The charges were eventually dismissed by the United States District Commissioner when the chief prosecutor failed "to establish as a fact that the issue of *The Star* complained of really went through the United States mail." According to *The Star*, "this failed because no post office employee would state, on oath, that the particular paper in question was handled by them." The attorney then introduced books and records purporting to be the official documents of the local post office, but "when certain employees and clerks admitted that these records and books had been doctored, the attorney withdrew them as exhibits and then withdrew them from the case." The case was eventually dismissed.[113]

Several weeks later, *The Star* editorialized on the turbulence it had encountered as a political heretic; the picture painted by the words of Thompson may well serve as an epitaph of the efforts and life of the Huntington socialist paper. The editorial read:

> The presence of a press that dares to call a spade or a society debauch by its right name, is not wanted by the gang of parasites that have made Huntington its stomping ground since time out of mind. . . . Midnight arrests without reason or warrant; ridiculous exhibitions of military and police forces in a cowardly and contemptible effort to humiliate and intimidate the worker, all rankle in the blood, and an outraged working class may one day demand payment of this debt with interest.[114]

The life of *The Star* concluded in January, 1915, with the merger of the Charleston socialist paper, *The Labor Argus*. *The Star* claimed that the policies of the two papers were so nearly identical and the territory covered so adjacent that "there was really no longer any reason why both papers should continue, and we have decided to give a concrete example in practice of what we preach so continuously—'cooperation.'" The main office of the *Argus Star* was maintained under the auspices of Thompson with a branch office in Charleston in charge of Charles Boswell. According to *The Star*,

> The *Argus Star* will have the undivided editorial efforts of the fearless writers who have made the two old papers as terror to would-be tyrants and oppressors in the past, and we confidently expect to make the paper the most religiously read and widely discussed publicity medium in the state of West Virginia.

The Socialist Printing Company concluded on July 11, 1922, when it was dissolved by the Decree Circuit Court of Kanawha County for the failure to pay corporation taxes.[115]

Epilogue or Prologue?

In 1916, Allen Benwon, a pacifist journalist, was nominated for President by the American Socialist Party. For the first time since its genesis in 1898, the party's candidate was not Eugene V. Debs. Various explanations have been offered for this turn of events; Debs was ill and the party desired a younger man to seek the office.[116] Perhaps to this list can be added the conflict, feud, and resentment that developed in the party because one small socialist press dared to challenge the word of "Mr. Socialist."

In 1917, the United States became a belligerent in the "war to end all wars." The Wilson war administration, in an effort to "make the world safe for democracy" ruthlessly suppressed the heretical presses throughout the nation. In less than two years, over fifty socialist journals were prohibited from publication.[117] For daring to castigate the "war efforts" of Governor Henry D. Hatfield, the socialist paper of Huntington, West Virginia was suppressed. Four years later, for daring to castigate the "war efforts" of President Woodrow Wilson, numerous national socialist publications met the same fate. In the early 1920s, the ideological differences in the American socialist movement became apparent. The revolutionary left-wing split from the Socialist Party to form the Communist Party. The ideological differences which confronted the socialist members of the United Mine Workers and caused the bitter feud between the editor of *The Star* and the National Executive Investigating Committee was a small sampling of this confrontation one decade later.

From 1910 through "Mr. Wilson's War," the names Ludlow, Patterson, and Butte were but a portion of the nomenclature that sounded in the industrial frontiers of the United States, and have been resounded in the nation's history books. Often absent from this symphony of names is the coal strike that occurred in the Paint Creek–Cabin Creek Districts of West Virginia. An industrial conflict which resulted in personal and financial tragedy in the State of West Virginia played a dramatic and potent role in the life of a small socialist newspaper.

Notes

1 The original name of the paper was *The Socialist and Labor Star*. In April, 1914, the name was changed to *The Labor Star*. For consistency and clarity the paper will be referred to as *The Star*. This was the name applied to the newspaper.

2 *The Labor Star*, April 3, 1914.

3 State Corporation Papers of The Socialist Printing Company, July 3, 1912. Files of Secretary of State Book 84, 195.

4 Nathan Fine, *Labor and Farmer Parties in the United States* (New York: Rand School of Social Sciences, 1928), 240; *Rand School of Social Sciences, American Labor Yearbook* (New York: 1916), 144–146; During childhood, the nickname "Henry" became attached to the future editor, and this stayed with him for the rest of life. *The Star* always referred to him as W.H. Thompson, and when it did print his entire name it included the "H." to mean Henry. Later in life, when his radical background jeopardized the status of his job and family, he used various pen names. These were usually a deviation of his real name and some member in the family, generally, an ancestor. Personal interview with Francis Allen, the daughter of Wyatt Henry Thompson. Columbus, Ohio, August 6, 1971.

5 Ralph Chaplin, *Wobbly: The Rough-and-Tumble Story of an American Radical* (Chicago: University of Chicago Press, 1948), 120; Mrs. Francis Allen, August 6, 1971; *The Labor Star*, May 1, 1914.

6 Chaplin, *Wobbly*, 116–130; Mrs. Francis Allen, August 6, 1971; Philip S. Foner, *History of the Labor Movement in the United States IV*, (New York: International Publishers, 1965), 155; Chaplin's two major works were *When the Leaves Come Out* (1917) and *Bars and Shadows* (1919). Later he wrote his autobiography which is cited in this paper. For a selection of Chaplin's poems and songs, see the first two books, Joyce L. Kornbluh (ed.), *Rebel Voices: An I.W.W. Anthology* (Oakland: PM Press, 2011), and Charles Patterson, "Paint Creek Miner," (Huntington: Appalachian Movement Press, 1970).

7 Personal interview, Francis Allen, August 6, 1971; Leslie H. Marcy, "Hatfield's Challenge to the Socialist Party," *International Socialist Review*, XIII (June, 1913), 884.

8 The financial losses were: the coal operators, $2,000,000; the miners, $1,500,000; United Mine Workers of America, $602,000; taxpayers

of Kanawha County, $100,000; property destroyed, $10,000. The total cost was $4,612,000. See Lawrence R. Lynch, "The West Virginia Coal Strike," *Political Science Quarterly*, XXIX (December, 1914), 642; Charles F. Carter, "West Virginia Coal Insurrection," *North American Review*, CXCVIII (October, 1913), 469.

9 For additional reading and reference, see Howard R. Lee, *Bloodletting in Appalachia* (Morgantown, West Virginia: McClain Printing Company, 1969); Winthrop Lane, *Civil War in West Virginia*, (New York: B.W. Huebsch, 1921); William C. Blizzard, "Martial Law Crushed Paint Creek Strikes in 1912–1913," Charleston, West Virginia, *Sunday Gazette-Mail*, June 16, 1963, Section G, 7–9; Kyle McCormick, *The New-Kanawha River and the Mine War of West Virginia*, (Charlestown: Matthews Printing, 1959). Also see the two articles cited above, Lunch, "Coal Strike," *Political Science Quarterly*; and Carter, "Insurrection," *North American Review*.

10 "Digest of Report on Investigation of Paint Creek Coal Fields of West Virginia," Committee of Education and Labor, March, 1914, 6.

11 Selig Perlman and Philip Taft, *History of Labor in the United States 1896–1932*. (New York: Augustine M. Kelley, 1966), 329; United States Bureau of Mines, Department of Interior, *Mineral Resources of the United States for the Calendar Year 1912*, 193, Vol. II, 36, 233.

12 Perlman and Taft, *History of Labor*, 326.

13 "Digest of Report" Education and Labor, 5.

14 Chaplin, *Wobbly*, 119–121, U.S. Congress, Senate, Subcommittee of the Committee on Education and Labor, *Conditions in the Paint Creek District, West Virginia*, Hearing 63rd Congress, 1st Session, (Washington: Government Printing Office, 1913), 2098.

15 *United Mine Workers Journal*, (editorial), April 24, 1913, 1; "International Executive Board on the West Virginia Situation," *United Mine Workers Journal*, May 15, 1913), 4.

16 Wyatt H. Thompson, "How a Victory was Turned into a Settlement," *International Socialist Review*, XIV (July, 1913), 12–17.

17 Although this writer is using Thompson's interpretation of the settlement, this accusation is seconded by articles in the *New York Times*, the *Charleston Gazette*, and the *Huntington Herald-Dispatch*.

18 This accusation is affirmed by the *Kanawha Citizen* (Charleston, West Virginia), which was the only newspaper to provide daily coverage of the convention.

[19] Wyatt H. Thompson, "Strike Settlement in West Virginia," *International Socialist Review*, XIV (August, 1913), 87; Wyatt H. Thompson, "Victory," *International Socialist Review*, 13; Fred H. Merrick, "The Betrayal of West Virginia Rednecks," *International Socialist Review*, XIV (July, 1913), 18–20: Perlman and Taft, *History of Labor*, 335.

[20] U.S. Senate, "Hearings" Part III, 2098; Harold W. Houston, "Amended Return of Socialist Printing Company," Hatfield v. Graham, State Court of Appeals of West Virginia. October, 1913, March 31, 1914.

[21] *The Socialist and Labor Star*, June 6, 1913.

[22] *The Socialist and Labor Star*, June 21, 1913; Thompson, "Strike Settlement," *International Socialist Reviews*, 87; "Miners on Paint Creek and Cabin Creek Anxious to Renew Strike," *United Mine Workers Journal*, June 19, 1913, 1; "Sanction of Miner's Union is Given to Paint Creek and Cabin Creek Strike," *United Mine Workers Journal*, July 3, 1913, 1.

[23] Thompson, "Strike Settlement," *International Socialist Review*, 88; "Agreement Made in Good Faith," *United Mine Workers Journal*, June 19, 1913, 5.

[24] "Paint Creek Settlement," *United Mine Workers Journal*, July 24, 1913, 4; Wyatt H. Thompson, "The War Is Over," *International Socialist Review*, XIV.

[25] Ibid., 162.

[26] *The Socialist and Labor Star*, May 2, 1913, 1; *Wheeling Majority* (Wheeling, West Virginia), May 1, 1913; Boswell was arrested and court-martialed, with Mother Jones, and charged with conspiracy to murder non-union miners and that the socialist activities of *The Labor Argus* "incited riots inside the strike area," *Charleston Gazette*, February 14, 1913, 1.

[27] Leslie H. Marcy, "Hatfield's Challenge to the Socialist Party," *International Socialist Review*, XIII (June, 1913). 882.

[28] Ibid., 882, 883; Chaplin, *Wobbly*, 128.

[29] *Wheeling Majority*, May 8, 1913.

[30] Ibid.; U.S. Senate, "Hearings" Part I, 204, 206.

[31] U.S. Senate, "Hearings" Part I, 204, 205; *The Socialist and Labor Star*, May 2, 1913.

[32] This statement was in reference to "Devil Anse," the leader of the famed Hatfield family of the Hatfield-McCoy feud.

[33] *The Socialist and Labor Star*, May 2, 1913.

[34] Ibid.

[35] *Huntington Herald-Dispatch*, May 10, 1913; Marcy, "Hatfield's Challenge," *International Socialist Review*, 883.

[36] *Herald-Dispatch*, May 10, 1913.

[37] One of the men was a reporter for the paper. The reason for his arrest was either for "bootlegging" strike materials inside the strike zone or for guarding the plant. A fifth man had left the paper several months before the attack, but through "neglect" his name was left on the masthead of *The Star* from which the authorities selected their victims. His arrest was not pursued.

[38] Thompson protested against this act claiming the military had "no right to deport him from his own county." Part III, 2093; *The Socialist and Labor Star*, May 30, 1913.

[39] *The Socialist and Labor Star*, May 30, 1913; *Herald-Dispatch*, May 9, 1913; *Huntington Advertiser*, May 9, 1913; U.S. Senate, "Hearings" Part III, 2092.

[40] *The Socialist and Labor Star*, May 30, 1913; *Advertiser*, May 9, 191; Houston, "Amended Return," 8. Two months after the raid, a man brought Thompson four pounds of "demolished type" that he had picked up over an area of four blocks from the plant; U.S. Senate, "Hearings" Part III, 2096.

[41] *The Socialist and Labor Star*, May 30, 1913. The extent of the damage was estimated at $2,000; Houston, "Amended Return," 7.

[42] *Wheeling Majority*, June 19, 1913.

[43] *Herald-Dispatch*, May 14, 1913. To the constant array of ironies, paradoxes, and hypocrisies of history belongs an editorial that condones a willful and purposeful disregard of "freedom of the press," the destruction of private property without reason, or warrant, and then castigates the victims of the assault as anarchists.

[44] U.S. Senate, "Hearings" Part III, 2101.

[45] *The Socialist and Labor Star*, May 30, 1913; *Wheeling Majority*, May 15, 1913; U.S. Senate, "Hearings" Part III, 2103.

[46] *Herald-Dispatch*, May 9, 1913. It should be pointed out that no warrants were issued by Governor or any other official. Senator Borah stated, "No complaint was ever lodged with any Justice of the Peace or any court or anything of the sort," U.S. Senate, "Hearings" Part III, 2095.

[47] Colonel George S. Wallace, "Brief for the Petitioners," Hatfield v. Graham, State Court of Appeals of West Virginia. October, 1913, March 31, 1914, 1, 2.

[48] U.S. Senate, "Hearings" Part I, 202; *Wheeling Majority*, May 15, 1913.

[49] *The Socialist and Labor Star*, May 31, 1913.

[50] *The Socialist and Labor Star*, June 13, 1913.

[51] Thompson, "Victory to Settlement," *International Socialist Review*, 15.

[52] Ibid.; *Herald-Dispatch*, May 28, 1913.

[53] *The Socialist and Labor Star*, June 27, 1913; Mary E. Marcy, "The Hatfield Whitewash," *International Socialist Review*, XIV (July, 1913), 54.

[54] *The Socialist and Labor Star*, June 27, 1913; *The Labor Star*, May 29, 1914; *The Socialist and Labor Star*, June 21, 1913. There was a parallel effort made to the Cabell County Grand Jury to have the persons involved in the suppression indicted for destruction of private property; the witnesses were refused admittance and the suit was dismissed; U.S. Senate, "Hearings" Part III, 2097, 2098.

[55] Hatfield v. Graham, 73 W. Va. Reports, 759–776.

[56] *The Socialist and Labor Star*, October 10, 1913; Wyatt H. Thompson, "Governor Hatfield Wins," *International Socialist Review*, XIV (December, 1913), 343. W. Va. Reports, 761–763.

[57] Houston, "Amended Return," 8.

[58] "Rule in Petition," West Virginia State Court of Appeals, Hatfield v. Graham.

[59] Nancy and May v. Brown, 71 W. Va. Reports, 519–67 (1912); Ex Parte Jones, 71 W. Va. Reports, 567–625 (1912).

[60] *The Socialist and Labor Star*, May 2, 1913; Edward J. Wheeler, "U.S. Senate Decides to Investigate West Virginia," *Current Opinion*, LV (July, 1913), 3, 4.

[61] "Digest of Report," Committee on Education and Labor, 2.

[62] Wallace, "Brief for the Petitioners," 1, 2.

[63] Ibid., 6–12.

[64] Houston, "Amended Return," 8–12.

[65] Ibid., 10–12.

[66] W. Va. Reports, 764.

[67] Ibid., 764–766.

[68] *The Labor Star*, April 3, 1913.

[69] Ibid.

70 Ibid.

71 Charles Fairman, *The Law of Martial Rule* (Chicago: Callaghan and Company, 1930), 227.

72 W. Va. Reports, 775–776; Robinson was, of course, praised by *The Star* for having the integrity and courage to defend the constitutional rights of the working class. Some persons and newspapers did not hold the Justice in such repute; they claimed that Robinson was seeking support of labor for the 1916 election in which he was the Republican nominee for governor. In the gubernatorial election, Robinson did receive endorsement from the American Federation of Labor, but in addition he was supported by several coal operator's associations and Hatfield; *The Labor Star*, April 3, 1914; *Herald-Dispatch*, May 11, 1916; *Herald-Dispatch*, October 14, 1916; *Herald-Dispatch*, October 25, 1916.

73 *Herald-Dispatch*, June 4, 1913, 1; *The Socialist and Labor Star*, June 13, 1913, 1.

74 "Minutes of Meeting of National Executive Committee of the Socialist Party of America," *The Party Builder*, XXIX (May 21, 1913), 5; Grace Silver, "National Committee Meeting, Socialist Party," *International Socialist Review*, XIII (June 6, 1913), 877–879.

75 Ray Ginger, *Eugene V. Debs* (New York: Collier Books, 1966), 338.

76 "Minutes of Meeting of National Executive Committee of the Socialist Party of America," *The Party Builder*, XXX (May 31, 1913), 4–7.

77 *Wheeling Majority*, May 22, 1913; "Minutes of National Executive Committee of the Socialist Party of America," *The Party Builder*, XXXI (June 7, 1913), 4. After the "Kern Resolution" was passed by the United States Senate, the National Executive Committee decided it not necessary to present the report to the President; *Herald-Dispatch*, May 29, 1913.

78 Silver, "National Meeting," *International Socialist Review*, 879–880; "Minutes," *The Party Builder*, 4; *Wheeling Majority*, May 15, 1913.

79 *Herald-Dispatch*, May 22, 1913.

80 *Wheeling Majority*, May 22, 1913; *The Socialist and Labor Star*, May 30, 1913.

81 *Wheeling Majority*, June 12, 1913; *Wheeling Majority*, June 19, 1913.

82 *The Socialist and Labor Star*, June 13, 1913.

83 *The Socialist and Labor Star*, June 21, 1913.

84 Ibid.

85 *The Socialist and Labor Star*, June 27, 1913.

[86] *The Socialist and Labor Star*, July 4, 1913.

[87] *Wheeling Majority*, June 19, 1913.

[88] Wyatt H. Thompson, "A Reply to Debs," *International Socialist Review*, XIV (August, 1913), 106–107.

[89] *The Socialist and Labor Star*, July 4, 1913.

[90] Mary E. Marcy, "The Hatfield Whitewash," *International Socialist Review*, XIV (August, 1913), 22.

[91] *The Labor Star*, August 7, 1914; Eugene V. Debs, "Debs Denounces Critics," *International Socialist Review*, XIV (August, 1913), 104–106.

[92] Ibid.

[93] Wyatt H. Thompson, "A Reply to Debs," *International Socialist Review*, XIV (August, 1913), 107.

[94] Chaplin, *Wobbly*, 122–125.

[95] Eugene V. Debs, "I.W.W. Bogey," *International Socialist Review*, XVIII (February, 1918), 395–396.

[96] James Winestein, *The Decline of American Socialism* (New York: Vantage Books, 1969), 34, 35.

[97] *The Labor Star*, July 31, 1914.

[98] Ibid.

[99] *Wheeling Majority*, June 19, 1913.

[100] *The Labor Star*, May 20, 1914.

[101] Personal interview, Francis Allen, August 6, 1971; *The Labor Star*, May 29, 1914.

[102] *The Labor Star*, August 14, 1914; *The Labor Star*, July 24, 1914.

[103] *The Labor Star*, May 29, 1914.

[104] *The Socialist and Labor Star*, May 30, 1913; *The Labor Star*, October 30, 1914; *The Labor Star*, October 9, 1914.

[105] *The Socialist and Labor Star*, March 20, 1914; *The Socialist and Labor Star*, March 27, 1914.

[106] *The Socialist and Labor Star*, October 3, 1913.

[107] *The Socialist and Labor Star*, March 20, 1914.

[108] *The Miners Herald* (Montgomery, West Virginia), August 30, 1913.

[109] *The Socialist and Labor Star*, July 24, 1914; *The Miners Herald*, March 27, 1914.

[110] *The Labor Star*, May 8, 1914.

[111] *The Socialist and Labor Star*, February 20, 1914; *The Labor Star*, April 24, 1914.

[112] *The Socialist and Labor Star*, February 20, 1914. Apparently it was permissible for the ladies to expose the subjects of interest, and the

various political and business leaders to view the exposed trophies, but *The Star* was wrong to write about it.

[113] *The Socialist and Labor Star*, February 20, 1914; *Herald-Dispatch*, February 16, 1914.

[114] *The Socialist and Labor Star*, February 27, 1914.

[115] *The Labor Star*, January 1, 1915; *Huntington Advertiser*, January 4, 1915; "Decree Warrant," Decree Circuit Court of Kanawha County, July 11, 1922.

[116] Ginger, *Debs*, 320–355; David A. Shannon, *The Socialist Party of America* (Chicago: Quadrangle Books, 1967), 90–92.

[117] Horace C. Peterson and Gilbert C. Fite, *Opponents of War* (Madison: University of Wisconsin Press, 1957), 95.

Bibliography

Primary Sources and Depositories

Department of Archives and History of West Virginia (Charleston, West Virginia).
Library of Congress (Washington, D.C.).
Marshall University Library (Huntington, West Virginia).
National Archives, Department of Labor (Washington, D.C.).
University of Wisconsin Library (Madison, Wisconsin).
West Virginia State Library Commission (Charleston, West Virginia).

Printed Primary Sources

Chaplin, Ralph H. *Bars and Shadows*. New York: Leonard Press, 1922.
_____. *When the Leaves Come Out*. Cleveland: published by the author, 1917.
_____. *Wobbly: The Rough-and-Tumble Story of an American Radical*. Chicago: University of Chicago Press, 1948.
Debs, Eugene V. *The Writings and Speeches of Eugene V. Debs*. New York: Hermitage Press, 1948.
Kornbluh, Joyce L. (ed.). *Rebel Voices: An I.W.W. Anthology*. Oakland: PM Press, 2011.
Patterson, Charles. *Paint Creek Miner*. Huntington: Appalachian Movement Press, 1970.
Radosh, Ronald (ed.). *Debs*. Englewood Cliffs: Prentice Hall, 1971.
Rand School of Social Sciences. *American Labor Yearbook*. New York, 1916.

Government Documents

Federal
Department of the Interior. United States Bureau of Mines. Mineral Resources of the United States, 1912, 1913.

United States Senate. Conditions in the Paint Creek District, West Virginia. 63rd Congress, 1st Session Senate Resolution 37. "Hearings Before a Subcommittee of the Committee on Education and Labor," Washington, D.C. 1913.
West Virginia State Supreme Court of Appeals.
Amended Return of Socialist Printing Company, Hatfield v. Graham, 2578.
Brief for Petitioners, Hatfield v. Graham, 2578.
Rule in Prohibition, Honorable H.D. Hatfield, et al., Petitioners, v. In Prohibition Honorable John T. Graham, Judge, et al., Respondents, 2578.
West Virginia Reports, Hatfield v. Graham, 73, 759–779.

State
Agreement for Incorporation, Socialist Printing Company, filed in office of West Virginia Secretary of State, Book 84, 195.
Certificate of Incorporation, Socialist Printing Company, filed in office of Clerk of Cabell County, Book 9, 135–136.
Decree of Dissolvement, Socialist Printing Company, filed in office of West Virginia Secretary of State, Book 84, 195.

Newspapers

Charleston (West Virginia) *Gazette*, 1913.
Charleston (West Virginia) *Kanawha Citizen*, 1913.
Girard (Kansas) *Appeal to Reason*, 1912, 1914.
Huntington (West Virginia) *Advertiser*, 1913, 1914.
Huntington (West Virginia) *Herald-Dispatch*, 1913, 1916.
Huntington (West Virginia) *The Labor Star*, 1914, 1915.
Huntington (West Virginia) *The Socialist and Labor Star*, 1913, 1914.
Montgomery (West Virginia) *The Miner's Herald*, 1913.
The *New York Times*, 1913.
Wheeling (West Virginia) *Majority*, 1913.

Periodicals

Articles

Carter, Charles F. "West Virginia Coal Insurrection," *North American Review*, CXCVIII (October, 1913), 455–469.

Chaplin, Ralph H. "Violence in West Virginia," *International Socialist Review*, XIII (April, 1913), 729–735.

Debs, Eugene V. "Debs Denounces Critics," *International Socialist Review*, XIV (August, 1913), 104–106.

_____. "I.W.W. Bogey," *International Socialist Review*, XVIII (February, 1912), 481–486.

Kintzer, Edward H. "Reconstruction in West Virginia," *International Socialist Review*, XIV (July, 1913), 23–24.

Lynch, Lawrence R. "The West Virginia Coal Strike," *Political Science Quarterly*, XXIX (December, 1914), 626–663.

Marcy, Leslie H. "Hatfield's Challenge to the Socialist Party," *International Socialist Review*, XIII (June, 1913), 881–887.

Marcy, Mary E. "The Hatfield Whitewash," *International Socialist Review*, XIV (July, 1913), 54–55.

_____. "Unions Repudiate Debs' Escort, Haggerty," *International Socialist Review*, XIV (July, 1913), 22.

Merrick, Fred H. "The Betrayal of West Virginia Rednecks," *International Socialist Review*, XIV (July, 1913), 18–22.

Silver, Grace. "National Committee Meeting, Socialist Party," *International Socialist Review*, XIII (June 6, 1913), 877–880.

Thompson, Wyatt H. "Governor Hatfield Wins," *International Socialist Review*, XIV (December, 1913), 343.

_____. "How a Victory Was Turned into a Settlement in West Virginia," *International Socialist Review*, XIV (July, 1913), 12–17.

_____. "A Reply to Debs," *International Socialist Review*, XIV (August, 1913), 106–109.

_____. "Strike Settlement in West Virginia," *International Socialist Review*, XIV (August, 1913), 87–89.

_____. "The War Is Over," *International Socialist Review*, XIV (September, 1913), 162.

Wheeler, Edward J. "U.S. Senate Decides to Investigate West Virginia," *Current Opinion*, LV (July, 1913), 3–4.

Journals
"Agreement Made in Good Faith," *United Mine Workers Journal*, June 19, 1913, 5.
Debs, Eugene V. "An Appeal to the West Virginia Miners," *United Mine Workers Journal*, June 26, 1913, 7.
"International Executive Board on the West Virginia Situations," *United Mine Workers Journal*, May 15, 1913, 4.
"Miners on Paint Creek and Cabin Creek Anxious to Renew Strike," *United Mine Workers Journal*, June 19, 1913, 1.
"Minutes of Meeting of National Executive Committee of the Socialist Party of America," *The Party Builder* XXIX (May 21, 1913), 3–8.
"Minutes of Meeting of National Executive Committee of the Socialist Party of America," *The Party Builder* XXX (May 31, 1913), 4–7.
"Minutes of Meeting of National Executive Committee of the Socialist Party of America," *The Party Builder* XXXI (June 7, 1913), 3–8.
"*New York World* Denounces in Editorial Action of the Majority of Supreme Court of West Virginia," *United Mine Workers Journal*, June 5, 1913, 1.
"Paint Creek Settlement," *United Mine Workers Journal*, July 24, 1912, 4.
"Sanction of Miner's Union is Given to Paint Creek and Cabin Creek Strike," *United Mine Workers Journal*, July 3, 1913, 1.
"Settlement Made with Paint Creek Companies, Full Recognition Conceded," *United Mine Workers Journal*, July 24, 1913, 4.
United Mine Workers Journal, (editorial), April 24, 1913, 1.

Personal Interviews

Allen, Francis, Columbus, Ohio; August 6, 1971.
Blizzard, William, Jr., Charleston, West Virginia; June 9, 1971.
McCormick, Kyle, Princeton, West Virginia; June 12, 1971.

Secondary Sources

Books
Fairman, Charles. *The Law of Martial Rule*. Chicago: Callaghan and Company, 1930.

Fine, Nathan. *Labor and Farmer Parties in the United States*. New York: Rand School of Social Sciences, 1928.

Foner, Philip S., *History of the Labor Movement in the United States IV*. New York: International Publishers, 1965.

Ginger, Ray. *Eugene V. Debs*. New York: Collier Books, 1966.

Lane, Winthrop D., *Civil War in West Virginia*. New York: B.W. Huebsch, 1921.

Lee, Howard B., *Bloodletting in Appalachia*. Morgantown: McClain Printing Company, 1969.

McCormick, Kyle. *The New-Kanawha River and the Mine War of West Virginia*. Charleston: Matthews Printing, 1959.

Perlman, Selig and Philip Taft. *History of Labor in the United States 1896–1932*. New York: Augustus M. Kelly, 1966 (Vol. IV, of John Common's Reprints of Economic Classics).

Peterson, Horace C. and Gilbert C. Fite. *Opponents of War*. Madison: University of Wisconsin Press, 1957.

Shannon, David A., *The Socialist Party in America*. Chicago: Quadrangle Books, 1967.

Weinstein, James. *The Decline of American Socialism*. New York: Vintage Books, 1969.

Index

"Passim" (literally "scattered") indicates intermittent discussion of a topic over a cluster of pages. Page numbers in *italic* refer to illustrations.

elections and voting: Mother
Jones on, 86
Engdahl, J. Louis, 219
espionage. *See* spies and spying
Estep, Francis F. "Cesco," 46–50
Estep, Maud, 46
Ethel, West Virginia, 19
evictions, 88, 89, 96, 97, 119, 127,
148, 191, 198–99

F
Fairman, Charles, 235–36
Fairmont Coalfield, 190
Fayette County, 141
fear, 77–78
fear of mine guards, 34
federal troops. *See* United States
Army
Felts, Albert, 97–99, 102, 103, 106
Felts-Baldwin Agency. *See*
Baldwin-Felts Agency
Felts, Lee, 106
Felts, Thomas, 122, 123–24
feuds, 133, 189, 199, 246
firearms, right to bear. *See* right
to bear arms
firings, 19, 26, 36, 38, 130, 135–36,
198
Foner, Philip, 220
Ford, Stanley, 157–65
Fortieth Infantry, 158
freedom of assembly, 149–50, 177,
193, 199
freedom of press, 225
freedom of speech: suppression
of. *See* censorship and press
suppression
Fry, Ezra, *81*, 127

G
Gallagher, West Virginia. *See*
Mucklow, West Virginia
Germer, Adolf, 237, 238
Gillespie, George W., 226
Glasscock, William E., 24, 41, 77,
232, 238, 239–40
Glen Alum, West Virginia, 118
Gompers, Samuel, 23
governorship: West Virginia
Supreme Court on, 234–35
Graham, John T., 231, 232
guards. *See* mine guards
guns, right to bear. *See* right to
bear arms
Guyandotte River, 10, 129

H
habeas corpus suspension, 24,
232, 234
Hamilton, Alexander, 225
Harbord, James G., 138
Harding, Warren G., 138, 142, 154,
157, 161, 162
Hatfield, Anse, 104
Hatfield, Bill, 110
Hatfield clan, 128, 129, 168, 189
Hatfield, Henry D., 26, 67–69,
222–23, 226–45 passim
Hatfield, Jessie Testerman,
106–10, *111*, 145
Hatfield, Sid, *81*, 96, *104*, 106
murder of, 3, 106–10, 112, 141,
145, 191, 199
Senate testimony of, 97–104
tombstone of, *115*
Haywood, Bill, 220
health care, 15, 20
Heizer, J.L. 131

When Miners March

By William C. Blizzard
Edited by Wess Harris

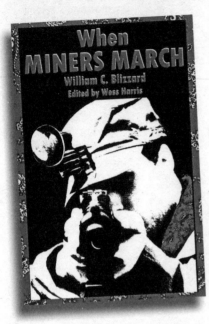

$21.95 • 978-1-60486-300-0 • PAPERBACK •
6x9 • 408 PAGES • LABOR/ HISTORY-U.S.

AN INSIDER'S LOOK AT THE LARGEST OPEN AND ARMED REBELLION IN U.S. HISTORY

The uprisings of coal miners that defined the Mine Wars of the 1920s were a direct result of the Draconian rule of the coal companies. The climax was the Battle of Blair Mountain, the largest open and armed rebellion in U.S. history. The Battle, and Union leader Bill Blizzard's quest for justice, was only quelled when the U.S. Army brought guns, poison gas, and aerial bombers to stop the 10,000 bandanna-clad miners who formed the spontaneous "Red Neck Army."

Over half a century ago, William C. Blizzard wrote the definitive insider's history of the Mine Wars and the resulting trial for treason of his father, the fearless leader of the Red Neck Army. This is a people's history, complete with previously unpublished family photos and documents. If it brawls a little, and brags a little, and is angry more than a little, well, the people in this book were that way.

> ## "An extraordinary account of a largely ignored but important event in the history of our nation."
>
> —Howard Zinn, author of *A People's History of the United States*